D1083794

Ulysses in Critical Perspective

The Florida James Joyce Series

Florida A&M University, Tallahassee
Florida Atlantic University, Boca Raton
Florida Gulf Coast University, Ft. Myers
Florida International University, Miami
Florida State University, Tallahassee
University of Central Florida, Orlando
University of Florida, Gainesville
University of North Florida, Jacksonville
University of South Florida, Tampa
University of West Florida, Pensacola

Ulysses in Critical Perspective

EDITED BY
Michael Patrick Gillespie
and A. Nicholas Fargnoli

Foreword by Sebastian D. G. Knowles

University Press of Florida
Gainesville/Tallahassee/Tampa/Boca Raton
Pensacola/Orlando/Miami/Jacksonville/Ft. Myers

Copyright 2006 by Michael Patrick Gillespie and A. Nicholas Fargnoli
Printed in the United States of America on recycled, acid-free paper
All rights reserved

11 10 09 08 07 06   6 5 4 3 2 1

A record of cataloging-in-publication data is available from the Library
of Congress.

ISBN 0-8130-2932-5

The University Press of Florida is the scholarly publishing agency
for the State University System of Florida, comprising Florida A&M
University, Florida Atlantic University, Florida Gulf Coast University,
Florida International University, Florida State University, University
of Central Florida, University of Florida, University of North Florida,
University of South Florida, and University of West Florida.

University Press of Florida
15 Northwest 15th Street
Gainesville, FL 32611-2079
http://www.upf.com

For Zack Bowen

With respect and affection

Contents

Foreword

I often wonder how new Joyceans get started in this field. There is so much work done on Joyce on so many continents and at so many conferences that it is nearly impossible to stay abreast of new material, let alone sort through what has already been written to test the originality of a new idea. As it was for another Ulysses on a different occasion, the margins of our experience of Joyce fade forever and forever as we move. We have, like Tennyson's traveler, reached both a natural point of reflection and departure: reflection, in passing Bloomsday's centenary year, and departure, in all that has transpired since the new millennium. New directions have been suggested by the National Library of Ireland manuscripts; there are new concerns about copyright, new waves in feminist and queer theory, new textual approaches that fundamentally alter the reader's relation to the text, new philosophies that call all in doubt. What is badly needed is an assessment of the current state of affairs, without excessive polemic in any particular direction, to allow a new generation of Joyce critics to follow knowledge beyond the utmost bound of human thought, instead of rowing around in circles.

So I was delighted when Michael Gillespie and Nicholas Fargnoli suggested this book. *"Ulysses" in Critical Perspective* removes much of the guesswork from Joyce studies, by taking the compass of the field's achievements and its future possibilities. The editors have divided the critical work on *Ulysses* to date into nine areas of inquiry: Reader Response (Riquelme), Narratology (Norris), Language Theory (Brivic), Feminism (Devlin), Queer Theory (Valente), New Historicism (Nadel), Genetic Criticism (Groden), Cultural Studies (Downing), and Bibliography (Brockman). These general rubrics are never laid out so baldly, for this is not a casebook for undergraduates but a work of reference and inspiration for scholars. The essays frequently move into wider territory: Riquelme and Norris write about language and style, Devlin and Valente about sexuality and politics, Nadel and Downing about history and culture. This allows the broader sections of the book to develop: the first two essays are largely concerned with close reading, the second three are grouped under theoretical approaches, and the last four study the text as a historical and temporal record. In all nine cases, the editors present leading Joyceans in the respective areas: indeed, in most cases these are the first and possibly the only people one could reasonably expect to be able to provide such a rich and reasoned overview of the subject at hand. Mick and Nick (as Gillespie and Fargnoli amiably style themselves) have chosen their Maggies well: each contributor is at the very top of his or her field.

"Ulysses" in Critical Perspective is both a retrospective arrangement, as a record of the major work on *Ulysses*, and a proleptic gesture, pointing to work still to be done. The Joycean scholar is here provided with an overview of what is past and passing, and an intimation of what may be to come. Anyone looking for a way to navigate through the secondary material on *Ulysses* written in the last several decades, and a guide to a newer world, should take this book on board.

Sebastian D. G. Knowles
Series Editor

Introduction

The Mime of Mick, Nick, and the Maggies

At the Dublin International James Joyce Symposium of 2004, Joyceans from all over the world gathered to commemorate June 16, 1904, and celebrate Bloomsday 100, the centenary of a day that never took place, or at least a day that never unfolded as recounted in *Ulysses*. Both the sincere enthusiasm of the varied participants and the contradictions inherent in their undertaking provide a ready stimulus for the cynical humor of those who delight in the eccentricities of academics, but that kind of response misses the point. The fascination that Joyceans feel for *Ulysses* comes from the seemingly inexhaustible aesthetic pleasure that the narrative provides. Like the description that Enobarbus applied to Shakespeare's Cleopatra: "Age cannot wither nor custom stale [its] infinite variety."

But academics are never content simply to experience a condition. We must dissect, analyze, and explain to the best of our ability without doing so ad nauseam. This feat can prove quite challenging when confronted with a work that simultaneously acknowledges and disavows the power of temporality and that situates itself within the "ineluctable modality of the visible" while at the same time producing the kinetic sensation of "walking into eternity along Sandymount strand" (*U*, 3.1, 17–18). The Dublin symposium, as others in the past, stands as just one alternative in a range of efforts to delineate the ever-expanding possibilities for meaning emerging from Joyce's text. In organizing this collection of essays of critical perspectives on *Ulysses*, our dominant concern was to explore diverse ways of understanding the range of elements that produce interpretative responses in readers.

That goal, however, does not assure immediate acceptance by readers interested in Joyce's novel. Despite the popularity of *Ulysses*, critical responses to the work have experienced a mixed reception. One of the papers at the Dublin symposium, "Past Its Sell-By Date: When to Stop Reading Joyce Criticism," seems to exemplify the exasperation that sometimes accrues. Despite the flippancy of its title and the implied cynicism in its contents, this sort of approach, nonetheless, provokes a useful question for anyone who reads *Ulysses*, or any of Joyce's other works for that matter: What useful and fresh interpretive insights does recent Joyce criticism provide? We hope, with the essays collected here, to point toward answers to that question.

Justifying criticism will always be a difficult enterprise. Reading is a highly personal endeavor, and the responses or interpretations (to our minds, synonymous conditions) that come out of engagement with Joyce's text are informed by a variety of subjective elements that vary greatly from person to person. Intratextual conditions—our past experiences with the novel, our familiarity with the allusions that pepper the narrative, our expectations for reading Joyce, and our theoretical inclinations—shape our responses in ways that vary from person to person and even within the individual from day to day. Further, countless mundane extra- and (non)textual concerns—the pollen count, receipt of a tax refund, music playing in the background, and any number of other factors—compound the uniqueness of our way of seeing the novel. Nonetheless, as the Dublin symposium attests, despite the subjectivity of any reading, we have a strong inclination to turn to others for insights or assistance in discerning meaning in *Ulysses*.

Readers have always juggled attention between their own views and those of others, and we suspect that the paper cited above was trying to offer guidance in the process. We take the position here that good criticism serves as a goad. From assignments read in graduate school to essays we have seen in the latest issue of *James Joyce Quarterly*, we benefit from the interpretations of others, but the specificity of that benefit can be difficult to pin down. More often than not it comes down to the ideas of others sparking reactions, sometimes positive and sometimes negative, from us. With this in mind, the essays collected here do not attempt to offer prescriptive interpretations or a converging focus of interpretations or even a converging focus. Rather, they seek to provide readers with diverse starting points for coming to an individual understanding of the role that the work of others has on our understanding of *Ulysses*.

In one sense, this hardly stands as an original project. *Ulysses* has been a topic of public commentary since Valerie Larbaud's December 1921 lecture at Sylvia Beach's Paris bookstore, Shakespeare and Company. Private critiques began even earlier as the letters of Ezra Pound to Joyce during the novel's composition indicate. From the first reviews of the novel by Edmund Wilson, Mary Colum, and T. S. Eliot, among others, and the seminal works by Stuart Gilbert, *James Joyce's "Ulysses": A Study* (1930), and Frank Budgen, *James Joyce and the Making of "Ulysses"* (1934), books and articles on *Ulysses* continue to appear at regular intervals, and a great many have significantly contributed to our understanding of a novel that an anonymous reviewer of the 1936 Bodley Head edition judged in a January 1937 issue of the *Times Literary Supplement* "obscure enough to have invited several interpretations." There is much to be said, then, for the opportunity to see a variety of perspectives based on a range of approaches to *Ulysses*. Unfortunately, there has not been such a collection of essays devoted exclusively to the novel since Bernard Benstock's *Critical Essays on James Joyce's "Ulysses"* appeared in 1989, and it has been at least thirty years since a number of groundbreaking collections—Clive Hart and David Hayman's *James Joyce's "Ulysses": Critical Essays* (1974), Thomas Staley's *"Ulysses": Fifty Years Later* (1974), and Staley and Benstock's *Approaches to "Ulysses": Ten Essays* (1970)—appeared and offered interpretive positions that challenged and engaged readers from the start.

No matter how timely those essays were three decades ago and no matter what their continuing impact, the interpretive landscape of Joyce studies has changed radically over the past three decades. Not only have several generations of Joyce readers come to maturity under the influence of these essays, but the range of theoretical approaches to reading *Ulysses* has markedly expanded. It now seems appropriate to give representatives of those generations the opportunity to trace the latest extension of the critical trajectory begun by Larbaud in 1921. The essays in this volume attempt to do just that.

Once this aim of assessing the current state of *Ulysses* criticism and of predicting the directions it was headed crystallized for the editors, the plan of the volume proceeded in a straightforward fashion with each essay in the collection offering both a retrospective and proleptic view of a particular approach. As the late Hugh Kenner was fond of saying, one of the things that *Ulysses* teaches us is how to read *Ulysses*. In fact, readings of Joyce's novel come down to rereadings that seek to reconcile experience with opportunity. An awareness of what has been said *about* the novel informs our sense of *where* many of our responses to it originate. But *Ulysses* does not cultivate passive reception and predisposed interpretations but rather engages us actively in the creation of meaning. The process takes the form of prolepsis (literally "flash forward"), narrating an event before it has actually occurred. It is a phrase introduced into narrative theory by Gérard Genette and popularly applied to Joyce by David Hayman. In *Ulysses*, prolepsis provokes readers to bridge gaps in the narrative created by this forward glance to anticipate and complete meaning. This concept fittingly encapsulates the imaginative strategy in Joyce's writing that draws us into the process of creating meaning from the text, and it seems equally applicable to speculations on the direction of criticism of the novel.

Focusing on a specific method for approaching *Ulysses*, each critic contributing to this volume dexterously combines these seemingly contradictory gestures of a backward glance and a forward projection. Each contributor comments on general achievements from a personal point of view, and each conjectures on the direction that a particular approach may take. Like any task undertaken by separate individuals, emphasis on specific elements varies from essay to essay. The contributors have stamped each approach not only with an interpretation of *Ulysses* but also with a unique perspective on reading the novel. And that is as it should be, for no definitive reading of the novel exists and no reading can stand alone. The most effective criticism remains a highly personal reflection that does not provide absolute answers but serves as inspiration for further reading and as a basis for dialogue with others. Divided into four broad, but interrelated, interpretative perspectives, this volume attempts to serve that end—that is, to stimulate and engage readers in an ongoing dialogue of reading and interpreting *Ulysses*.

Part 1, "The Words on the Page," begins with John Paul Riquelme's "'Preparatory to anything else': Joyce's Styles as Forms of Memory—The Case of 'Eumaeus.'" Concentrating on the "Eumaeus" episode, Riquelme attends to the elements of language and scrutinizes the active (and necessary) role of memory in reading *Ulysses*. In "Narratology and *Ulysses*," Margot Norris, after providing a brief overview of the genesis of modern narratology, details approaches concentrating on narrative issues in *Ulysses* and speculates on how a continued discussion of narratological theory can enhance our understanding of *Ulysses* and how *Ulysses* can in turn enhance narratology.

Part 2, "Perspectives of the Readers," contains three essays. The first, "Joyce and the Invention of Language" by Sheldon Brivic, looks at the linguistic dynamic of excess and multiple meanings in *Ulysses*, a work that defies a single authoritative interpretation. Brivic anticipates that further discussion of the novel may focus on how readers invent meaning (language) when reading *Ulysses*. In "En-Gendered Choice and Agency in *Ulysses*," Kimberly Devlin summarizes selected feminist approaches to *Ulysses* before examining the themes of gender, choice, and agency. Future feminist studies of the novel, Devlin suggests, may point to even greater political relevance of *Ulysses* by stressing the connection that these themes have to our conception of male and female and of the masculine and the feminine. Joseph Valente's essay, "*Ulysses* and Queer Theory: A Continuing History," concludes part 2. Valente explains what queer theory entails and surveys the history of the theory in Joyce studies with attention given to *Ulysses* criticism. He conveniently situates queer theory and *Ulysses* into three critical conceptual stages or waves that can be traced back to Frank Budgen and that can anticipate a fourth characterized by an association between homosexuality, shame, and social reprobation.

Part 3, "Pre- and Post-Publication," consists of four essays. The first, Gregory M. Downing's "Joycean Pop Culture: Fragments toward an Institutional History and Futurology," argues that popular culture provides an important interpretative context for Ulysses, a *Sitz im Leben* without which the novel cannot be fully appreciated. Downing predicts that popular culture will broaden its attraction to future readers of Joyce's novel. "Historicizing *Ulysses*," by Ira Nadel, delineates and appraises the invaluable contribution historicism provides (and will continue to provide) the reader of *Ulysses*. In reference to the work itself, Nadel pays particular attention to historicism and textual criticism. In "Before and After: The Manuscripts in Textual and Genetic Criticism of *Ulysses*," Michael Groden provides a detailed look, assessing the use of manuscripts in *Ulysses* studies from the perspectives of scholarly editing and textual criticism, on the one hand, and from genetic criticism and manuscript study, on the other. These critical perspectives, Groden proposes, will play an even greater role in *Ulysses* scholarship in years to come. William Brockman's "*Ulysses*: Bibliography Revisited" clarifies the different bibliographical approaches to the study of *Ulysses*. Though concentrating on the importance of establishing the primary bibliography of the novel, Brockman does not exclude secondary bibliography of the work. Included is also a chronological checklist of editions, imprints, and important reissues of *Ulysses*.

Allow us to close with a note on the title of this introduction. In *Finnegans Wake*, Shem and Shaun engage in a dramatized version of the Dublin children's game "angels and devils," or "colors," in an effort to gain the attention and affection of Issy and the Maggies. While we two editors of this volume share the given names of the title characters in that performance, our function here is markedly different. Instead of taking on the roles of actors, the editors, for better or worse, have assumed the parts of directors. Further, our task has proven to be far simpler than that facing Shem or Shaun. Rather than trying to please the willful and petulant Maggies, we worked with a group of critics who were universally enthusiastic, energetic, and generous. Assembling this collection has been a particular pleasure, and we are grateful to all the contributors for making it so.

I

THE WORDS ON THE PAGE

"Preparatory to anything else"

Joyce's Styles as Forms of Memory—The Case of "Eumaeus"

JOHN PAUL RIQUELME

. . . As from his small window
The astronaut sees all that he has sprung from,
The risen, aqueous, singular, lucent O
Like a magnified and buoyant ovum—
Or like my own wide pre-reflective stare

All agog at the plasterer on his ladder
Skimming our gable and writing our name there
With his trowel point, letter by strange letter.
—Seamus Heaney, "Alphabets"

The affirmation of the word yes is the affirmation of memory.
—Jacques Derrida, "Ulysses Gramophone"

Reading's Dual Perspectives

My title is drawn from the opening of the "Eumaeus" episode of *Ulysses*, but preparatory to turning to that episode and to some general and historical matters concerning close readings of Joyce, I want to draw your attention to a response to Joyce by a later Irish writer who has read him closely, Seamus Heaney.[1] Heaney's "Alphabets," which presents the development of the Irish artist from early childhood, proceeds against the backdrop of Joyce's portrayals of the young artist in Ireland.[2] Although Heaney provides his own version of the artist's stages of development, he takes over from Joyce a complex double vision that asks us to stand in two places at once, as the Irish artist appears also to have done, whether that be the artist who writes the works or the one represented in them. In the texture of the poem's language, Heaney's response to Joyce includes his linking *A* with *O*, *alpha* with *omega*, as letters representing the ends of the Greek alphabet but also suggesting beginnings and endings in general and specifically the beginnings and ends of literary creation. *A Portrait of the Artist as a Young Man* ends with its artist character's entries in his journal, which may well turn out to be not just the narrative's end but the beginning of later writing. And *Finnegans Wake* famously recirculates, its closing words inviting us to read them as continuous with its opening.

The *Wake* also links the letters *A* and *O*, at times in verbal plays, including the abbreviated name of the writer "jas jos" (*FW* 184.2) in syllables that suggest plural forms of words meaning *yes* (as in the German *ja*). The informing presence of *A* and *O* is evident "letter by strange letter" in the words of the closing stanzas of "Alphabets," quoted as one of this essay's epigraphs: "*a*stronaut," "*a*queous," "*a*gog." Like Joyce, Heaney mixes in his style elements with diverse linguistic and cultural origins (here Greek, Latin, and Middle English) that become linked through surprising juxtapositions in a pervasively Irish context.

Engaging closely with Joyce's writing involves attending both to the small elements of its language, down to the individual letters, and to the larger structural arrangements, such as the linking of ends and beginnings, sometimes discernible in the arrangements of those letters. Our responses to Joyce can be dual in an extreme way as we take note of the small and the large, which often turn out not to be at odds, though they differ in scale.

Heaney also captures in the closing stanzas another doubled element in Joyce's writings, their dual temporal perspective, which is at once prospective and retrospective. He does so by setting simultaneously in parallel and in contrast an adult, as an explorer of space, and the child, in awe of language, that the artist once was and may in certain regards continue to be. Lower and higher, future and past, forward and back have become revolving positions. The astronaut looks up and back at the earth "risen" like the sun. At the same time, the poet in his writing looks retrospectively at the child, who gazes up from the ground at the adult act of writing and who presumably also looks prospectively at it as the future beyond early childhood. Any persuasive close reading of Joyce will recognize and account for these kinds of doubled perspectives, the small and the large in mutually defining relation and the act of looking back as inseparable from a looking forward.

The sections that follow attempt to capture the energetic motions and directions that reading *Ulysses* closely can involve as responses to the book's challenging, but also often funny, diversity of perspectives. They do so first by suggesting that *Ulysses* invites us to understand it through memory of various kinds, then by providing a selective overview of close reading's place since World War II in critical debates and critical writing about modern literature, especially Joyce. To illustrate how close reading attentive to memory could proceed in the wake of earlier efforts to read Joyce closely, I collect and comment on aspects of "Eumaeus" as a step toward interpreting the book's concluding "Yes." Because of the multiple positions inscribed in Joyce's language, I read *Ulysses* as making the experience of mixtures compellingly available to us by means of style. The mixtures evoked by *Ulysses*, however, are not only or primarily aesthetic in character; they are also political and historical. The book's styles resist being understood as unmixed or unadulterated language; they are neither purely literary nor otherwise unalloyed. The stylistic details provide no coherent basis for accepting aesthetic, cultural, political, or racial purity as attractive or possible. Even Molly's "Yes" is mixed.

Close Reading's Memories

As I have begun to suggest, when we attend to the details of language in reading closely, we engage in acts of memory, including remembering works by other writers. A book called *Ulysses* projects the reasonable expectation that we have read or will read and remember earlier relevant texts, including especially Homer's *Odyssey*, but also, as it turns out, works by Shakespeare, Oscar Wilde, W. B. Yeats, George Meredith, and many other writers. The array of pertinent texts, however, is not literary in a high cultural sense only; it also includes nursery rhymes, street ballads, and other works of popular culture.[3] To ignore their presence is unjustified in our response to the styles of *Ulysses*. This text-oriented view is at odds with the principles of formalist close reading associated with New Criticism, which became important in universities within the English-speaking world during the 1950s. By formalism, I mean an attitude toward literary works that views them as self-contained entities whose integrity, unity, and significance are defined by elements of form, especially the arrangements of language, that constitute them. One commentator describes as follows the approach of New Criticism as "practical criticism or 'close reading,' in which the poem or literary text is treated as a self-sufficient verbal artifact":

> By careful attention to language, the text is presumed to be a unique source of meaning and value, sharply distinguished from other texts or other uses of language (particularly scientific language). Accordingly, the meaning of the poem is not conveyed by any prose paraphrase and is valued as the source of an experience (for the reader) available in no other way. For this among other reasons, opponents of the New Critics have frequently charged that they ignore history, ideology, politics, philosophy, or other factors that shape literary experience. (Searle 692)

Other commentators have suggested more strongly that Anglo-American formalism was politically, not just intellectually, motivated to reject Marxist and psychoanalytic perspectives as leftist (White 270–72). A formalist close reading that understands the work as a "verbal icon" or a "well-wrought urn" would not attend closely to historical and social contexts, the author's intentions, the audience's response, or other writing, whether literary or popular.[4] The narrow focus on form can result in a reading that is not only close but *closed* to the cultural history of texts that stands behind and within the work, and also closed to political implications. Such a reading assumes that we respond to a special kind of language, marked by its literariness, that makes up the work and that distinguishes it from other elements of culture. The assumption represses or forgets that the language of literature is not unalloyed and separate, since it emerges from and addresses cultural contexts in which it is always engaged. In the case of Joyce and other modern Irish writers, the contexts include the history of Ireland's domination by England.

Through a defining reliance on memory, Joyce's writings encourage us to remember in various ways and to recognize that remembering is part of moving forward, whether we are moving forward in the process of reading or moving forward in life, as we see the characters doing. Joyce's texts are constituted by and as memory, specifically by elements of form and narrative that rely on memory of at least four kinds: a broadly cultural, though often literary, memory for earlier works; a linguistically and structurally focused memory for details of form and narrative; the memory of individual characters; and a historical, social memory that may also be communal. The first I have already evoked by the example of Heaney: a cultural memory, often of a literary sort, that has registered, whether close up or from afar, details of other works that are significant precursors for the text at hand. In the case of *Ulysses*, those precursors can include Joyce's earlier writings, especially *A*

Portrait of the Artist as a Young Man, whose narrative focuses on Stephen Dedalus, and the stories of *Dubliners*, some of whose characters reappear in *Ulysses*.

The second kind of memory would be in its general qualities the kind that any literary text requires for cogent analytical response, a memory of the details of language and narrative that we encounter in the process of reading. Joyce's narrative in *Ulysses* asks us in particular to engage in acts of remembering that involve the sort of double temporal perspective we find in Heaney's "Alphabets." The double perspectives are retrospective and proleptic. We recognize references to earlier moments of *Ulysses'* narrative and form in a proliferating sequence that includes multiple retrospective recognitions of those earlier moments as proleptic, moments that have pointed forward to the one we currently inhabit in the reading process and almost surely also to moments yet to emerge.[5] As my comments on "Eumaeus" will illustrate, the effect is something like being in an echo chamber in which multiple reverberations with diverse origins make varying, combined demands on our attention. This need not be a confused or confusing situation, since many kinds of sense can be made of the converging, diverging elements.

The third type of memory that we recognize, and in the case of Joyce's narrative also come close to experiencing, is the memory of individual characters. Internal to the narrative, the characters engage in personal recollections. Not only do we realize that remembering is occurring when the recollections are presented in a detailed and intimate way; we may begin to share the characters' memories because in our attentive reading, we remember them, too. Once we become sufficiently acquainted with aspects of a character's interior life, we can begin to recall some large and small, past and present contexts for brief references that we have encountered before. Frequently in *Ulysses*, cultural memory and individual memory coincide when a character's remembering includes details from a literary or a popular text. These two kinds of memory mingle and merge for the characters and for us. Stephen's thoughts about the present and the past, for example, often include literary references.

A fourth type of memory relevant for reading *Ulysses* is historical memory. This type depends on our knowing facts and texts that help us make sense of references to historical situations and their language when we encounter them in *Ulysses*. But it requires more than just mastery of facts unconnected in our own experience that we can extract from encyclopedias and other reference works if we do not already know them. It requires as well the recognition of overlapping contextualizing narratives, frequently with significant political dimensions, that provide frames for understanding the action and the often challenging formal aspects of *Ulysses*. Central to the framing narratives constituting the historical memory that *Ulysses* invites us to exercise is the history of relations between Ireland and England, a history that includes the story of Charles Stewart Parnell (which comes up centrally in "Eumaeus"), the Home Rule movement, other aspects of Irish nationalism, and the place of England as an imperial power whose military forces, including Irish soldiers, occupy strategic outposts such as Gibraltar. The exercise of a historical consciousness in the reading of *Ulysses*, or the generating of one through the reading process, can have simultaneously individual and communal dimensions. This can be the case when the memories of individual characters, which we partially share, or other memories evoked in the reading process are bound up with Irish history in ways that bring to the fore an Irish nation in the process of emergence. We recognize that process of emergence in the narrative at times and in styles that extend and transform the resources of the English language in ways that are not anticipated in the history of English fiction. By leaving the English novel in his wake, Joyce redefines its limits and opens up possibilities that are political as well as aesthetic.

Remembering Close Reading's History

Whether we emphasize primarily the text's evocations of earlier works, our own reading experience as remembering and fitting together small and large elements retrospectively and prospectively, the characters' memories, or historical memory, memory as a determining element in responding to *Ulysses* provides rich opportunities for the reader. It also presents a challenge to formalist close reading, especially comparatively *closed* reading that excludes one or more aspects of memory that contribute to our experience of *Ulysses*. Reading informed by memory of various kinds tends not to be teleological. Its directions of movement and its results can be multiple and unpredictable. Rather than leading regularly to closure, it is likely instead to open new perspectives. In that regard, such a reading acknowledges the work's variable, fluctuating, temporal quality and resists understanding its form as spatial, stable, and determinate. In so doing, it aligns itself implicitly with an Irish writer who influenced Joyce, Oscar Wilde (1854–1900), and with critical and theoretical tendencies that emerged in the 1970s as effective challenges to New Critical formalism. Wilde claims in the first part of "The Critic as Artist" (1891), one of his dialogues on art, that literature is the highest form of art because its combination of language and narrative allows it to render the movement of human experience, which is a matter of mortality, that is, temporality (362–63). It is no coincidence that Wilde is mentioned at significant moments in *Ulysses*, during "Telemachus" and "Scylla and Charybdis." The latter episode bears a direct relationship to Wilde's dialogues on art and his writings about Shakespeare. They are part of the literary memory that *Ulysses* invites us to acquire and exercise in our close readings. Wilde's death after his imprisonment by the English is also part of the history of Ireland and England that *Ulysses* frequently expects us to remember.

In the 1960s and 1970s—three-quarters of a century after Wilde wrote "The Critic as Artist"—theory and criticism coming to the English-speaking world from Europe or inspired by European examples brought out literature's relation to process, including the generation of meaning through the temporal process of reading and through embedded relations to earlier works.[6] This was the period during which Umberto Eco, the Italian theorist strongly influenced by Joyce, published *Opera Aperta* (1962), concerning the concept of the open work. Joyce's writings are clear examples of open works, ones that trigger an overflow of implications not graspable in a critical response that identifies literature with the verbal icon and the urn of New Criticism. Wolfgang Iser's essays on fiction and the reading process, including his commentaries on *Ulysses*, were also being translated into English from German. Although he did not write about Joyce, the American critic Stanley Fish developed persuasive critical strategies for taking into account the temporal process of reading, which is sequential but also constantly under revision through retrospective adjustments and prospective surmises.[7] By focusing on what is, in effect, the reader's memory in the process of exercising itself, Fish rejects the New Critical tendency to present and interpret literature as spatial in structure, that is, as graspable in overview in a determinate, static configuration.

Conceptually, the difference between an emphasis on the reader and the New Critical emphasis on the work as an object involves the contrasts between time and space, the aural and the visual, and Echo and Narcissus. The temporal, the aural, and the echoic are matters of sequence and reverberation, which we experience in a series of moments. The spatial, the visual, and the self-reflecting gaze occur in an instant of time. In his seminal essay

"The Rhetoric of Temporality" (1969), the Belgian critic Paul de Man argues against spatialized attitudes toward literary texts by bringing out the temporality of the reading process as an encounter with echoic evocations of earlier works. He objects specifically to giving precedence to the concept *symbol* in responding to Romantic and post-Romantic writing, suggesting instead that what he calls *allegory* is equally important. The implications of allegory for literary interpretation are temporal, according to de Man, since they include the recognition that literary texts respond to earlier texts, usually multiply and variously, in a temporal, figurative, and conceptual process that needs to be accounted for in any persuasive reading. Other European critics writing specifically about Joyce were among the first to build interpretive arguments around what came to be called *intertextuality* in readings that went beyond earlier claims about Joyce's use of Homer as scaffolding.[8] In de Man's view, which can be taken as representative, by contrast with recognizing and remembering the precursor texts, critical reliance on *symbol* tends to stabilize and narrow the interpretive process through an emphasis on singular meanings that prevent the movement to and among precursors.[9] In his influential challenge to New Critical key concepts and readings, de Man argues, in effect, for the incarnation of literary memory in the texts and for our reading as an activating of that memory.

The positions taken by Wilde, Eco, Iser, Fish, de Man, and others provide a temporally oriented conceptual frame for questioning the largely atemporal tendencies of formalist close reading of the 1950s and 1960s. The New Critical emphasis on paradox as the holding together and resolving of oppositions and on literary works as spatial constructs of a formal kind found its primary exemplars in the interpretation of poetry.[10] But it also had a significant impact on critical writing about fiction. In his influential essay "Spatial Form in Modern Literature" (1945), which deals primarily with narratives by Joyce, Proust, and Djuna Barnes, Joseph Frank established the term *spatial form* in the study of modern narrative. He flatly states that "modern literature . . . is moving in the direction of spatial form." In his view, all the writers he discusses "ideally intend the reader to apprehend their work spatially, in a moment of time, rather than as a sequence" (10).

Frank argues for a totalizing perspective in which "the reader is forced to read *Ulysses* in exactly the same manner as he reads modern poetry, that is, by continually fitting fragments together and keeping allusions in mind until, by reflexive reference, he can link them to their complements" (20).

Luckily, despite Frank's assertion, literature forces nothing, though it can encourage or enable many things. Frank's description was meant as praise for Joyce's achievement and that of other modernist writers, and it was initially widely accepted. But many later critics and theorists eventually reversed the judgment of value by seeing in such a totalizing, reflexive process an exercise of power, including the power of a controlling, exploitative male in the act of gazing at women.[11] We need not accept Frank's identification of *Ulysses* with spatial form as definitive. In particular, we can question his concluding statement that "modern literature has been engaged in transmuting the time world of history into the timeless world of myth" (64). His position hinders the recognition of Joyce's engagement with time, history, politics, and mortality.

In its turn to "timeless" myth, the New Critical aversion to history finds a counterpart in the critical writings of William York Tindall, who also avoided history in his readings of Joyce by recourse to the *symbol*. I mention him in the context of close reading's development because an important commentator, Kenneth Burke, responded memorably in the 1950s to critical reliance on the *symbol* and to the formalist structuring of close reading by pursuing a more open alternative. Besides publishing two books about Joyce (Tindall 1950; 1959), Tindall directed over a dozen doctoral dissertations on Joyce at Columbia University by students who made careers as publishing scholars.[12] One of Tindall's points of origin was Edmund Wilson's groundbreaking work on Proust, Yeats, Joyce, and other early twentieth-century writers. Wilson's much admired *Axle's Castle* (1931) presented these writers as a twentieth-century resurgence of late nineteenth-century French symbolism, which he considered a second wave of Romanticism. Although important at the time and in its influence, Wilson's position on the continuity between modernism and Romanticism is subject to dispute. From Wilson's linking of modernism to symbolism, Tindall develops a mode of interpretation that depends on identifying symbols. Writing specifically of *Ulysses*, he designates as "symbolic" those elements he considers suggestive but that ultimately carry no "definite or fully demonstrable meaning" (1959, 131). Tindall's approach through *symbol* frequently yields speculative readings emphasizing archetypes and motifs, readings that are not tied closely to the text by careful examination of its language. His comments on the passage concerning horse and driver at the close of "Eumaeus," a passage I return to later, are typical:

> Horse and driver are suggestive. The horse creates "three smoking globes of turds" and the driver "humanely" waits "till he (or she) had ended." Is Stephen, creator of a three-part aesthetic theory, the horse, and Bloom the driver? (1959, 220)

In response to symbolic and to formalist readings, Burke, an American critical theorist, produced an alternative that anticipated the later European-inspired reaction against both. He did so in a close reading of Joyce's prose that presents its open character as the heterogeneous relations among its words. In "Fact, Inference, and Proof in the Analysis of Literary Symbolism" (1954), an essay about *A Portrait of the Artist as a Young Man*, although Burke retains the term *symbol*, he foreshadows the poststructuralist undermining of spatialized readings by treating the book's language as repetitions with a difference.[13] Calling his procedure "preparatory" (145), Burke works on the small level of the word in order to collect repetitions in *A Portrait of the Artist as a Young Man* and to begin making an index of repeated elements. Burke's provisional response to Joyce's writing is clearly opposed to strategies that ignore or reduce the variegated implications of the work's language. When Burke makes his list of key words, which he calls "facts," he explicitly refuses to assign a symbolic meaning to them first. The "inference," or interpretation, which comes later, is both "tentative" and responsive to "a constant demand for fresh inquiry" (150). The process is open rather than closed, temporal rather than spatial, because it never reaches complete closure. The result is an evocation of the literary text as echoic in the strong sense, not a manifestation of Echo as the repetition of the same but instead as repetition with significant differences that cannot be readily ignored. The differences allow for a variety of interpretations to emerge from close reading that is not tied to formalist or symbolic assumptions.

There have been many critical responses to *Ulysses* involving careful attention to the texture of its language not tightly bound to New Critical formalism. As a consequence, I can mention only highlights.[14] Since 1970, after the waning of the influence of the New Criticism and the rise of poststructuralism, readings that are, like Burke's, tentative and inferential in character by Fritz Senn and Hugh Kenner have been particularly distinctive and compelling. As the title of one of his collections of essays indicates, Senn's readings are "inductive scrutinies" that do not pursue the kind of totalizing view advocated by Frank. Senn's essays (1984; 1995) regularly take advantage of the perspective of the translator, who works with small but significant aspects and implications of the book's language. Rather than dealing with *Ulysses* as a matter of spatial form whose arrangement we can grasp with certainty in overview, Senn identifies the frequently dislocating effect of Joyce's locutions, which are more likely to dislodge us from an ostensibly stable point of vantage than to confirm what we think we know. Kenner's inductive readings of *Ulysses* are available in various essays and chapters and, at their most extensive, in his critical volume called *Ulysses* (1980; rev. ed. 1987). His best-known contribution to the understanding of Joyce's styles is the "Uncle Charles Principle," named for a character in *A Portrait*, which "entails applying the character's sort of wording to the character" (1978, 35). The principle captures memorably the way Joyce's interior monologues frequently ask us to move in a fluctuating manner between the character's perspective and the narrator's. That movement involves the text's enabling of a dual or variable, rather than a singular, response by inviting us to stand in more than one place. In line with the Uncle Charles Principle, however, Kenner tends to rely on assumptions about the psychological presence of characters beyond the first six episodes of *Ulysses*, even though later episodes move extravagantly away from representations of character and thinking.[15]

With his principle, Kenner responds to what is more formally known as narrated monologue or free indirect style (Fr., *style indirect libre*; Gr., *erlebte Rede*), an ambiguous merging of first-person and third-person language that Joyce was the first to develop extensively in English. Several significant critical studies focusing on free indirect style primarily in European authors (by Cohn, Pascal, and Banfield) appeared around 1980. These emerged as part of stylistics, a literary offshoot of linguistics, which had gained in importance in literary studies because of structuralism's interest in language. The work of these linguistically oriented comparatists was followed by book-length studies (Lawrence, Riquelme, and Gillespie) that attended to the styles of *Ulysses*, both small elements and structural features, from perspectives influenced by structuralist and poststructuralist thinking. At about the same time, feminist theorists and critics interested in style explored the extent to which Joyce's writing could be described as an antipatriarchal *écriture feminine* (feminine writing), a term used by Hélène Cixous and other French feminists.[16] Poststructural theory from France inspired some critics, including Derek Attridge in *Peculiar Language* (1988), to interpret Joyce's language as comparatively untethered to representations of character or gender.[17] For

Attridge, the styles of *Ulysses* anticipate in significant regards the more extreme, stranger language of *Finnegans Wake*.

More recently critics such as David Lloyd and Andrew Gibson have attended to the interplay among language, history, and anti-imperialist politics in *Ulysses*. Writing about *Ulysses* in the context of Ireland's relations with England, Lloyd has suggested that the book's style is adulterated. By that he means that the writing is mixed or hybrid in a way that reflects the encounter between the English and the Irish in a principled resistance on Joyce's part to a homogeneous style that would smooth over disruptive elements. Lloyd emphasizes the "internal heterogeneities" that mark the "interpenetrating discourses" in Joyce's stylistic "blending" of disparate elements through "modulations among different registers" (107–8). The mixing resists totalizing perspectives, including both English imperialist and Irish nationalist insistence on opposing kinds of cultural purity. As Lloyd describes them, the disruptive mergings of Joyce's writing are not reducible to New Critical paradox, which holds opposites together in a resolving way. Focusing in more detail than Lloyd on the anti-English aspects of *Ulysses*, Gibson presents abundant evidence that Joyce's styles call up a variety of English discourses in order to undermine them.[18] The book's frequent incongruities, which often contribute to the writing's humor, carry political implications.[19]

"Eumaeus": Toward a Temporal Reading through Memory and History

What follows is a "preparatory" and illustrative attempt to read aspects of "Eumaeus" closely and inferentially with attention to the four aspects of memory that I outline above. That opening word of the episode alerts us to the significance—both orienting and disorienting—of time in "Eumaeus." The episode's multiple temporal elements and effects, called up by its language, encourage a reading informed by memory in its cultural, analytic, personal, and historical aspects. Many such readings are possible. The paths of memory and language we are offered are so numerous that a straight-ahead process of reading is hardly possible. No two memory-informed readings by different readers or by one reader will be identical, though they will have some features and tendencies in common. We can follow one forking path through and beyond "Eumaeus" by beginning to index references to memory itself.[20] In doing so, it is important to include instances of remembering in which words for memory do not explicitly appear. As anyone who has prepared an index for a book realizes, an index is not simply a list of words that literally occur, because topics, ideas, events, and people can be central to specific passages and yet not explicitly named. The implied references are no less present.

The narration's language in the episode's opening paragraph, which is also the opening of the book's third part, invites us to remember earlier episodes, either because objects and events we have encountered before are mentioned or because words and phrases trigger our recollection. As Hugh Kenner pointed out, the words *brushed, shavings,* and *bucked* in the first sentence send us back to the opening of part 1, the "Telemachus" episode, in which a character named Buck uses a brush as he shaves (1978, 35). That first episode also comes up when the narrator mentions later in the paragraph that Stephen has "forgotten" his "soapsuddy handkerchief" (*U*, 16.19–20). It is not clear whether the narrator only or Stephen has recognized this act of forgetting, which may be a representation not of the character's thinking but of an absence that is not on his mind. Frequently, the episode's language presents an indeterminate relation between the narrator's language and the character's thoughts. The fact that the first word pertaining to memory in the episode concerns forgetting suggests, together with later lapses and mistakes of memory, that the episode proceeds often by indirection, mistakes, and omissions.

Bloom rather than the narrator continues the evocation of earlier incidents from the narrative in the second paragraph when he relates his encounter with a "sandstrewer" that occurred in "Circe." His fleeting reference, however, is likely to remind us that the incident near the opening of "Circe" is bizarrely presented (*U*, 15.184–95) in language that echoes Bloom's encounter with a tram in "Lotus-Eaters" (*U*, 5.131), one that he also remembers in "Lestrygonians" (*U*, 8.349). As do many of the book's passages, these opening paragraphs make it possible to invoke numerous previous moments as part of our interpretive response. The multiply retrospective orientation has a prospective counterpart as well because "Eumaeus" closes with Stephen and Bloom's encounter with another street vehicle, not a sandstrewer or a tram but a horse-drawn "sweeper" that Bloom "jocosely" calls a "steamroller" (*U*, 16.1780). Bloom's warning to Stephen near the end of "Eumaeus" can send us back to "Lestrygonians" again, where he cautions the blind stripling about a horse-drawn van on the street (*U*, 8.1086).

The textual space in which these details of language and action reverberate does not constitute "spatial form" in Frank's sense, which carries Cartesian and Euclidean implications for a stable observer. This space turns back on itself in various ways that are non-Euclidean and temporally diverse. What is preparatory and forward looking also takes us back and then projects us forward to various points in the text that can have other antecedents. As a consequence, the process of close reading through indexing will take us, as it now has, unexpectedly to other moments that are not in the strict sequence of the words. When that happens, it can be time to dwell on a particular moment, in this case the episode's closing.

When they encounter the sweeper at the end of "Eumaeus," while Stephen sings and the horse defecates, Bloom and he cross the street "Side by side" (*U*, 16.1880), stepping over the mire. As the last in a series of difficulties with memory he has in "Eumaeus," Stephen misremembers the line of a song by Johannes Jeep, which is "*Welches das Schiff in Unglück bringt*," not "*Und alle Schiffe brücken*" (Gifford 562). He does so just at a moment in which the style evokes doubled, even multiple, perspectives that are also "Side by side." These perspectives emerge not primarily because the language reminds us of earlier episodes but because it refers to texts and history from outside the book's narrative. The closing presents the driver "in his scythed car" watching blankly and not hearing what Stephen and Bloom are saying: "The driver . . . merely watched the two figures, *as he sat on his lowbacked car*, both black, one full, one lean, walk towards the railway bridge, *to be married by Father Maher*" (*U*, 16.1885–88). After the narrator tells us what they are discussing ("sirens" and "usurpers, historical cases of the kind"), we learn that "the man in the sweeper car or you might as well call it in the sleeper car who in any case couldn't possibly hear because they were too far simply sat in his seat near the end of lower Gardiner street *and looked after their lowbacked car*" (*U*, 16.1891–94).

The references to the car create incongruous fluctuating perspectives. Because it is described as "scythed," the vehicle suggests a war chariot presumably of a kind used in the distant past by Celts and Britons (Gifford 562); the chariots of the Greeks in the Trojan War are also possibly implied. The martial reference is followed by the italicized language from a popular song by the Irish composer Samuel Lover (1797–1868) about love and marriage, "The Low-Backed Car" (Gifford 562–63; Bowen 1975, 321–22). The phrases from the song are inserted without explanation directly into the narration of scene and action. It is not clear that either Stephen or Bloom is thinking about the words, which can give rise to a laugh because of the homosocial replacement of the song's man and woman by the pair of men, as well as the substituting of the sleepy male driver for the song's Peggy as the car's occupant. The sung rhythms and rhymes are so strong in the passage that the final sentence could be set up roughly as rhyming verse:

> the man in the sweeper car
> or you might as well call it in the sleeper car
> who in any case couldn't possibly hear
> because they were too far
> simply sat in his seat
> near the end of lower Gardiner street
> and looked after their lowbacked car.

We also encounter, among other effects, the internal rhyming of "hear" and "near." In its texture, the prose has moved toward song, which it nearly becomes. Stylistically, we have a prose discourse mostly in roman type that contains a poetic discourse in italic type, but despite the lack of transitions between the two, the poetic and the prosaic cannot be easily separated. Like the full and the lean black figures, they are "Side by side" (*U*, 16.1880) in a "*tête à tête*" (*U*, 16.1889), different, and yet strangely linked. At the same time as we encounter the stylistic linkage, the sweeper car, which is also jokingly a "sleeper" car, in an urban setting has become associated with martial precursors and with an image from a popular song that evokes a rural locale and love. Even the martial reference to a "scythed" car turns out retrospectively to be an allusion to the song that occurs before the italicized phrases from the song alert us to the presence of the earlier text. In the second verse of Lover's song, we hear of Mars's "hostile scythes" and "warlike cars." The song also anticipates Molly and memories of Howth with its comparison of Peggy, a "blooming girl" in "blooming grass," to a "flow'r" (Bowen 1975, 321). Even the "god of Love" in "The Low-Backed Car" is "blooming" (Bowen 1975, 322).

In the midst of experiencing in the final paragraphs the infusion of the Irish song's stylistic effect, we hear that the characters are discussing "sirens" and "usurpers," which are elements of Odysseus's experience. Because of earlier details in this and other episodes, we associate "usurpers" with the story of Charles Stewart Parnell, which is central to "Eumaeus." Parnell as Kitty O'Shea's lover is a usurper, as are those who take his place politically after he falls. In "Scylla and Charybdis," Stephen sets "usurping" in parallel with "false" and "adulterous" when he presents Shakespeare's domestic and artistic situation (*U*, 9.997–98), which is bound up for Stephen with the adulterous relations between Hamlet's uncle and his mother. In "Telemachus," we encounter "Usurper" (1.744) as a single-word paragraph in Stephen's thoughts about Buck Mulligan. The potential relevance to the closing of "Eumaeus" is emphatic because of parallel placement: the single word is the closing paragraph of part 1's opening episode. There and later the word evokes the suitors in the *Odyssey*. The word *sirens* in the final paragraph of "Eumaeus" has an immediate antecedent in Stephen's singing of lines from another Jeep song in the closing pages, lines that are typographically presented with the German word *Sirenen* centered on the page in italics. *Sirens* also occurs as an adjective earlier in the episode (*U*, 16.1382) when Bloom is apparently retelling to himself, in one of the episode's longest paragraphs, the story of Parnell's adultery and his fall (*U*, 16.1358–1410). Outside the episode, the word takes us back to, among other places, the "Sirens" episode and to the sirens of the *Odyssey*, who induce forgetting by their singing. And it takes us forward to the book's open ending in Molly Bloom (as can many elements and close readings of *Ulysses*).

Because of its inclusions, the style in the closing and in earlier portions of "Eumaeus" induces the opposite of forgetting. Besides inviting us to remember earlier moments in the episode, in the book, in other works, and in Irish history, it introduces into English prose other languages, phrases, and references that are either not literally English or not culturally of English origin. The presentation in italics of words that are linguistically or culturally of German, French, and Irish origin emphasizes typographically the presence of the non-English elements. And by the episode's end the texture of the prose has become so filled with repeated sounds that it starts to take on the character of verse. It sings with an Irish voice that amalgamates disparate materials, as does Heaney's style at the end of "Alphabets." English prose has been infiltrated and transformed in the direction of Irish musical language that includes German, French, and Greek elements and connections. Although T. S. Eliot's *The Waste Land* is a sparer, sterner work, Joyce's mixing of languages and styles with various high cultural and popular origins resembles the juxtaposing of diverse elements in Eliot's poem. And it points toward the amalgamation of elements in *Finnegans Wake*.[21] The mixture violates expectations because an ostensibly unruly or undomesticated element has intruded into English prose style and changed it. As Andrew Gibson has argued, the language of "Eumaeus" resists English attitudes toward pure, appropriate, and correct language within "a colonial politics of discourse" (224–25). The episode's style is the vehicle for bringing together disparate elements that, like the very different but now linked characters, "one full, one lean," "both black," exhibit a forward motion in a "Side by side," implicitly nonhierarchical structural relation. The Irish element is not subordinate to other stylistic elements with which it has been juxtaposed and merged. In fact, it has the last word in the temporal sequence of the language. Because of its exuberance and humor, the Irish element also has the last laugh.

Between the mention of Stephen's forgotten handkerchief on the first page of "Eumaeus" and his misremembering of the line from Jeep's song on the last page, there are numerous mentions and instances of forgetting, re- membering, recollecting, and repicturing. I list only a few examples to estab- lish the recurrence. In part because of their length, as we shall see, central to the passages involving memory are those about late nineteenth-century Irish history, especially Charles Stewart Parnell, and those about Molly Bloom. In his confusion early in the episode, Stephen has difficulty remembering and recognizing his father's friend Gumley, who is working as a watchman (*U*, 16.106–9). Discovering pieces of biscuits in his pockets, Stephen "tried to recollect" (*U*, 16.186) what happened to his earnings and only "dimly re- membered" (*U*, 16.190) how the biscuits came into his possession. When Bloom warns him about not trusting Mulligan, Stephen does not respond because his "mind's eye" is "busily engaged in repicturing his family hearth the last time he saw it" (*U*, 16.269–70). Bloom later recognizes the "street- walker" (*U*, 16.704) who looks in as the one he had seen earlier in the day on Ormand Quay at the end of "Sirens" (*U*, 11.1252–60), and he remembers that she knows his connection to Molly. In their conversation, "Stephen has to make a superhuman effort of memory to try and concentrate and remember" (*U*, 16.754–55). Bloom's "recollection" about how little a temperance coffee shop paid Molly is "painful" (*U*, 16.797), and when "he remembered reading" something, "he couldn't remember when it was or where" (*U*, 16.802–3).

In the episode's middle, Bloom and the sailor who calls himself Murphy show mementos of a visual kind: the sailor's picture postcard from South America depicting native women with infants, the shape-changing tattoo of the Greek Antonio with the number 16, and Bloom's photograph of Molly Bloom.[22] While Bloom holds the card in his hand, his thoughts about pos- sible trips to Mullingar, to London, and to Irish tourist destinations, including Howth, present details of his family life that we have already encountered in some form. His daughter, Milly, lives in Mullingar; his trip to England would include scouting for a concert tour for his wife as part of the imaginary "Tweedy-Flower grand opera company" (*U*, 16.525); his thoughts about Howth carry implicit personal associations in addition to the "historic associations" (*U*, 16.558) mentioned. The details have prospective as well as retrospective orientations because they anticipate aspects of the book's closing episode. When Stephen and others in the cabmen's shelter are passing around the postcard, the sailor's mention of "the park murders of the invincibles" (*U*, 16.590–91) triggers Bloom's vivid recollection of the event, which occurred in 1881, an event in which Skin-the-Goat, the keeper of the shelter, may have been involved. But immediately after Bloom "vividly recollected" (*U*, 16.604–5) the murders, he asks the sailor if he knows "the Rock of Gibraltar." He has Molly as well as Irish history on his mind. The remainder of the episode continues to mention Molly and history, especially events involving violence, in proximity, anticipating the linking of Molly with imperial Gibraltar in "Penelope."

Bloom brings his conversation with Stephen around to Molly by combining the knives from the murders with Gibraltar. He moves by association from the sailor as "Sinbad" (*U*, 16.858) to the Italians who were arguing outside and then from "that stab in the back touch" (*U*, 16.865) finally to the "passionate temperaments" of "Spaniards," including his wife, "born in (technically) Spain, i.e. Gibraltar" (*U*, 16.878–79). "Technically" applies by implication to Ireland as well. The mention of shipwreck "off Daunt's rock" (*U*, 16.906) brings the Rock of Gibraltar into association with Ireland, before another kind of wreck, the fall of Parnell, becomes the center of attention in Skin-the-Goat's nationalist statements and Bloom's internal responses to them (*U*, 16.983–1080). The keeper's remarks about the beauty of Ireland and the inevitable fall of "mighty England, despite her power of pelf on account of her crimes" (*U*, 16.999–1000), recall the Citizen's statements in "Cyclops" and the speech about reforestation in the newspaper office of "Aeolus." (Newspapers play a role later in the episode.) In his thoughts, Bloom compares political violence to violence in response to marital infidelity when he thinks first about his "admiration for a man who had actually brandished a knife" (*U*, 16.1058–59) in a political cause but distances himself from "those love vendettas of the south" (*U*, 16.1061) in which the husband stabs his unfaithful wife.

From this point on in the episode, historical and domestic situations become intertwined around memories and hopes in relation to the common element of adultery and its aftermath. When the shelter keeper recalls Parnell's loss of political power and reflects on the possibility that he would return, Bloom feels "rather surprised at their memories" (*U*, 16.1307–8) and skeptical about the advisability of returning to a situation in which others "ruled the roost" (*U*, 16.1328). But he also thinks that "You had to come back" (*U*, 16.1331–32), a statement that applies to Odysseus and to himself, as well as Parnell. Bloom's meditation on returning merges with his memory (*U*, 16.1333–39) of having seen Parnell once during a raid on a newspaper office, when Bloom picked up Parnell's hat for him.[23] A few pages later (*U*, 16.1495–1528), the narrator uses similar phrasing to repeat the details of Bloom's recollected encounter with Parnell, now by contrast with the incident involving John Henry Menton's hat at the end of "Hades."[24] We might conclude that the narrator has forgotten that the details have already been told. In the second version, however, by mentioning "history repeating itself with a difference" (*U*, 16.1525–26), the narrator reflects implicitly on the events and on the repetition in the narration. The statement refers to the difference in the widely separated events involving Menton today and Parnell before his death, but it suggests as well the relation between Odysseus and Bloom, Parnell's adulterous situation and Bloom's, the narrator's repeating with a different perspective the details mentioned only a few pages earlier, and Bloom's own altered versions of events from earlier in the day.

Between the two presentations of the incident involving Parnell's hat, one of the men in the shelter mentions having seen a "picture" of Kitty O'Shea, "Fine lump of a woman" (*U*, 16.1354). Bloom then "reflected upon the historic story" (*U*, 16.1361) of Parnell's adultery, which he retells in detail to himself, and he shows Stephen "a faded photo" of Molly (*U*, 16.1425) that he does not put away until they leave the shelter (*U*, 16.1648). As Bloom comments in "Hades" (*U*, 6.966–68), photographs serve as aids to memory; in effect, they keep people and images from dying away. Bloom's personal memories and his recollection of Parnell's history, both political and personal, have merged when "Looking back" becomes linked but also contrasted with "coming back." "Looking back now in a retrospective kind of arrangement" (*U*, 16.1400–1401) allows for the recognition that "coming back" (*U*, 16.1402) would be difficult or impossible because things change. "Coming back" refers simultaneously to multiple returns: Parnell's, Odysseus's (in the

Odyssey and in *Ulysses*), and the husband's, the last to a domestic situation in which his place has been usurped. For Bloom, "coming back" is not a retrospective matter but the step he is about to take, as well as the situation he is in as a version of Odysseus. Because Bloom thinks that Kitty O'Shea "was Spanish or half so," subject to the "passionate abandon of the south, casting every shred of decency to the winds" (*U*, 16.1409–10), he associates her with Molly, whose picture he shows. In effect, the story of recent Irish history and the story of his own domestic life have become versions of each other, and the common feature is adultery, in which he and Parnell play different roles, though both may be "coming back."

The details are not presented in a melodramatic or solemn way, largely because the language generates laughter rather than pathos or some other unalloyed sentiment. In particular Bloom's recollection of Parnell's story and his crossover to his own occur as incongruous language. When the shelter keeper talks about Parnell, like the Citizen in "Cyclops," he speaks declaratively about political violence and clashes between antagonistic forces. By contrast, the language presenting Bloom remembering Parnell includes a stylistically laughable statement, filled with clichés, about Parnell's supporters having "effectually cooked his matrimonial goose, thereby heaping coals of fire on his head, much in the same way as the fabled ass's kick" (*U*, 16.1399–1400). And when Bloom suggests to Stephen that O'Shea was Spanish, he misunderstands Stephen's allusion to a nursery rhyme as a literal claim that she was "The King of Spain's daughter," a claim Bloom obligingly declares to be "Possible" (*U*, 16.1419).

The presentation of adulterous situations as the story of Ireland and the story of the Blooms could be angry, bitter, and single-minded in the mode of the Citizen and the shelter keeper. Instead, Joyce's tour de force in creating an adulterated, impure style of linguistic ineptitude keeps the details from coalescing into the tale of a wrong that requires a bloody revenge, though it does require response. The episode continually gives us mixed rather than pure uses of language, surprising conjunctures, and incongruous perspectives, like those of the concluding paragraph of "Eumaeus." When it triggers our laughter, the language does not provide one or a few fixed objects of irony. In order to do that, it would have to establish a stable, detached point of vantage from which we could exercise our judgments as ironic observers. That kind of spatialized point of vantage is not available. Because the style has moved so far from realistic representation, our laughter is not concentrated on realistically presented characters who are making mistakes. Instead of laughing *at* something in a narrow way, we are laughing *because* of the style. The reader's situation bears comparison to the audience's laughter at Bottom and the other rustics during their performance of scenes from a tragic play in the final act of *A Midsummer Night's Dream*. There we also laugh because of incongruous and inept language. But we recognize as well that the blunders are aspects of a carefully crafted mask worn by accomplished actors, and in *Ulysses* by an accomplished writer, pretending to be inept performers whose statements are so malappropriate that they generate infectious ripples of laughter. Because of the virtuoso performance of stylistic ineptitude in "Eumaeus," the exuberance and excess of the laughter is affirming rather than ironic. Through the style's incongruities, we reach a moment like the one Stephen Dedalus experiences in the library, when "he laughed to free his mind from his mind's bondage" (*U*, 9.1016).

Moving Toward the Strange Affirmation of Yes(terday)

The movement of the episode, and the book, is toward Molly Bloom, whose photograph triggers Bloom's various recollections about her looks, her background, the statues he saw earlier in the day, and things she said in the morning concerning their life, among other matters. The photo provides "a speaking likeness in expression but it did not do justice to her figure" (*U*, 16.1444–45). The body is not adequately presented, in part because dimensions are lost in a photographic image. The loss involves not only the third dimension in space but also the dimension of time that is the province of memory, of the body as it ages, and of history. As Bloom looks at "the slightly soiled photo creased by opulent curves, none the worse for wear" (*U*, 16.1464–66), he thinks that "the slight soiling" (*U*, 16.1468) makes it more attractive. The soiling is the mark of time's passage on the photo, but Bloom knows that the subject of the photo has also aged: "at the moment she was distinctly stouter. And why not?" (*U*, 16.1479–80). The word *creased* could suggest that the photo has been folded, but the creasing is figurative, not literal, caused by the rich curves of the body. The body has been creased in advance of its representation on paper, whether or not the paper has ever been folded. Although the photo is apparently worn, as is the now older body whose curves are represented, the value of the photo and of the curves is unaffected by the deterioration.

The photo as "speaking" likeness anticipates our encounter with Molly in "Penelope," where various photos are also mentioned.[25] The movement of the narration and of Bloom toward Molly's "Yes" is simultaneously forward and backward. "Yes" is part of Bloom's memory and of hers concerning their lovemaking on Howth. But the repeating of "yes" is also prospective for them and for the reader until we encounter its repetitions with a difference in her thoughts. The considerable force of Molly's final, capitalized "Yes" as an exuberant verbalized recollection goes beyond the "speaking likeness" of the photo but not absolutely beyond it. Either stamped on the photo or in Bloom's memory in a way that intrudes into the narration of "Eumaeus" is the photo's origin as an object and an illusion that has been executed aesthetically: "Her (the lady's) eyes, dark, large looked at Stephen, about to smile about something to be admired, Lafayette of Westmoreland street, Dublin's premier photographic artist, being responsible for the esthetic execution" (*U*, 16.1433–36). Her "Yes" comes close to expressing the voice of the passionate body, evoked in "Eumaeus" by "Her . . . eyes" (an evocation tempered by the parenthetical insertion of "the lady's"), as something spontaneous and virtually independent of context except for the context that the body provides. "Yes" expresses the body remembering in an extreme instance of individual recollection. But the word is verbal, not just corporeal; it is remembered and textualized language rather than voice and "eyes." The memory that it inscribes involves a premeditated act rather than a purely immediate, spontaneous one. As with the photo, someone is responsible for the execution. That someone is Molly Bloom as well as Joyce. Instead of being pure and unalloyed, this "Yes" is as mixed as many other elements of style in *Ulysses*.

Molly's "Yes" has origins that have not been masked, forgotten, or obliterated. As a consequence, it is no more singular and self-contained than the diverse language assembled into the closing of "Eumaeus." Both closings are internally riven. "Yes" is the recollected answer to a question that Molly remembers having triggered not uniquely and not without forethought but as part of a process of repetition over time. In that regard, her "Yes" is a counterpart for the response given late in "Ithaca" to the question, "If he had smiled, why would he have smiled?" (*U*, 17.2126). That response presents the in-between quality of a moment that is simultaneously "the last term of a preceding series" and "the first term of a succeeding one" (*U*, 17.2128–29). The prior stages to "Yes" include her thinking "well as well him as another," based in part on her experiences with other men. And they include her intentionally asking "him with my eyes," a word that, as Jacques Derrida has pointed out (1998, 84), suggests its homonym "ayes" and contains already within it the word *yes*, which we see in the typography of the printed page. Her eyes are not literally looking at us, but we look at her word *eyes*, and the implied *yes* looks back at us. As with the linking of alpha and omega in the multiple yes of *jas jos*, the embedding of *yes* in *eyes* can bring us back to Heaney's presentation of an encounter with language in which, by looking back and looking forward, we recognize its strange quality and, by implication, our own.

As an instance of language's inherently strange character, Molly Bloom's memorable language in *Ulysses* stages our chameleonic ability to respond multiply, ambivalently, and ambiguously through memory.[26] Her asking on Howth may be a repetition enabled by memory, since her eyes "asked him" "to ask again." Perhaps she and Bloom had been in a similar situation before. But "again" can also be understood as attached to "yes": "again yes" rather than "ask again." Having experienced "Yes" that time on Howth, possibly earlier, and perhaps many times in various ways since, Molly wishes, because of her memory of the repetitions, to experience it "again." "Again yes" anticipates the phrase "again wake" evoked by the title of Joyce's next book. *Yes* is also the first syllable of *yesterday*, a word that Molly uses earlier in the episode when she thinks "its just like yesterday to me" (*U*, 18.821) in another passage in which she "promised him yes" (*U*, 18.822). The promise to "him" is not for Bloom on Howth but for Lt. Mulvey on Gibraltar, a place of cultural crossovers.[27] By means of memory, Molly stands simultaneously in more than one location. There is no unattractive soiling or loss of value in the premeditated, repeated character of Molly's "Yes," which is heterogeneous, not univocal or pure. We understand it as, among other things and in various ways, the book's final stylistic invitation for us to experience the compelling inevitability of remembering and of repeating with a difference. In that act of repeating, to which we are given access by means of reading as remembering, a translation occurs. We are memorably translated back, forth, and among various yeses, including: a "yes" on Howth (an Irish location), the "yes" of "yesterday" on Gibraltar (an English outpost of Empire), and yeses that persist now as new but still recognizable mixed forms on Eccles St. Together these repeated yeses open onto an unpredictable future that the book makes proleptically available in the retrospective and prospective movements of its language. Molly Bloom's large ayes are the end. And they are preparatory.

Notes

1. This essay and the version delivered in San Diego at the 2003 MLA convention are in memory of Hugh Kenner (1923–2003), the *aeglaeca* of modernist literary studies. For the sake of convenience I refer to the episodes of *Ulysses* by the Homeric names that most critics use. From the perspective of close reading, however, the practice is unwarranted, since no titles are provided for the episodes in the text.

2. Heaney's comments and his readings from his own poems at the opening session of the Bloomsday 100 (Nineteenth International James Joyce) Symposium on June 13, 2004, eloquently confirmed Joyce's importance for the poet's career. In his remarks, which I heard after having written this essay, Heaney explicitly affirmed Joyce's influence on him, and he read poems that make Joyce's presence in his writing clear. They included "Alphabets" (269–71) and "The Strand" (406). The speaker in the latter asserts that his father made a line with an "ashplant," a kind of walking stick, on Sandymount Strand, just south of Dublin harbor, that will not "wash away." Both the location and the ashplant link the father with Stephen Dedalus, who walks along Sandymount Strand in the "Proteus" episode of *Ulysses* and carries an ashplant in *Ulysses* and in part 5 of *A Portrait of the Artist*. In section 12 of Heaney's "Station Island," Joyce walks with an ashplant (244). In effect, in his poetry Heaney has identified Joyce as a primary forebear.

3. Herr and Kershner provide critical commentaries on Joyce and popular culture in relation to *Ulysses*.

4. The terms *verbal icon* and *well-wrought urn* come respectively from William K. Wimsatt and Cleanth Brooks, who used them as title phrases for books listed in the bibliography.

5. I present elsewhere a reading of this kind for aspects of *A Portrait of the Artist as a Young Man* (Riquelme 2004, esp. 117–20).

6. Stanley Fish, for example, mentions retrospectively (21) his encounter with Roland Barthes' *S/Z* (published in French in 1970) while he was formulating the argument of "Literature in the Reader: Affective Stylistics" (1970).

7. See in particular "Literature in the Reader: Affective Stylistics" (Fish 21–67) and "What It's Like to Read *L'Allegro* and *Il Penseroso*" (Fish 112–35).

8. See, for example, Topia.

9. In the wake of the challenge to the adequacy of *symbol*, younger Joyce critics began to question the use of the term by the previous generation. See, for example, Herr, who asks "who is to say that 'symbol' is the correct term for the meaning-bearing components of Joyce's fictions?" (1986, 283).

10. Cleanth Brooks's *The Well-Wrought Urn* (1947) was highly influential as a model of New Critical readings of poetry from the Renaissance through the twentieth century.

11. Laura Mulvey's "Visual Pleasure and Narrative Cinema" (1975) is an early, influential moment in this reversal of value.

12. See Richard F. Peterson, "A Reader's Guide to William York Tindall" (Dunleavy 106–19).

13. Burke's procedures anticipate the approach of some poststructuralist critics of fiction, including, for example, J. Hillis Miller in his treatment of the various nonconverging instances of "red" in Thomas Hardy's *Tess of the d'Urbervilles* (1982, 122–27).

14. For a more detailed discussion of criticism from 1970 to 1998 focusing on discourse and the reader, see the second chapter of Gillespie and Gillespie (23–45). Their first chapter also provides more background than I can here concerning earlier Joyce criticism.

15. I take issue with Kenner's assumptions concerning the relation of Joyce's language to character in his reading of "Circe" (Riquelme 1983, 140–42). Attridge raises similar objections to Kenner's claim (Kenner 1978, 37–38) that the style of "Eumaeus" is one that Bloom could be capable of producing (Attridge 1988, 174, 183).

16. Derek Attridge surveys and comments on some prominent attempts to present Joyce's style as either antifeminist or feminist (1989).

17. In his "Introduction: Language(s) with a Difference," Milesi argues for the continuing importance of language-oriented interpretations of Joyce in the wake of recent critical emphases of a historicizing kind on gender, nation, and history (1–27, esp. 10 20).

18. By emphasizing the "adulteration of Englishness" as "central" to *Ulysses* (Gibson 264), Gibson tends to slight the affirming and the comic aspects of the mixture that Joyce creates out of the crossover between English, Irish, and other cultural elements, which contribute to a new idiom that goes beyond parody and irony.

19. For a brief linguistically oriented commentary on "Eumaeus" that brings out the humorous effects of the language, see Wales, esp. 124–27.

20. For a different kind of indexical response to the episode, see Senn's "'All kinds of words changing colour': Lexical Clashes in 'Eumaeus'" (1995, 156–75), in which he collects instances of word repetition and considers the interplay of literal and figurative. At the end of that essay, Senn focuses briefly on "the reader's memory" (173). Christine O'Neill (1996) comments on Senn's contributions to the reading of Eumaeus in a thorough sketch of responses to the episode through 1994. See also n. 23.

21. As others have also claimed, including Kenner (1978, 37), Attridge (1988, 183), and Senn (1995, 174).

22. Derrida comments on some aspects of the postcard (1998, 73–75).

23. Senn indexes the word *pick* in "Eumaeus" in "Syntactic Glides" (Milesi 35).

He also suggests there that the repeated narration of the encounter with Parnell is reminiscent of the Homeric "repetition of certain formulaic passages" (Milesi 35).

24. Kenner reads the two similar passages concerning Parnell as first Bloom's thoughts, in effect his silent rehearsal, followed by his spoken version addressed to Stephen (1987, 132). There is, however, no clear indication that Bloom speaks the second version, which is narrated in third person. The use of the word *inwardly* (*U*, 16.1529) in the opening sentence of the next paragraph suggests that Bloom has not been speaking.

25. Ewa Ziarek discusses the photos in "Penelope" as emblems of mechanical reproduction that seem, in her reading, to be at odds with a more organic erotic memory. In my view, the apparently opposing elements are not separable.

26. Attridge explores the "peculiar language" of *Ulysses* with particular reference to "Eumaeus" as springing "from the propensities and liabilities of language itself" (1988, 183). The peculiarity of Joyce's writing involves more specifically the multiple affiliations and embodiments that we experience as forms of memory. "Language itself" does not provide sufficient explanation for the style's eccentricities.

27. Gibson convincingly presents Gibraltar in "Penelope" as racially mixed and "hybrid" in contrast to contemporaneous English presentations of it as imperially and monolithically British and Protestant (260–61).

2

Narratology and *Ulysses*

MARGOT NORRIS

Mieke Bal begins the introduction to her second edition of *Narratology: Introduction to the Theory of Narrative* as follows: "*Narratology* is the theory of narratives, narrative texts, images, spectacles, events; cultural artifacts that 'tell a story.' Such a theory helps [one] to understand, analyze, and evaluate narratives" (3). The genesis of modern narratology is generally attributed to two twentieth-century intellectual movements—Russian formalism and French structuralism. The term *narratology* was introduced by Tsvetan Todorov in his 1969 study of Boccaccio's *Decameron*, although this work was preceded by the protonarratological study of the morphology of the Russian folktale by Vladimir Propp in 1928. Narratology's linguistic ancestry can be found in the Moscow Linguistic Circle, whose scholars explored the nature of oral and written language as early as 1915.

One of the Circle's most important theorists was Roman Jakobson, who contributed greatly to linguistic theory's understanding of *deixis* (means of expression whose interpretation is relative to the context of the utterance). His work was complemented by that of Emile Beneveniste, a French linguist whose work on such language "shifters" as pronouns and verb tense also influenced literary theory. The French structuralists—particularly Claude Lévi-Strauss, Roland Barthes, and Gérard Genette—helped to make narratology an important focus just as critical theory was beginning to gain attention and acceptance in literary study in the 1960s and 1970s.

Since that time the structural approach to narratology has achieved wide currency in the academy. Michael Kearns cites the following as "the books normally used as texts in courses on narrative theory": "*Narrative Discourse* [Genette], *Narrative Fiction* [Rimmon-Kenan], *Narratology: Introduction to the Theory of Narrative* [Bal], *Story and Discourse* [Chatman], and *Narratology: The Form and Function of Narrative* [Prince]" (6). In addition to the branch of narratology concerned chiefly with the technical analysis of narrative texts, much attention has also been given in recent years to exploring the social, cultural, and political contexts in which readers and audiences encounter narratives. The attention to context has produced expansion into the fields of "rhetorical narratology" (Kearns), "speech-act theory," (Austin, Searle, Miller), and "reader-response" and "reception" theory (Jauss, Iser). Given the high degree of narrative innovation and experimentation that Joyce's writing, and particularly *Ulysses*, has brought to literature, the Joycean text has enjoyed a privileged status as exemplar in some aspects of narratology over the years.

While narratological theory has offered critics precise concepts and taxonomies for understanding the unusual storytelling styles and devices in the novel, *Ulysses*, in its turn, has challenged the field and offered interesting test cases for refining its concepts. In the first part of this consideration of narratology and its relation to Joyce's *Ulysses*, I plan to look at critical studies that have explored the narrative challenges of *Ulysses*—with and without explicit benefit of theory. In the second part of my study, I will look to the future, and consider both how narratology can continue to contribute to our understanding of Joyce's narrative experiments in *Ulysses*, and how *Ulysses* can continue to contribute to the field of narratology itself.

One of the earliest narratological studies of *Ulysses* was produced by a critic who was also a theorist of narrative—the Austrian scholar Franz Stanzel, whose *Narrative Situations in the Novel: "Tom Jones," "Moby-Dick," "The Ambassadors," "Ulysses"* appeared in translation in 1971. Stanzel's work departed somewhat from the more rigorously formalistic approaches that characterized narratology in the 1970s by addressing not only the generic features of narrative but also the contexts in which stories are told, that is, their *narrative situations*. Narrative context includes audiences and readers in their relation to narration. Stanzel's chief narratological focus is something he calls "mediacy of presentation," which allows him to distinguish two principal types of narration. These are *authorial* narrations, in which an authorial medium guides the reader's imagination of the narrative situation, and *figural* narrations, in which the reader is allowed to feel like a witness of a narrative situation without any mediation.

These relatively simple initial distinctions display their usefulness in discussing *Ulysses* when they allow Stanzel to give a highly specific description and analysis of the work's experimental departures. For Stanzel, the experimental narratological turning point in *Ulysses* comes in "Wandering Rocks," the chapter in which Joyce introduces *segmentation* as a structuring principle. By dispensing with the beginnings and ends of the narrated sections, Joyce's mode of presentation in these chapters eliminates all authorial interpretation and commentary. But Stanzel notes that even though the different scenes of "Wandering Rocks" are strung together without commentary or transition, they nonetheless contrast with one another—and it is their contrast that gives rise to varied interpretive effects. As Stanzel elegantly puts it: "Authorial commentary is replaced by a process of rearrangement in which the fictional material interprets itself. The author's personal intrusion, which always takes place by narration—that is, by the words and voice of the authorial narrator—is now abstracted, depersonalized; it attains visible form in the geometry of the novel's structure" (125). Stanzel traces this experimentation into the later chapters, for example, "Sirens," where he sees "the mimesis of reality" moved "away from the words' meanings and into the body of the word itself, into the sound and sight pattern of the language" (127).

Stanzel's validation of Joyce's experimental techniques of the later chapters of *Ulysses* effectively reversed their disparagement in *The Classical Temper*, S. L. Goldberg's influential 1961 study of *Ulysses*. But both before and after Stanzel, American critics were also developing similar mechanisms for addressing the problematic narrative disjunctions in the second half of the book. Appearing just before Stanzel's English translation, David Hayman's 1970 *"Ulysses": The Mechanics of Meaning* also tracked the shifts of style in the novel and connected them to a specific narrational function. He gave this function a name—although so unobtrusively that it is not even listed in the book's index. He called it the *arranger*. Hayman describes this narrative device as an "invisible yet consistently identifiable speaker" who "[plays] on our need to naturalize and explain the strange and elusive" yet "[asserts] his independence, his freedom from the rules he himself has established." The arranger is construed as something like a transcendent multitasking narrative activity. "By the book's second half he will have become a creature of many faces but a single impulse, a larger version of his characters with a larger field of vision and many more perceptions to control, the figure I am calling the arranger" (78).

This *arranger* became popularized some years later by Hugh Kenner, who adopted Hayman's term even as he proceeded to depersonify this unusual "consciousness," which he considers "the most radical, most disconcerting innovation in all of *Ulysses*":

It is something new in fiction. It is not the voice of the storyteller: not a voice at all, since it does not address us, does not even speak. We do not hear its accents, we observe its actions, which are performed with a certain indifference to our presence.... For the tale of Bloomsday is not in the old sense, nor in any sense, "told": it is mimed in words arranged on pages in space. (1980, 64–65)

By the time Hugh Kenner published his revised edition of *Ulysses* in 1987, French structuralism, with its possibilities for conceptualizing narration as a depersonalized process, had already become firmly established as a force in literary criticism, and narratology as a theoretical field had flourished.

One of the first full-length critical studies of *Ulysses* using some early narratology was published two years after Stanzel's translation. Erwin R. Steinberg's 1973 *The Stream of Consciousness and Beyond in "Ulysses"* explores just one aspect of Joyce's narrative technique by offering a highly specialized analysis of the use of stream of consciousness in the novel, with particular attention to its psychological aspects. Steinberg carefully distinguishes *stream of consciousness* from silent soliloquy or interior monologue (as in "Penelope"), *spoken* monologue or soliloquy (as in "Cyclops") and *erlebte Rede*, or *narrated* monologue, a technique narratologist Dorrit Cohn finds chiefly in Joyce's *A Portrait of the Artist as a Young Man*. But Steinberg's most interesting analysis concerns the role of what he calls a "prespeech level" of thought in stream-of-consciousness narration, which he finds predominantly in "Proteus" and "Lestrygonians." It is this "prespeech" level that makes stream of consciousness "difficult, if not impossible, to read; for it would be a mass of psychological images, sensations, and perceptions which would provide little or no orientation or method of organization for the reader" (253). Consequently, even in "Proteus" and "Lestrygonians," two chapters in which the action consists largely of the thinking process of the characters, the stream of consciousness is *simulated* rather than pure, he argues. Steinberg's analysis of *Ulysses* achieves much of its technical sophistication by appeal to the field of cognitive psychology.

This choice of theoretical influence is particularly striking in light of the short-lived prominence of psychoanalytic theory, both Freudian and Jungian, in literary study in the 1960s and early 1970s.[1] But psychoanalytic theory, with its heavy emphasis on the psychically mediated interpretive consciousness of the reader, made little appeal to the function of narration and narrative as a determinant of reader response. Such approaches as Norman Holland's were soon eclipsed by the more phenomenological direction of the Konstanz scholars of aesthetic reception, and Wolfgang Iser's 1974 study *The Implied Reader* included an important analysis of *Ulysses*. Iser draws on an eclectic range of scholarship in this study, including the work of the phenomenological philosopher Roman Ingarden. Iser's later theoretical work, his 1978 *The Act of Reading*, also draws on speech-act theory, with its emphasis on the effects of communication. In the case of *Ulysses*, Iser is particularly interested in the text's foregrounding of its own narrativity as its salient phenomenon. He writes of the text's abrupt narrative alternations:

> In the middle of a third-person narrative we are suddenly confronted with statements in the first-person, which strike the reader so forcibly that he soon becomes more conscious of narrative patterns than of things narrated. And so here, as elsewhere in the novel, one gets the impression that one must constantly differentiate between the linguistic possibilities of style and the possible nature of the phenomena concerned. (*The Implied Reader* 205)

The direction of both Stanzel and Iser in treating the segmentation, disjunction, and discontinuity of narrative in *Ulysses* as a major development in the modern novel swept aside the criticism promoted by Goldberg—that Joyce's more radical narrative experiments produced a self-indulgent and sterile artifice. Stanzel and Iser cleared the way for recognizing the novel's self-reflexive attention to its narrative innovations as a sign of its postmodernity, its veering from fiction into metafiction.

Three of the major narratological approaches to *Ulysses* in the 1980s—the critical studies of Karen Lawrence, John Paul Riquelme, and Michael Patrick Gillespie—continued the project of celebrating the novel's narrative play. Their books treat its narrative complexity as "radical stylistic and modal changes" (Lawrence), "oscillating perspectives" (Riquelme), and signs of a "hermeneutical circle" and paradigm shifts (Gillespie) that produce, in their view, the highly dynamic interpretive challenges of *Ulysses*. Although Karen Lawrence is chiefly concerned with narrative expressivity in her 1981 *The Odyssey of Style in "Ulysses,"* her strategy actually points to the nature of narrative when she "narrativizes" the stylistic experiments in the novel. By focusing on stylistic *change* throughout the work, she uses this crucial element of *story* to tell her own *story* of the vicissitudes of style as the "odyssey of style in *Ulysses*," as she calls it. The result is her analysis of how the work's "radical stylistic and modal changes" (5) transform the work from a novel about characters into a novel about novel writing. Lawrence writes:

> One can describe Ulysses as a book that changes its mind as it progresses and forces a corresponding change of mind in the reader. The segmented quality of Ulysses—the discontinuity of the narrative as it dons various stylistic 'masks'—can be treated as successive breaks in "narrative contracts" and successive rhetorical experiments rather than segments in a spatial whole. (6)

Lawrence proceeds by discussing how the narrative norms established in the first part of *Ulysses* give way to a "series of aesthetic experiments" in the second half of the work. "It is as if Joyce had asked himself, 'What if I write everything in two styles?' ("Cyclops"); 'What if I write only in clichés?' ("Eumaeus"); 'What if I imitate music in language?' ("Sirens"). Part way through *Ulysses* we witness the breakdown of the novel as a form and the creation of an encyclopedia of narrative choices" (10).

True to its title, *The Odyssey of Style in "Ulysses"* treats narrative and narrative techniques in the context of that aesthetic disposition of language we call "style." The study consequently makes little direct appeal to narratology as a theory, and does not generally use narratological concepts as analytical instruments or tools. But Lawrence's approach nonetheless reflects a solid grounding in theories of narrative discourse that had been developing between the 1950s and the 1970s, spearheaded by such figures as Wayne Booth, Gérard Genette, Seymour Chatman, and Dorrit Cohn. The deeper background supplied by Russian formalism (Roman Jakobson) and structuralist and poststructuralist theory (Roland Barthes, Derrida, Lévi-Strauss, Todorov, Foucault) is also evident in occasional citations, and shapes the sophistication of Lawrence's analysis without drawing particular attention to its theoretical erudition.

John Paul Riquelme's *Teller and Tale in Joyce's Fiction* appeared in 1983, not long after Karen Lawrence's book. Dealing with the range of the Joycean oeuvre, this study is broader in scope but more specific in its focus on narration and narrative. Although Riquelme disputes some of Lawrence's formulations of Joyce's narrative shifts and experiments, he too points to "oscillating perspectives," as his subtitle makes clear, and finds "the story of writing" "inscribed implicitly throughout *Ulysses*" (226). His strategy for exploring

Joyce's narrative experiments is finally heuristic—eschewing theory, per se, in favor of a series of illuminating metaphors for narrative function. The most original of these is his discussion of the Möbius strip as a figure illustrating the effects of repetitions, variations, and transformations in the narrative of *Finnegans Wake* (25–28). For *Ulysses*, Riquelme points to homelier tropes, "the pattern in the carpet" or "the spectrum of a coat of many colors" (133) to suggests the complexity of the "polytropes" in which Joyce's novel is written. He also borrows some of his narrative metaphors from *Ulysses* itself, including the cracked looking glass (137), and takes others from mythology, such as the descent into the underworld. Still others are borrowed from other critics, such as Hugh Kenner's metaphor of splicing (139)—especially effective for indicating some of the dramatic shifts in "Circe." And to describe the narration of "Penelope," Riquelme invokes Roland Barthes' concept of "the grain of the voice." "In that special singing, we hear the physical, fleshly apparatus at work as part of the performance and not covered over. . . . our reading is listening in which we hear our own interior speech as writing" (228).

Between the narratological treatments of *Ulysses* published in the early 1980s and those of the late 1980s, a 1986 essay by Monika Fludernik appeared in the *Journal of Narrative Technique* that offers a highly focused, technically sophisticated revisitation of "Narrative and Its Development in *Ulysses*." Fludernik is herself a theorist of narrative trained by Franz Stanzel, and she uses his analysis of mediation to dispute earlier notions of an "initial style" and of radical narrative changes and ruptures that culminated in the characterization of a "first half/second half dichotomy" in the book (16). Her application of Stanzel's notions of mediation allows her to analyze the narrative changes in the later chapters of the novel as produced by progressive "distanciations" that are already introduced and prepared in the earlier chapters. "I have tried to show that there is more continuity in the development of the narrative than is generally conceded," Fludernik concludes (35).

Fludernik attends chiefly to narrative "telling" without attention to effects on the reader—a problem to which Michael Patrick Gillespie returns in his 1989 *Reading the Book of Himself: Narrative Strategies in the Works of James Joyce*. Like Lawrence and Riquelme, Gillespie argues that the text's multiplitude of perspectives and the disjunctions and inconsistencies are "essential components" of its structure. Mikhail Bakhtin's concepts of heteroglossia and polyphonic discourse therefore serve as particularly valuable inspirations for Gillespie's approach to the experimentalism of *Ulysses*. But

Gillespie shifts to the reader responsibility for "reconciling [the text's] multitude of voices by amplifying or muting elements of the discourse in an effort to achieve a balanced impression of the aesthetic experience" (155). Gillespie's figure for this reconciliation process is the hermeneutical circle:

> The fluctuations present a paradox analogous to the image of the hermeneutical circle—the whole receives its definition from the parts, and reciprocally, the parts can only be understood in reference to the whole. Ulysses, however, expands the implications of this trope. Although the perspective that forges the circle creates a provisional interpretation upon which all of the elements are centered, the elements themselves undermine the authority of a single point of view. Irreconcilable antinomies continually call for a recentering and continually question the legitimacy of any reordering. (155–56)

Gillespie finds in "Aeolus," particularly, a shift toward what he calls the "postmodern paradigm" with its metafictional emphasis.

Two other studies that included Joyce among a range of other writers appeared in the late 1980s and 1990s. Derek Attridge's 1988 *Peculiar Language: Literature as Difference from the Renaissance to James Joyce* deserves mention because its theoretical focus is grounded precisely in the work of the linguists whose early contributions laid the foundations of modern narratology.[2] But although Attridge quite deliberately invokes the theories of Roman Jakobson in approaching the language of the novel, his attention is directed chiefly to its poetic qualities and effects rather than to its narrative challenges.

Richard Pearce's 1991 *The Politics of Narration: James Joyce, William Faulkner, and Virginia Woolf* appeals mainly to the work of Mikhail Bakhtin and Julia Kristeva to support its critical aims in approaching the three experimental novelists of its title. Pearce announces his project: "I will show how the authorial voice employs traditional conventions to make power relations seem natural, speaks through other narrative voices, co-opts or lends its authority to voices that would seem to challenge it. I will also show how the authorial voice is challenged, disrupted, and subverted by rebellious voices" (18). In discussing Joyce, he makes a particularly interesting appeal to what he calls the "body-text" in the work:

> Countering the authorial voice is the voice of the body-text, functioning like voice in speech as it modifies, contradicts, or adds meaning that

goes beyond the meaning of the words. In so doing it leads us to regard the printed text itself as a source of signification. The voice of the body-text makes itself felt rather than heard by intruding the materiality, or physicality, of the print and in shaping "an epic of the human body." (60)

Pearce's work anticipates the particular attention paid to voice and orality in the most important narratological study of the Joycean text to appear at the turn of the millennium: Willi Erzgräber's *James Joyce: Oral and Written Discourse as Mirrored in Experimental Narrative Art*, published in an English translation in 2002.[3] Erzgräber cites the work of Bakhtin as a major inspiration. But he also draws specifically on new research on the relationship between oral and written discourse grounded in an article by Peter Koch and Wulf Oesterreicher with the long title "Language of Immediacy and Language of Distance: Orality and Literacy in the Area of Tension between Linguistic Theory and History of Language" (11). Although this ambitious study addresses the major works of the Joycean oeuvre, it nonetheless contains detailed discussion of narration and dialogue in every chapter of *Ulysses*. Erzgräber comes to the following conclusion about Joyce's management of the tension between the oral and the written in his works: "Joyce does not give preference to either oral or written discourse. . . . Joyce defends neither a phonocentric nor a logocentric concept of language" (395).

What will be the direction of narratology in the future? More specifically, what can narratology contribute to the study of Joyce's *Ulysses* in the future?[4] Gerald Prince published an essay in the 1990 *French Literature Series: Narratology and Narrative* titled "On Narratology (Past, Present, Future)," in which he suggests some future directions for the theoretical field. Several of these may offer particularly interesting new approaches to *Ulysses*. For example, Prince identifies the chief difference between narratology's origins and its modern direction in the late twentieth century as "pragmatics"—the address to such contextual factors of narration as gender and positionality. Susan Sniader Lanser and Robyn Warhol are cited as pioneers of feminist narratology, and perhaps their work could offer new inroads into the relation of narration and gender in *Ulysses*. Ross Chambers's work on narrative "oppositionality"—which was used to excellent effect in Tanja Vesala-Varttala's work on *Dubliners*—could possibly also serve study of the *Ulysses* narrative.

Monika Fludernik has recently explored "The Genderization of Narrative" in a group of late twentieth-century texts; given her long-standing work on Joyce, she would be superbly qualified to explore narrative genderization in *Ulysses* as well. Is gender in the narrative of *Ulysses* a cut-and-dried matter—with all narration identifiable with a masculine voice or a masculine persona with the exception of the Gerty MacDowell section of "Nausikaa" and Molly Bloom's soliloquy in "Penelope"? The answer may be *no*—if gender is construed as a position in the symbolic order rather than as an essential character. Joyce's critiques of masculinism in such chapters as "Cyclops," for example, could be localized in certain habits of narration and storytelling—such as authoritativeness and belittlement—that may be more complicated than they appear. Conversely, Bloom's and Molly's discourses could betray oscillating genderizations with respect to how they are positioned by others, and how their own discourses allow them to position themselves in relation to persons and institutions to which they either grant or deny respect. Of course, it is "Circe," with its gender-bending transmutations, which would challenge us most acutely to determine precisely how habits of reportage, expression, and rhetorical aim are linked to gender in a nonrealistic genre.

Another area of future narratological investigation noted by Prince that could be adapted to future *Ulysses* criticism concerns the study of narrative domains and narrative worlds. "Many narratologists now consider that a story can be characterized as a universe consisting of one or more worlds," he writes (7). These include "actual worlds" (which "may or may not be similar to our own 'real' worlds"), "relative worlds" (idealized models of worlds, for example), "epistemic or knowledge worlds" (what characters know or believe), "wish-worlds," "moral worlds" (what characters consider good or bad), "obligation worlds" (specifying group values), and "alternate worlds" (creations of the mind, such as dreams, fantasies, hallucinations, fictions). Narratology could thus provide tools for exploring the relations between the worlds that intersect in a given story as properties of internalized narrative genres.

One could argue that such work has already been done—for example, on the effect of Gerty MacDowell's appropriations of the "feminine" genres of romance novels and advertisement on the narration that describes her. But criticism of this kind has been inflected chiefly by a literary vocabulary and by psychoanalytic (Lacan) and metaphysical (Girard) theories of the relationship of self and world. Prince's model may provide a far more flexible schema for exploring narrations in *Ulysses* that are *not* imitative or parodic. For example, what could be learned by analyzing the relationship between "actual worlds" and "relative worlds" in Bloom's psycho-narrations? What does it mean for a single individual to live in a social world whose corruptions, abuses, and hypocrisies are clearly visible to him while he continually imagines utopian alternatives? How does one distinguish the humane and humanitarian scenarios Bloom produces from the sadomasochistic fantasies that coexist with them in his thoughts? Do these worlds coexist in the same narrating mind as separate spheres governed by different laws? Looking at the registers of multiple worlds in the varieties of narration in *Ulysses*—external, focalized, interior, and so on—could greatly expand our understanding of the relationship between narration and its experiential limitations and possibilities.

Another suggestion by Gerald Prince for future narratological study lies in the area of *tellability*. He cites Marie-Laure Ryan's plot model that "predicts that tellability is a function of unrealized strings of events (unsuccessful actions, broken promises, crushed hopes, etc.), that it increases as the narrative goes back and forth between the competing plans of [different] characters" (10). It would be intriguing to consider how significantly such factors serve as motors for both plot and its tellability in *Ulysses*. For example, what effects do Stephen's failure to pray at his mother's bedside, and Bloom's failure to produce a son, have on the telling of their story in *Ulysses*?

Prince gives the problem of *tellability* a further complication by aiming its focus specifically on what he calls "the disnarrated: all those terms, phrases, and passages in a narrative that refer to what *does not* take place" (10). Would Stephen's ruminations on history in "Nestor" fall into the category of the *disnarrated*? "Had Pyrrhus not fallen by a beldam's hand in Argos or Julius Caesar not been knifed to death. They are not to be thought away. Time has branded them and fettered they are lodged in the room of the infinite possibilities they have ousted. But can those have been possible seeing that they never were? Or was that only possible which came to pass?" (*U*, 2.48). More significantly, to what extent does the failure of Charles Stewart Parnell to achieve Home Rule for Ireland haunt the figures and turn countless of their stories into species of ghost stories? One could argue that all of *Ulysses* may be seen as a narration that creates itself out of a *disnarration*—out of a world of narrative possibilities that were foreclosed for one reason or another and never occurred. What if Ireland had not become priest-ridden or had remained independent of Britain? Could Joyce have written *Ulysses* as he did, or would *Ulysses*, in that case, have become *untellable*? Clearly Prince's notion of the *disnarrated* could prove a provocative concept for exploring *Ulysses*.

In addition to these intriguing possibilities suggested by Gerald Prince for the future of narratology, I would like to propose my own list of interpretive questions and challenges in *Ulysses* that may be fruitfully addressed with the concepts and tools of narratology. The question of *plot* in relation to narration strikes me as a particularly neglected aspect of the novel whose complications come into clearest focus by imagining an artificial model of a first-time, or "virgin," reading of *Ulysses*. A reconstruction of a virgin reading—that is, a linear reading from beginning to end limited to the knowledge incrementally unfolded by the narration(s)—foregrounds such aspects of the narration in relation to temporality as suspense, secrets, repression, surprise, advance, delay, illumination, and indeterminacy. Unlike classical retrospective narrative, which tells of events in the past, a salient feature of narration and plot in *Ulysses* is that the novel for the most part tells of events simultaneous with their occurrence. In other words, *erzählte Zeit* (story time) and *Erzählzeit* (narrative time) generally overlap in *Ulysses*—as they do in cinematic narrative. Uri Margolin explains some of the effects this produces:

> In simultaneous narration, factivity is inevitably reduced. While punctual, momentary actions and events can be reported with certainty, long-range, multi-staged ones, as well as most cause and effect relations, remain within the realm of mere possibility, since they have not yet reached their completion at the moment of utterance. Their outcomes are still undecided, and they may or may not succeed, be accomplished or achieve their goals. (52)

In *Ulysses*, the simultaneous narration produces a singular suspense in the course of a virgin reading. The reader remains uncertain until the last chapter whether or not Molly Bloom's assignation with Blazes Boylan will indeed culminate in adultery. How this information is delayed in the presence of a frequently seemingly omniscient narrator is itself an interesting narratological conundrum that obliges us to explore not only the manipulation of focalization in the text but also its interpretive significance.

The function of narration in producing, preserving, and betraying secrets not only *of* the characters and from the characters but also *from* the reader is itself worthy of investigation not only for *how* it is done but also for *why*. The focalization of the narration on Bloom in "Calypso," for example, reveals that Molly Bloom's letter from Boylan contains a secret that Bloom suspects but to which he has no direct access. But the same focalization also shows Bloom hiding a slip of paper in his hatband without revealing its meaning to the reader. "He peeped quickly inside the leather headband. White slip of paper. Quite safe" (*U*, 4.70), the narration tells us, but without explaining what the card says, what it is doing in the hatband, and from what it is quite safe. Since third-person narrators are generally considered immune from unreliability ("We cannot question the reliability of third-person narrators, who posit beyond doubt or credulity the characters and situations they create" [W. Martin 142]), we need an alternative formulation for the kind of selective narrative disclosure we receive in "Calypso."

One useful model for measuring narrative transgressions or irregularities in *Ulysses* may be offered in the work of Paul Grice, whose essays from the 1960s through the 1980s were collected in a 1989 volume titled *Studies in the Way of Words*. Grice is a philosopher of language whose special focus is the logic of ordinary language, and particularly, that of conversation—a language activity whose tacit contractual character he formulates as a series of maxims. He begins with the overarching maxim that he calls the "Cooperative Principle": "Make your conversational contribution such as is required, at the stage at which it occurs, by the accepted purpose or direction of the talk exchange in which you are engaged" (26). The Cooperative Principle entails rules governing quantity, quality, relation, and manner of talk in conversation. The first maxim of quantity requires that speakers make their contribution "as informative as is required (for the current purposes of the exchange)" (26). The parenthetical qualification may hold a possible clue to what the "Calypso" narrator is doing when he refuses to tell us why Bloom hides a slip of paper in his hatband. The information about the card in the hatband is not needed until "Lotus Eaters," when Bloom uses it to collect his letter from Martha Clifford. The narrator therefore defers its disclosure until then, while giving us the information more urgently useful in "Calypso"— that Molly is not the only Concealer in the Bloom household, and that the husband too has secrets from his wife.

However, "Calypso" elsewhere violates Grice's first maxim of quantity: "Make your contribution as informative as is required (for the current purposes of the exchange)." The narrator neither tells us nor shows us in this first introduction of Leopold Bloom that he is a Jew. This information, however, is required if we are to understand a curious moment in the shop of Dlugacz, the pork butcher, when the two men, alone in the shop, transact a peculiar ocular exchange. "A speck of eager fire from foxeyes thanked him. He withdrew his gaze after an instant. No: better not: another time" (*U*, 4.186). Because we know nothing yet of Bloom's Jewishness, we lack the context required to make sense of this scene, which we subsequently interpret retrospectively as an overture by two Jews to breach their ethnic closet. But without this context the reader is caught in a situation to which Grice has given the name of *implicature*. The imaginary conversation Grice uses to illustrate implicature begins with A asking B how C is getting on with his job in the bank, and receiving the answer, "*Oh quite well, I think; he likes his colleagues and he hasn't been to prison yet*" (24). Grice writes, "At this point, A might well inquire what B was implying, what he was suggesting, or even what he meant by saying that C had not yet been to prison" (24). This example of implicature draws our attention to the ability of some utterances to say something in a way that suggests meanings beyond what is actually said in the words.

The unspoken but implied meaning becomes available to the interlocutor by way of a shared context that gives a sense to the implied matter or *implicatum*, as Grice calls it. The consequence of lacking the context in the example of the ocular exchange between Bloom and Dlugacz is that the reader is obliged to make a risky and possibly self-incriminating inference—perhaps that the exchange signals an overture to breach a different kind of closet, possibly a homosexual closet. Once identified and analyzed, Grice's implicature is seen to play significant roles throughout *Ulysses*. For example, the whole "Throwaway" incident becomes enmeshed in implicature—beginning with a hidden context, the Gold Cup race, that causes Bloom's innocent offer of the paper to be construed as an implied tip on the dark horse. The consequence of Bantam Lyons's erroneous inference is carried forward throughout the day until it culminates in near disaster in "Cyclops" when another false context triggers the anti-Semitic outburst against Bloom. I suspect that Joyce has implicature play a huge role in the function of prejudice in its various forms in *Ulysses*.

Grice's maxims may be used in coordination with other narratological concepts to help us analyze puzzling features of narration in *Ulysses*. Grice's maxims of quantity—give as much information as necessary for the conversational situation, but do not make your conversation more informative than is required—are clearly violated in "Ithaca," for example. There we are alternately given too much information, as in the famous treatise on the waterworks, and too little—as when the narration withholds Stephen's motive for singing the anti-Semitic ballad of "Little Harry Hughes" to Bloom. These quantity maxims formulate a rule for the phenomenon Gérard Genette terms *paralipsis* (holding back of information that would be logically produced under the type of focalization selected) and *paralepsis* (information in excess of what is called for by the logic of the type selected).

While their combination in "Ithaca" remains puzzling, we have already seen paralipsis combined with paralepsis produce high narrative irony in "Nausicaa." There Gerty's narration dwells endlessly on clothing and cosmetics while eliding information about Gerty's lameness until it is revealed in a dismissive and ostensibly inconsequent aside. Such examples also clarify the border of the domains of the narratologist and the critic.

Even though narratology describes, catalogues, and integrates narrative and narrational features into communicative systems whose rules can then be determined and articulated, it leaves to literary critics the explanations for authorial selection and practice and its consequence for the reader. Grice's maxims identify and illuminate such conversational violations as irrelevance, prolixity, and ambiguity that can help analyze the increasing narrative excesses and other deviations of the later *Ulysses* chapters. The violations of the overarching Cooperative Principle of conversation clearly apply also to the compacts between narrators and readers. But while these rules of the logic of conversation and narration can help the critic analyze more systematically *how* they are violated in Joyce's experimental storytelling, the critic must supply the *why* or motive for his narrative transgressions. The function of narratology as an instrument of knowledge or a tool for application remains a vexed question even among its foremost theorists.[5] But I believe nonetheless that narratology still has much to contribute to the arsenal of theories, methods, and approaches that can help the critic illuminate the treasure trove of human understanding in the discourses that make up Joyce's *Ulysses*.

Notes

1. Norman Holland's early theoretical model of reader response, *The Dynamics of Literary Response*, appearing in 1968, drew heavily on Freudian theory and its corresponding therapeutic model for conceptualizing the reading experience.

2. Attridge's book contains two chapters on *Ulysses* that announce their linguistic focus in their titles: "Literature as Imitation: Jakobson, Joyce, and the Art of Onomatopoeia" (127–57), and "Literature as Deviation: Syntax, Style, and the Body in *Ulysses*" (158–87).

3. Amy Cole's translation of this text is extremely lucid and readable. See also Sylvia Beeretz's engaging (but nontheoretical study) "'Tell us in Plain Words': Narrative Strategies in *Ulysses*," published by Peter Lang in 1998.

4. A 1999 GRAAT volume called *Recent Trends in Narratological Research* suggests several possibilities that might be useful for exploring *Ulysses*—including new considerations of unreliable narration; order and narrative; dimensions of space in narrative; and parody.

5. Mieke Bal's "Afterword: Theses on the Use of Narratology for Cultural Analysis" comments on this question by noting, "Although it is common usage to talk about concepts as 'tools' for analysis, understanding is not an operation that can be instrumentally performed" (221).

II

PERSPECTIVES OF THE READERS

3

Joyce and the Invention of Language

SHELDON BRIVIC

As Stephen Dedalus launches into his Shakespeare theory in *Ulysses*, he thinks to himself, "Folly. Persist" (*U*, 9.42). Gifford and Seidman's *"Ulysses" Annotated* does not mention it, but this refers to a line from Blake's *Marriage of Heaven and Hell*, "If the fool would persist in his folly he would become wise" (Erdman 1965, 36), parallel to the nearby proverb "The road of excess leads to the palace of wisdom." The importance of excess in Joyce's work increases steadily from the "scrupulous meanness" of *Dubliners* to the outpouring of *Finnegans Wake*. And it progresses from the short, simple opening chapters of *Ulysses* to the expansive later chapters. Such a development toward excess may also be seen in the works of Jacques Lacan, who began with a relatively contained outlook and moved toward emphasis on excess in a final phase influenced by Joyce to aim at the unaccountable.

The principle of increasing expansion into possibilities beyond calculation may also be traced through the history of *Ulysses* criticism. The earliest studies, such as Stuart Gilbert's *James Joyce's "Ulysses"* (1930), Frank Budgen's *James Joyce and the Making of "Ulysses"* (1934), and Paul Jordan-Smith's *A Key to the "Ulysses" of James Joyce* (1934), tended to be confident that they were giving the true explanation. A major step toward realizing that Joyce's work could not be encompassed by one consistent viewpoint was Arnold Goldman's *The Joyce Paradox: Form and Freedom in His Fiction* (1966). Since then, the best books on *Ulysses* tend to be aware that their views are partial and uncertain. Colin MacCabe's *Joyce and the Revolution of the Word* (1979), influenced by Lacan, see Joyce's works as rejecting the idea of a single dominant language and aiming at continual reinterpretation, so that the Joycean text refuses any narrative father or overall authority (14, 25, 66). Derek Attridge's *Joyce Effects* (2000) calls into question the most central and certain views of Joyce's works—such as the Homeric parallels in Ulysses or the idea that the *Wake* is a dream—seeing these merely as possibilities among a vast number of other perspectives.

The two best books on *Ulysses* in the last five years do not combine consistency with comprehensiveness. Paul Schwaber's *The Cast of Characters* is consistent but not comprehensive. It uses psychoanalysis to focus on sibling rivalry, which is clearly not the central concern of Ulysses, though Schwaber shows that it is more pervasive than one would think. Andrew Gibson's *Joyce's Revenge* sees virtually every page of *Ulysses* as an allegory of resistance to British and Roman Catholic imperialism. Gibson is comprehensive but not consistent. He privileges resistance, but the multiplicity appears in his exhaustive analysis of trends in thinking about social issues in Joyce's time. The subtle interplay of historical forces in *Ulysses* is Joycean because the levels of input cannot be reduced to a clear formulation. Speaking of the "Scylla and Charybdis" episode, for example, Gibson emphasizes Stephen Dedalus's attack on the glorified English bard Shakespeare, but he adds that Stephen's subversion of "bardolatry will not explain the full variety and subtle complexity of the literary practices informing the chapter," practices Gibson calls "irreducibly multiple" (76). Juxtaposing Schwaber's analysis with Gibson's indicates the need to coordinate the psychological and the historicist wings of Joyce criticism, and the idea of excess may serve to do so.

Lacan says, "in what Joyce writes, there's always more," and sees an extension or excess linked to Joke's prose. According to Lacan, "That each chapter of *Ulysses* is given as support a mode of framing, termed for instance 'dialectical,' 'rhetorical' [or] 'theological,' is for him linked to the very materiality of what he narrates" (May 11).[1] Joyce's attachment of every discourse to a further level is central to how Joyce inspires Lacan to a new theory of the *sinthome* in his volume of seminars on Joyce, *Le sinthome*, of 1975–76, which presented a major change of course for Lacan.

The *sinthome*, Joyce's symptom as the saint of man, is represented by Lacan as a splicing of the functions of ordinary language to a further level. Joyce as artificer gives us not life as it is already known, but life supplemented by expertise, life as it could be further known. The splicing of the ordinary to a further level is an artificial attachment that displaces and undercuts the normative structure of perception or subjectivity. This normative structure, for Lacan, involves three registers of language looped together: the Imaginary, the Symbolic, and the Real. To give a loosely approximate idea of what the registers designated by these three terms are like, they may be seen as analogous to the body (Imaginary), language (Symbolic), and surprise (Real). The self-possession of the body, the system of language codes, and the element of surprise operate on three different levels, and cannot be reconciled. Yet it is impossible to be conscious without using all three, and they intertwine their inputs to form our perceptions of reality. In Joyce's writing, however, their attachment to something beyond ordinary discourse dislodges the stability of their connections (Harari 71–104, 202–5).

Each chapter of *Ulysses*, after what Karen Lawrence, in *The Odyssey of Style in "Ulysses"* (60), calls the "initial style" of the early chapters, distorts the idea of neutral discourse by attaching it to further levels, such as journalism and music. Usually there is more than one extra level at a time, so that in "Oxen of the Sun," each sentence may refer to a Homeric parallel, to stages of the development of the fetus, and to the history of English literature.

In relation to the depiction of realistic action, these levels amount to or operate as errors. For example, when the narrative gets infected with music in "Sirens": "Shrill with deep laughter, after bronze, they urged each each to peal after peal, ringing in changes, bronzegold, goldbronze, shrilldeep, to laughter after laughter" (*U*, 11.174–76). These shifts always represent the action on a deeper level, for the reverberation of "laughter" is sustained by "after," and the echoes expand into "each each" and "laughter after laughter." This continues to express the uproarious expansiveness of the scene, for Joyce never gives up on some level of representation. The break in the link between language and what it tries to describe is delineated as a scene of artifice. The chain of echoes that runs through the passage not only expresses feeling in the scene but speaks for the activity of an artisan. This *sinthome* distorts the illusion of objectivity to make representation more real by making it mistaken.

Perceptual mechanisms like these invariably interrupt the surface continuity of the narrative: when one hears the echo of "after," or any "technique" of Joyce's, the forward movement of the story goes astray. Language is subjected to a series of errors to reframe its apparatus. Jean-Michel Rabaté says in *James Joyce and the Politics of Egoism* that the *Wake* consists of nothing but a series of errors (206–7), and *Ulysses* moves in this direction as its extra levels grow more intrusive. One implication is that as we move through our day, errors infiltrate our consciousness more and more. This effect is enhanced because Bloom has an orgasm and Stephen gets drunk, rendering both of them somewhat groggy for the balance of the day. Their experience could not be represented without a massive influx of slippage.

There are also errors the reader makes unceasingly because (s)he is not informed. Gibson, for example, cites a series of Dublin literary controversies that are continually referred to in "Scylla and Charybdis" (61–68). These controversies of 1904 were largely forgotten when *Ulysses* was published eighteen years later—or became legal in America twelve years after that. Perhaps fewer than one hundred readers of *Ulysses* in the twentieth century were aware of these controversies, which were not revealed to Joyce criticism until the twenty-first.

Jacques Derrida said in "Two Words for Joyce" (1984) that Ulysses and the *Wake* far exceeded the greatest complexity of which computers were capable; and this suggests the likelihood that the average reader of *Ulysses* knows less than 10 percent of the information submerged in the book. The more the reader learns, the more (s)he realizes that (s)he is virtually always making several errors at once by embracing a small fraction of what each phrase contains. This is like the psychosexual act of taking a part object for the whole body. It may be as much of a slip as if, meaning to shake someone's hand, you shook his foot.

Lacan says that the slip is the foundation of Freud's notions of the unconscious and of jokes (February 17), and the same seminar locates the *sinthome* as the place where the knot of Real, Symbolic, and Imaginary slips, unsettling perception and subjectivity. The *sinthome*, which Lacan aligns with artifice, builds awareness through distorted ways of seeing. While it may be asked whether there is any way of seeing that is not distorted (or torted), the *sinthome* as a symptom is inherently temporary and tentative. One only has a symptom when a disorder is active, just as one is only musical when music overwhelms one in "Sirens," or hallucinatory when one is intoxicated in Nighttown. The slip is a mental state that ends when it takes place, and every active symptom slips away from normality. It is out of control because it knows enough to know that it doesn't know what it is doing.

Stephen understands creativity as a slip. His first original image appeared on his first page when he displaced the green of the song from the place onto the rose (*P*, 7). Lacan's argument is based on Stephen's Shakespeare discussion. When Stephen says, "A man of genius makes no mistakes. His errors are volitional and are portals of discovery" (*U*, 9.228–29), he implies that through self-attention one can see volition as a slip that reveals the structure of thought as tentative and reparable. Here volition is opposed to rational clarity, which precludes will by dictating one's choice. Volition generally transgresses an established framework, so it is generally sinful, and this is why Stephen keeps insisting that the soul is born in sin (*P*, 103, 172, 203). One implication of original sin for Joyce is originality, inventing the new.

While the *sinthome* is temporary, it stimulates the illusion that it can be passed on as a signifier, which is the basis of phallic authority. Stephen never forgets the green rose, which is uniquely his, and so provides the basis of a sense of mission, a direction of being sent (apostolic): "But you could not have a green rose. But perhaps somewhere in the world you could" (*P*, 12). By forging in the smithy of his soul an Irish consciousness, he will create the consciousness of Ireland based on his individuality or *sinthome*. This is why Ireland can only be important because it belongs to him (*U*, 16.1164–65).

Individuality always consists entirely of the symptomatic abnormality that differentiates one from the nonexistent imaginary abstraction of the norm. The individual eccentricity of the author passes into his work as the neurosis of the father is reproduced in the irrational behavior of his child: "through the ghost of the unquiet father the image of the unliving son looks forth"(*U*, 9.380–81). Bloom feels that the "angry" Simon Dedalus is right to impose himself on his son: "Noisy selfwilled man. Full of his son. He is right. Something to hand on" (*U*, 6.74–75). What the bad enough father has to pass on to his son is his *sinthome*, his symptom as it operates as an artifice by being memorable. So that just as Stephen develops himself only by sin, the artist transmits his *sinthome* only by being mistaken, by creating the new.

The slip is related to what Roberto Harari, in *How James Joyce Made His Name*, sees as a movement from signifying to invention in the late works of Lacan and Joyce. The early Lacan, like Freud or Joyce the realist, thought that words to describe the symptom could capture or really signify it. The late Lacan sees that experience consists of the constant invention of new words. A word never has the same meaning twice, and Joyce aims to represent this realistically in the *Wake*, which approaches an ideal in which every word is new. In his effort to make each word new, Joyce frees himself from the law of the Father, which is the foundation of established language, the basis of the pretense that anything can be equal to anything else. This pretense is always false in actuality, though it may carry authority as an abstraction that allows calculation and control.

Lacan addresses actuality when he says that the Name of the Father can be bypassed, as long as use is made of it (April 13). As Harari indicates, this means that insofar as the author takes on God's power to create by naming things, he need not keep depending on the existing sediment of godhead

(302)—which now appears as something to be parodied, to be departed from insofar as it is coherent, as it pretends to be equal to itself.[2]

In *Joyce the Creator*, I examined how Joyce played the role of God in his works and concluded that he played this role most effectively by multiplying his identity, generating obscurity, and disappearing so that his characters and events would be free of his control (96–102). I now emphasize that Joyce assumes God's role in order to vanish into incomprehensibility. During his religious phase, Stephen realizes that the mysteries of the trinity are easier for him to accept "by reason of their August incomprehensibility than was the simple fact that God loved his soul" (*P*, 149), making it explicit that incomprehensibility is what attracts him most in religion. Such incomprehension is valued because it generates exaltation by surpassing what is knowable. In fact it avoids confronting God the Father by covering him with a screen of unknowing. A similar perplexity is linked by Stephen to the Virgin Mary: "How could a woman be a tower of ivory or a house of gold?" (*P*, 35). Her generative power releases discourse from what can be known, so the questioning metaphors that describe her actually work by being unresolvable, by a symptomatic unease. Stephen's attempts to explain these metaphors by Eileen Vance's physical resemblances to ivory and gold (*P*, 36, 43) are shadowed from the start by drastic inadequacy: the point of the Litany is not that Mary has white skin or blond hair. By being an understanding of something that it does not understand, a metaphor becomes a symptom.

It is by focusing on incomprehensibility that original thinkers have expanded human consciousness into areas formerly occupied by divinities. For example, people used to believe that thunder was caused by the deity, but by investigating the unknown, they discovered scientific causes. Likewise, much of the area formerly occupied by fate can now be understood by analysis. Stephen's vocation is prefigured early in *A Portrait of the Artist as a Young Man* when he meditates: "It was very big to think about everything and everywhere. Only God could do that" (*P*, 16). This leads to the relentlessness with which Joyce expands human consciousness into the unknown: "What was after the universe?" (*P*, 16). Competing with God is a forceful modification of competing with your peers to impress God, a step closer to the source of power. This step begins when one sees a slip or symptom or problem.

In the *Wake*, Shaun says that Shem boasts of the "idioglossary he invented under hicks hyssop" (*FW*, 423.9). This means that he created his own language rather than using the existing ones linked to divine authority. *Hys-*

sop can mean holy water, and "under hicks hyssop" probably means "drunk" (his highship hiccoughs), but it also means "under him himself" rather than under the conventional assumption of God that has generally claimed to validate language. Actually, Shem's claim to invent his own words may only constitute a recognition of what everyone does. Lacan maintains that each person creates his or her own language "to the extent that at each moment one gives it meaning . . . gives the language one speaks a little prod, without which it would not be living" (April 13). *Ulysses* enacts this principle as its discourses constantly exceed reasonable models. There cannot be a neutral style that is not driven by something further. Each person has his or her own frame of reference in the background, which is thoroughly incomprehensible to anyone else.

Even in the first two chapters of *Ulysses*, which appear to be among the most straightforward, the initial style is perturbed by undercurrents and extra levels, in addition to an increasing use of interior monologue. As in *A Portrait of the Artist as a Young Man*, Stephen is generally depicted here in narrated monologue, which may also be called free indirect discourse, and which is presented in the third person by a voice that uses his language and discourse.

It has been observed that this makes it hard to distinguish Stephen's words from those of his author.[3] But Stephen is working on authoring himself, or turning his life into fiction, from the time he records his first three epiphanies at an age around thirteen in the second chapter of *A Portrait of the Artist as a Young Man* (*P*, 67–69). In the epiphanies, people express more than they know, so that Stephen takes on the potential to see more than he could have. Moreover, the epiphanies are arranged as a sequence of three scenes with no transition, each starting with "He was sitting." Stephen's artifice here takes over the narrator's role by installing Stephen's form. Narrated monologue is a step toward stream of consciousness, the protagonist moving toward taking over its telling; and this is carried further when the character as narrator controls the form, which is true of most episodes in *Ulysses*. For example, the rhythm of "Lestrygonians" is the rhythm of Bloom's digestion.

While lecturing on esthetics, Stephen tells Vincent Lynch that the tragic or dramatic emotion faces two ways—toward pity, which unites with the sufferer, and toward terror, united with the secret cause (*P*, 204–5). This may indicate that the narrated monologue in which he appears speaks for both his consciousness and the authorial consciousness he constantly strives to comprehend, most conscious when he is "*reading the book of himself*" (*U*, 9.115). The passages in *A Portrait of the Artist as a Young Man* and *Ulysses* that are ironic about Stephen are never separate from Stephen's consciousness, which is extremely self-critical: his "thinking" consists of "a dusk of doubt and selfmistrust" (*P*, 177). "selfmistrust" combines two opposed points of view in one word.

The idea that Joyce has an ironic attitude toward Stephen needs to be correlated with Stephen's smolderingly ironic attitude toward himself. Lacan says that Stephen is "Joyce as he imagines himself (and who, since he's not a fool, he's not in love with—on the contrary, he need only mention Stephen and he starts giggling)" (December 16). If he were to believe in himself, he would mutilate his subject into the paralyzed state of identity by reducing it to what can be believed in.

In *Ulysses*, Stephen's narrative about himself has grown more radically divided, and he increasingly takes control of it by being written or writing his consciousness more and more brilliantly. An example of how far from himself he can get appears on the third page of "Telemachus": "Pain, that was not yet the pain of love, fretted his heart" (*U*, 1.102). This seems quite external to Stephen's thinking, for it focuses on consciousness he lacks; yet it cannot be extricated from that thinking, which is here preoccupied with brooding on "love's bitter mystery" (*U*, 1.253). Dorrit Cohn sees Stephen's narrated monologue as "suspended on the threshold of verbalization" (103). Stephen's narrator contributes excesses of brilliance and self-criticism, two functions that can never exist without each other. Through them Stephen advances toward telling himself—narrating, calculating, and differentiating an identity that he re-creates continually. Stephen's earliest memory is his father's fairy tale, so from the start the child's discourse is hitched to a tradition from which it needs to awaken through a progressive alienation.

In "Proteus," the third episode, the illusion of neutral discourse is demolished as Stephen's thoughts are overwhelmed by a drive to change language that leads to a new dialect or accent or even language with each paragraph. This discourse is unprecedented in a level of freedom that allows it to shift in any number of directions, enlarging the subject. But Stephen is moving toward such expansion from the opening paragraphs of *A Portrait of the Artist as a Young Man*, where he first changes his father's story about Baby Tuckoo and then changes the song that Simon sings, "Lily Dale," by making the rose green. Each unit of narration consists of Stephen's departing from an established framework, or sinning, and this remains true for Stephen in *Ulysses*.

The sinful effort to break the frame casts the subject into the Imaginary, a realm of physical feelings. By this shift, he loses the cohesion formed through the Symbolic realm of language; so the moment of artistic realization disintegrates Stephen's unified subject in order to realize the work. He enters the work of which his life is increasingly a creation as he values his experiences more esthetically, living in his imagination.

Stephen tells Lynch that the artist disappears into his work in the dramatic phase: "The personality of the artist passes into the narration itself" (*P*, 215). The process of Stephen's disappearance into *Ulysses* begins at the end of "Proteus" and leads to a series of climaxes: the end of "Scylla and Charybdis," the last episode that takes place in Stephen's mind; the end of "Circe," which leaves him groggy; and the middle of "Ithaca," in which he departs from the novel (*U*, 17.1231). Stephen's progressive withdrawal is a departure into the text insofar as he gains the potential to write the novel. This withdrawal is accompanied by a process in which Bloom is possessed by Stephen's mind as Bloom's life is more and more dominated by its technical extensions. Through this process the artist that Stephen will become, the one that creates the work, is esthetically realized in the text as a combination of Stephen, Bloom, and Molly.

Bloom has hardly any idea of the esthetic and linguistic bases of the techniques that increasingly shape and critique his consciousness, but these techniques bear the signatures of Stephen's mind. After Bloom enters Stephen's world by joining the medical students in "Oxen of the Son" and then going to Nighttown, Bloom's consciousness becomes wildly distorted by avant-garde constructions. In "Oxen," the history of English prose style—which Stephen is (or will be?) absorbed in—shapes and voices Bloom's thoughts. In "Circe," the sexual perversions that Stephen has cultivated and theorized about blossom as extensions of Bloom's subjection to cultural dominance. Finally Bloom's own discourse is revealed as fatuous in "Eumaeus," after which it appears only in the form of an abstract catechism in "Ithaca." What could be more Dedalian? It speaks for the son who lives in art; and it suggests that Bloom is infected by Stephen's symptomatic self-criticism.

Stephen, who is described in his own terms in "Ithaca" as "moving from the known to the unknown" (*U*, 17.1013) is attached to a principle of incomprehensibility that demolishes established reality, the "ruin of all space" (*U*, 2.9). This incomprehensibility may be the most fascinating feature of Joyce's work, and Joyce expends great mental energy in generating it. The strongest form in which his investment in his work can appear is as incomprehensibility, the difference between intentions.

Bloom is summed up in terms of which he has no direct comprehension as proceeding "from the unknown to the known" (*U*, 17.1019–20). In attaching himself to extra levels, he seeks stability, while Stephen seeks incoherence. But just as Bloom's marriage to Molly leads him to disturbance, so his efforts to find reassurance in such ideological systems as science and commerce end up spurring him toward the need for disorder made manifest by his following Stephen. The extra level of discourse always breaks up coherence, but Stephen, who is caught in rationality, welcomes this breakup; while Bloom the outsider tries to avoid incoherence because he's caught in it.

Stephen gives Bloom coherence because Stephen serves Bloom as an ideal. Bloom follows Stephen because Bloom's narrative is dominated by the specter of Boylan, for whom Bloom is continually sacrificing himself to give Molly freedom. By following Stephen, Bloom develops his sensitive side in order to bear his cuckoldry and to provide Molly, as he does, with his alternative fantasy, a fantasy the Blooms can share more easily than they can share Boylan. To do this Bloom, as a follower of Stephen, makes Stephen his master, as a son tends to be the master of his father.

The fact that each technical innovation is a series of slips is made especially clear in "Eumaeus," the chapter in which Stephen and Bloom undertake (or possibly bury) communication. "Eumaeus" is made up of a series of errors that express the exhausted disorientation of the pair, especially Bloom. These errors ludicrously displace and render arbitrary the normal cognitive apparatus, so that Bloom and Stephen cannot perceive each other in ordinary terms, but this may help them to do so in extraordinary terms. Grammatical mistakes suspend the frame of language, so that what is expressed goes beyond the rules. This is one way, perhaps the most fundamental way, that the individual exceeds the law of the father by inventing his own language. Lacan gives credit to Eve for inventing the sin of originality (Nov. 18).

Expanding on narrated monologue in the first paragraph of "Eumaeus," Bloom's voice speaks of Bloom from a distance in the third person: "it occurred to him as highly advisable to get a conveyance of some description which would answer in their then condition, both of them being e.d.ed, particularly Stephen, always assuming that there was such a thing to be found" (*U*, 16.15–18). Bloom, or his narrator—and it seems that he is feeling narrated —makes "assuming that there was such a thing to be found" modify Stephen rather than the cab Bloom seeks. The error brings out one of Bloom's main concerns: he is not sure that there is such a thing as Stephen to be found. His difficulty in believing in Stephen puts Dedalus in a sacrosanct position as the Other toward which language is projected and from which it proceeds. In creating the surreal notion that Stephen can't be found, Bloom is actively artistic—and satirizes himself under Stephen's influence—without realizing it.

Bloom has reason to believe that Stephen is "educated, distingue and . . . far and away the pick of the bunch" (*U*, 16.1477–78). Yet all of the signs of Stephen's drunk, dirty, incoherent, and rude appearance go against the idea of his distinction in Bloom's terms. So Bloom has to assume that "such a thing" as the genius Stephen is to be found despite all the evidence: "though you wouldn't think he had it in him yet you would" (*U*, 16.1478). Stephen is causing him to read an extra level sinthomatically.

It is because Bloom cannot comprehend Stephen that Bloom cannot find "a conveyance of some description which would answer in their then condition," that is, a style suitable for their encounter. He keeps struggling through the chapter to find language that will be intelligent enough for Stephen. The result of his efforts is that, as Lawrence points out, everything he says "misfires" (167). Bloom is already riding a conveyance that answers their state, a discourse hitched to incomprehensibility. By going astray, Bloom invents an idiolect uniquely his that escapes the containment of prefabricated structure by never getting anything right. Bloom feels narrated because he is belaboring his thoughts to be literary for Stephen's sake, and he soon thinks of publishing an account of their meeting (*U*, 16.1230). Though Stephen does not hear it, Bloom thinks that "a conveyance of some description" is an elegant phrase for a cab that would impress Stephen, who would find it grotesquely pretentious. Stephen, as the master that Bloom's language serves, operates as his author. He appears to be the supposed master of the incomprehensible that inspires Bloom to exceed himself.

The usually Bloomian narrative of "Eumaeus" keeps qualifying itself, starting with "Preparatory to anything else," "generally in orthodox Samaritan fashion," "very badly," and "not exactly"—all in the first four lines. This is a parody of the effort to develop a meta-language, a discourse that will avoid error by considering everything; yet all of the qualifications end up increasing errancy since they never quite fit. "Always assuming there was such a thing to be found" is a logical effort to qualify the conveyance sought (cab or discourse) so as to improve the chances of finding it or making it correspond to actuality. Yet this line renders the desired carrier less probable by granting that it is an assumption. Language's mechanisms for specifying can unsettle perception by imposing a strain. The need to coordinate perceptual functions (such as pronoun references) works against the privileged focus of immediacy. Bloom is being too careful, extending care in all directions without keeping track of where his care should be channeled. Yet his errors yield insights.

The lack of coordination here is not (as convention would have it) a distortion of the situation, but the actuality of the situation in which meaning is always already changing. Bloom enacts this readily, but the understanding of it can only come through Stephen, who envisions such change in the radical form of synesthesia: "He could hear, of course, all kinds of words changing color like those crabs about Ringsend" (*U*, 16.1143). This harks back to Stephen's thoughts on the colors of words on the beach in *A Portrait of the Artist as a Young Man* (*P*, 166). The dynamism of language becomes visible through its alienation by the filter of color.

Stephen seems to be completely missing here the logical meaning that Bloom is trying to convey, but Stephen's recognition of what Bloom's language is doing may be more important than Bloom's advice. There is a recognition that cannot be reached without error, the recognition of change. Through the error that reveals change, coherent perception is involved with a farther field that works by not being coherent, by exceeding definition. The dizzy effort to cover every qualification operates through a scattering of errors. They are seeds of creation, though as with most seeds, most of them perish. Their life and death lay the basis for the next stage of questioning, which echoes their deaths in its emptiness.

In the following chapter, "Ithaca," the burden of error is suspended, as is the possible relation of Stephen to Bloom. Perhaps consciousness is always suspended between a question and an answer, but in this case, the two men are asking each other to reply. Every relationship forms in a space of inquiry between people, and all claims to knowledge in Lacan are directed at the Other, the idea of otherness represented by the individual other to whom we speak.

Harari, summing up the vision Lacan shared with Joyce, says that "instead of doing what we can ourselves, we always first put our faith in a constructed universe, created by God . . . a totality . . . that guarantees the existence of the Other" (125). Humanity has always claimed knowledge and meaning by positing this Other, a divine or linguistic totality in whose context meaning can be clarified. Under the influence of Joyce, Lacan envisions a process of continuous invention that does away with the need for a patriarchal God by doing without determinate knowledge and meaning.

The subject of Stephen and Bloom as question and answer cannot be resolved so as to join the desire to know and the claim of knowledge. Indeed, the vast entirety of human knowledge, from the galaxy to the atom, is evoked when the two men part, evoked mainly in terms of what cannot be known (*U*, 17.989–1157). As Harari argues (73), Joyce's epiphanies always reveal the incomprehensible, and "Ithaca" makes *Ulysses* add up to an enormous epiphany of unknowing.

While it is true that the answers in "Ithaca" address their questions, the main issues, such as the bond between the two men, are not resolved, making the bulk of the scientific facts effectively peripheral. If "Eumaeus" attached its discourse to error, "Ithaca" makes error impossible by answering every question precisely. But the truth that is sought lies in the realm of error, of the *sinthome*, of the makeshift, the jury-rigged. Lacan says that between people, "There is no relation except where there is *sinthome*" (March 16), perhaps because it is a sense of something beyond comprehension that brings the relationship to life.

The mathematical catechism shows the distance of scientific logic from the feelings of the protagonists; yet "Ithaca" also suggests by extending beyond Bloom's knowledge the realm of possibility. That all of these facts and ideas form a factitious universe toward which Bloom's thoughts reach suggests his potential to form a virtually infinite series of terms. When he thinks of his daughter's dreams or of the operation of the stars, he is inspired by the presence of Stephen, who may provide the charge behind the questions, though he does not articulate them.

Stephen stirs Bloom's thoughts of the poet he might have been, and Bloom remembers all of his attempts in this vein. The crucial point at which Bloom had his main opportunity as a poet was when he was asked to write a song for the annual pantomime of Sinbad the Sailor and prevented himself from doing so by indecisions and distractions (*U*, 17.555). After this there is no further reference to his writing poetry. At the end of the chapter, when Bloom falls asleep, he's described as weary because he has traveled with a long series of variations on Sinbad: "Sinbad the Sailor and Tinbad the Tailor and Jinbad the Jailer" (*U*, 17.2122). Gifford mentions that some of these forms actually appeared in Sinbad pantomimes (606). This list suggests that Bloom has traversed the possibilities of language that go beyond what is acceptable or knowable, that he has worked through the field of poetry. Lacan's idea of the *sinthome* helps us to see how Joyce portrays the common man as rich in poetry.

"Ithaca" ends by asking where Bloom's traversal of endless permutations of language has taken him and answering with a black dot. This black dot may be seen as an aperture leading to Molly. Bloom reaches a suspension between possibilities that is represented by Molly insofar as she projects the question of Bloom's validation, a question that is lost in her contradictions. Molly's freedom as a women centers on his and her doubt about her commitment to Bloom. Her strength draws on the extent to which he needs to believe in her feeling for him in order to survive, even her strength in rejecting him.

Virginia Woolf says in *A Room of One's Own* that in order to have confidence in themselves and maintain their identities, men need to see themselves as superior and to see women as inferior mirrors that reflect them twice their size (35). In this sense, Molly's femininity is an attachment to Bloom and to what Weldon Thornton calls the implied author of Ulysses (22–24). But Bloom and this author are both uncertain about their identities as men, and this uncertainty is attached to the ways in which Molly escapes definition and devotion—including her ability to assume the male role by taking a lover, something conventional women were not supposed to do. Her ability to leave him acts as the extra level or *sinthome* that stimulates the relationship. Joyce portrays both her cultural entrapment in the position of woman and the opening through which she can attain freedom.

As a typical feature of Joyce's flaunting of his parodic divinity, he makes every episode of *Ulysses* begin by referring back to the previous one, even when the figures involved in the new episodes have little knowledge of what preceded them. As Molly maps out the operation of her power in her first hundred lines, she says, "A young boy would like me Id confuse him . . . drawing out the thing by the hour question and answer" (*U*, 18.84–88). The thought of Stephen leads her to equate attraction with confusion, and this leads her to refer to the question-and-answer hour of "Ithaca" as the dynamics of desire. She exists for the male subject mainly as the distance between Q. and A., and this is why critics have long recognized that the suspension of doubt that allows her the freedom of self-contradiction is a major goal of the narrative.[4]

The Whitmanesque freedom to contradict oneself blazoned forth by Buck Mulligan in the first episode (*U*, 1.517) is projected here through femininity as a symptomatic attachment. It corresponds to Keats's idea of negative capability, the ability to remain suspended between possibilities without needing resolution.[5] The Q. and A. process of "Ithaca" is negated by the black dot, for the object of desire is the sign that the point of the question is not to be answered. Desire aims to reach the maternal space in which contradictions do not matter. The period is the point of a sentence, but Molly's nonsentence keeps displacing its point.

She characteristically enjoys the feeling of slipping from one connection to another, a movement that she sees as the substance of the nature she affirms: "all sorts of shapes and smells and colors springing up even out of the ditches" (*U*, 18.1562–63). Nature as movement consists of the appearing of unexpected forms in unexpected places. Slavoj Zizek says of the object of desire (Lacan's *objet petit a*) that it can only be reached by aiming at something else, as a by-product (77). Molly's constant displacement of frames constitutes the root of attraction that draws one through the novel in a relentless pursuit of newness.

The advance of her discourse at each moment expresses the tentative nature of the *sinthome* because her phrases are not affixed to a coherent sentence structure that would frame their meaning clearly or solidly; just as her logic, which has not been schooled, does not maintain or even try for determinate lines of causality. Her thoughts do not claim the solid certainty that men have been educated to pretend to. Her final affirmation clarifies her continual state by suspending her between the four men to whom she says yes, Bloom, Mulvey, Blazes Boylan, and Stephen. Her multiplicity as the vital component of Bloom's subject completes the book by maximizing the suspension of the *sinthome*.

Future studies of *Ulysses* may develop insights related to the idea that each person invents her own language, and to how the proliferation of each discourse is made possible by a series of temporary attachments. These attachments continually draw discourse out of the enclosures of normal reality to reveal that normal reality is an abstraction rarely enacted. Language lives in its excess, and this excess is the meeting point of the individual and the social, of psychology and politics. The ways in which the individual exceeds established definitions indicate the faults in the social structure that need to be reformed. The revolutionary increase in consciousness that Joyce aims at centers, as Colin MacCabe demonstrated, on progressive destabilizations of language.

Lacan says, "One thinks against the signifier" (May 11), and the life of the mind in *Ulysses* is a series of transgressions of the established systematic frames of language. Such invention leaves behind the stability of the imaginary first cause, so it does without the authority of God and tradition by taking it on. This excess in the mentality of language is a psychological dynamism that supports revolution in the most fundamental way. It is especially important to emphasize the revolutionary aspect of Joyce at a time when the government of the United States is returning to a theocratic imperialism not unlike the one Joyce rebelled against a century ago, with its heart of darkness made inevitable by its self-righteousness.

Notes

1. From 1975 to 1976, Lacan delivered a series of lectures on Joyce under the title *Le sinthome*. Some of the French texts of these seminars were published in Jacques Aubert's collection *Joyce avec Lacan*, and more appeared in the journal *Ornicar?* I listed sixteen French sources that added up to almost all of the seminars in my introduction to a special issue of *James Joyce Quarterly* that I edited with Ellie Ragland-Sullivan. Recently Luke Thurston was generous enough to give me his translation of *Le sinthome*. Since this is unpublished, I cite references to the dates of the sixteen individual seminars during the 1975–76 academic year. Each seminar tends to be about eight pages long.

2. A. Nicholas Fargnoli noted that God gave Adam the power to name animals (Genesis 2:19–20). In line, however, with Lacan's emphasis on how language creates reality, Harari discounts Adam's naming, arguing that it was originally God who gave things names when he created them: "Thus, when God offers the animals to Adam so that he can name them, He clearly locates him in a position of impotent dependence, masked as some kind of foundational naming. The language of Adam, in sum, is nothing but an occurrence regulated, supervised, and supported by an uncontestable and imperious judge, in a situation of implied examination" (27).

3. Critics who speak of the difficulty of separating the author from the character in narrated monologue, or separating Joyce from Stephen, include Riquelme 2004, 56–60; Brivic, *Veil* 48–51; and Goldman 1966, 95, 97. A statement of the danger of

confusing Stephen with Joyce is made by Wollaeger. Gillespie speaks of Joyce's use of a character's discourse for narration as "free indirect discourse" (1989, 10 16); but Thornton points out that "free indirect discourse" and "narrated monologue" are two terms (French and German) for the same arrangement (62–63). I prefer "narrated monologue" because it seems to me to state more clearly that the narration speaks for the character.

4. Critics who see Molly's uncertainty as the goal of *Ulysses* include Tindall 1959, 36–37; Ellmann 1972, 174; Riquelme 1983, 228; Brivic, *Veil* 128–47.

5. Keats defines negative capability in his letter to George and Thomas Keats of December 21, 1817 (103).

4

En-Gendered Choice and Agency in *Ulysses*

KIMBERLY J. DEVLIN

Part I

Joyce's structural template for *Ulysses*, Homer's *Odyssey*, does not offer a san-
guine message for feminists who ask what its female plotline implies about
choice and agency—the central thematics of Penelope's story. On the one
hand, Penelope appears to have a very clear-cut choice: she can either remar-
ry or continue to wait and hope that her husband is still alive and en route
to Ithaca after a twenty-year absence. Furthermore, with the first option, she
has multiple choices: according to one of the translations Joyce used, the one
by Samuel Butler, the number of suitors courting her is 108 (280)—produc-
ers of contemporary prime-time television would have a heyday with the
scenario ("Penelope Decides"—watch and predict the winner!). But if one
looks deeper at the female plotline of the epic, one notices some disturbing
qualifications of Penelope's apparent agency. According to Athene, Penelope's father will have the ultimate choice, if she opts for remarriage: the goddess informs Telemachus, "if your mother's mind is set on marrying again, let
her go back to her father, who will find her a husband and provide her with
all the marriage gifts that so dear a daughter may expect" (9). Athene also
tells Telemachus that if Odysseus is dead, the son has the right to force the
widow's hand: you can "celebrate his funeral rites with all due pomp, build a
barrow to his memory, and make your mother marry again" (10). Permanent
widowhood is not foregrounded as an option, even though the suitors are
supposedly uniformly boorish. Penelope is surrounded by potentially coer-
cive men, and her agency turns out to be almost nonexistent. She can only
choose not to choose, postponement or deferral emerging as her dominant
female strategy for surviving in a patriarchal culture.

Ulysses will reintroduce the themes of en-gendered choice and agency,
but before I explore them in the second part of my essay, I have been asked
to take a backward glance at Joyce's modernist epic in the context of more

general feminist concerns. A retrospective look at the impact of feminist perspectives of *Ulysses* is difficult for two reasons: first, such interpretations have burgeoned over the years; second, they have merged with other approaches in fruitful yet complex ways. I thus hope to provide in my retrospective discussion not an exhaustive catalogue but instead a summary of several feminist approaches to *Ulysses* that I find intriguing. These approaches produce provocative arguments that I would recommend to students and/or readers of Joyce in general who are interested in the evolution and merging of feminisms within Joyce's text as well as the various ensuing interpretations. For readers who want a more comprehensive retrospective look at the convergence of *Ulysses* and feminist perspectives, study and follow the footnotes in the secondary sources I discuss below: they will take one back to other key discussions of the epic in feminist (or, in some cases, prefeminist) contexts.

Bonnie Kime Scott's *Joyce and Feminism*, published in 1984, was the first major piece of scholarship to place the author and his writing in a gynocentric sphere. The first half of Scott's book examines a series of historical issues that enable the reader to develop a sense of Joyce's feminine and/or feminist contexts, both experiential and literary. One chapter traces the schism inherent in the cultural backdrop of Joyce's development from childhood to maturity. On the one hand, he saw the limited choices available to women living in the late Victorian era—most personally, of course, through his mother and five sisters. On the other hand, he was exposed simultaneously to women taking assertive roles, alongside their male counterparts, through nationalist organizations (such as the Ladies' Land League or the Daughters of Ireland) and the emergent Irish Suffragette Movement. Joyce's most personal contacts with political activism were Francis and Hanna Sheehy-Skeffington (the former becoming McCann in *A Portrait of the Artist as a Young Man*), a couple who were adamant advocates of equal education (primarily through coeducation) in Catholic universities. Scott persuasively argues that if Joyce's early literary education in feminism came from men (in writers such as George Moore, George Bernard Shaw, Gerhart Hauptmann, and Henrik Ibsen), his later experiences emerged from active contact with a set of feminist women (Harriet Shaw Weaver, Sylvia Beach, Adrienne Monnier, and others): Scott elaborately depicts them as the "midwives to his life and works" (107) in their roles as publishers, financial backers, promoters, and literary critics. In between, as John McCourt has demonstrated, are the influential women Joyce met in Trieste, who, as *Giacomo Joyce* shows—forced him "because of their sophistication, education, beauty and sexual ease—to reconsider his rather reductive early visions of the feminine and replace them with the fuller versions of womankind we find in the later fiction" (4–5).

Scott also provides the reader with brief sketches of the important women in Joyce's life (his mother, his aunt, his sisters, his wife, and his daughter), working with unfortunately scant sources. Her discussion of Lucia Joyce raises a key question—and some tentative answers—about a curious choice Joyce's daughter supposedly made, or at minimum, approved of as a parental decision (see 80): namely, the question of why Lucia gave up dance, a crucial creative outlet for her, the abandonment of which left her with a damaging sense of purposelessness. Female choice—and the lack thereof—will emerge as one focus of my later discussion of *Ulysses*. (For a more thorough account of Lucia's interest in and study of dance, see Shloss, particularly chapters 4–7. The complexity of the putative decision to abandon dance is discussed in detail on pp. 160–62 and 180–83. Shloss convincingly argues that there were many contributing causal factors in Lucia's failed dancing career—two of which were parental neglect and indifference to her aspirations. According to Helen Fleischman, Nora's intimidations of Lucia—motivated by jealousy—were a particularly strong deterrent.)

Scott's discussion of Joyce in his feminine and/or feminist contexts is admirable in its even-handed treatment of the author, recording the strains of male condescension and sexism in his writings and conversations, but also noting his unequivocally feminist statements. When Scott turns to interpretations of female characters (specifically Emma, Molly, and Issy) in the later sections of her book, she is similarly judicious. The analysis of Molly Bloom, for instance, explores both her symbolic and realistic dimensions as well as the range in her attitudes—those that come from a conventional matron, others that articulate liberal feminism (162). She notes Molly's insistence on "women's right to sexual freedom" (163) and the important ongoing thematic of her questioning of causality, "the refrain which asks, who made life the way it is for women?" (169). Two questions that Scott's analysis raises center on the accuracy of two assertions: first, her assessment of Molly's singing career ("Molly's lack of accomplishment as a professional . . . seems undeniable from 'Penelope'" [162]), and second, her claim that Molly is "more acted upon than acting" (178). Related to the issue of choice mentioned above, these assertions force us to think more closely about Joyce's representation in *Ulysses* of female agency.

Suzette Henke's *James Joyce and the Politics of Desire* (1990) offers a feminist-psychoanalytic approach to Joyce's works. The discussion of Molly Bloom implies a partial lack of female agency insofar as the female protagonist is examined as a hapless victim of maternal abandonment, an abandonment that has left unconscious psychic scars. For Henke, agency works predominantly through unconscious processes: the loss of Lunita Laredo in infancy and the consequent lack of maternal nurture lead Molly to seek out—in a reaction-formation—a spouse who provides the care and unconditional, nonjudgmental mother-love she has been deprived of as a child. (For a discussion of the ambiguities surrounding Lunita Laredo and Molly's upbringing on Gibraltar, see Herring.) This is a provocative explanation for Molly's strong and perduring affection for Bloom, her infidelity notwithstanding. Henke implies, however, that Molly does have clear and conscious agency in the act of infidelity itself: "Even as Molly celebrates Boylan's stud performance . . . her seduction of such a 'swell' is filled with ulterior motives" (151). The main motive is the excitation of conjugal jealousy through her attractiveness to a rival; a secondary one is Molly's sense that "cuckoldry is precisely 'what [Bloom] wanted'—a masochistic penance expiating marital 'omissions'" (153). In Henke's reading of Molly, a character emerges who is driven alternately by residual childhood trauma and devious intentional manipulations to regain the emotional and sexual attentions of Bloom, "'the strange wild lover' of youthful reverie" (159).

The "Nausikaa" episode of *Ulysses* is another chapter that has received recent feminist reevaluation. Margot Norris, in her book *Joyce's Web* (1992), combines a feminist point of view with cultural critique to examine the secondary myth embedded in Joyce's re-creation of the "Nausikaa" section of the *Odyssey*: the legendary trial of Paris, appropriately referred to as "the prototype for some of the most resistant sexist rituals in our contemporary culture," specifically, of course, the beauty pageant (180). The young women on the beach in Joyce's reenactment of this contest become victims of choice, as they rigorously compete for Bloom-as-Paris's gaze, a gaze that emerges as a biased and distortional lens. Norris effectively demonstrates the ways that "ethno-centrism, social construction, and gender politics" invariably shape and deform aesthetic ideology (177). Her larger project in this chapter of *Joyce's Web* focuses on "Nausikaa" as a critique of art's relationship to social and educational hierarchies, insofar as the classics and myth—and, in particular, an individual's access to them—are based on a system of class inclusions and exclusions: "The Gerty MacDowells and Leopold Blooms of the world have the same cultural and spiritual aspirations that are set forth by high art, and their constraints in pursuing them are produced not by innate limitations (stupidity or indifference) but by historical constraints"—in Gerty's case (like that of Joyce's five sisters), a deprivation of education (168).

Garry Leonard has also discussed "Nausikaa" at length in his groundbreaking work *Advertising and Commodity Culture in Joyce* (1998), where he deploys an admixture of feminist criticism (the arguments of Luce Irigaray and Teresa De Laurentis); psychoanalytic theory (the works of Jacques Lacan); and cultural critique in general. His central feminist concerns focus on mandates to women within patriarchal cultures to commodify and package their femininity according to guidelines provided by advertising, women's magazines, and other popular "textbooks." Paradoxically, these figurative instruction manuals "assure Gerty that femininity is innate, even as they inform her what she has to buy to construct it" (101). Advertisements present products as solutions to what Lacan calls "want-in-being," helping to create the illusion of self-coherence through gender codes. They are also, interestingly, a secular form of religion insofar as they aim to convert, to induce worship (as saints and the Virgin Mary are replaced by commodities), and to promote hope, belief, and trust. Within this system, women ultimately become the equivalent of the mass-produced commodities themselves, marketed for the male consumer, and a certain uniformity in the "winning" masquerade of femininity follows. This cultural framework of consumerism enables Leonard to convincingly reinterpret Gerty's trademark obsession with style: it indicates not simple-mindedness (the easy interpretative conclusion) but instead shrewdness. The impetus of the obsession is not vanity but resilient self-preservation: "Gerty's appearance is her career," the objective of which is to secure at least minimal economic security and to maintain social respectability as someone's wife (115–16). This leads to a very shrewd point on Leonard's behalf about the doubled message of Gerty's cultural primers on "proper" femininity: "The women's magazines that Gerty reads are in fact rather grim economic manuals; the sugary sweet rantings about 'true love' and domestic bliss serve to mitigate the dire warning, contained in some form in every column and every advertisement, that a woman who fails to successfully masquerade as a 'woman' may be forced to submit to public auction in the sexual marketplace"—most obviously and depressingly, as a prostitute or streetwalker (127–28). In its final sections, Leonard's analysis also perceptively exposes the sexist hypocrisy, from a feminist vantage, of the ideological message inherent in the lyrics of "Those Lovely Seaside Girls," one of *Ulysses'* major pop-cultural leitmotifs.

Discussing the gamut of major characters in the novel, Vicki Mahaffey has written a provocative essay entitled "*Ulysses* and the End of Gender" that appears in *A Companion to James Joyce's "Ulysses."* Although the essay is characterized as "A Gender Perspective on *Ulysses*" (151), it contains elements of reader-response criticism, insofar as it discusses common readerly expectations—conditioned or acculturated by earlier reading experiences—about male and female protagonists. Readers approach texts with various notions, which may function only unconsciously, about what constitutes a hero or a heroine. The truth behind this observation can be supported by an occasional response from first-time readers of *Ulysses* (who do *not* necessarily know the ending): after reading "Ithaca" and "Penelope," some students express surprise that Molly actually "did it" with Boylan, or "went through with it," that she unequivocally sexually consummated her flirtation. This surprise may spring from a readerly en-gendered assumption that "proper" heroines should not be promiscuous or disloyal and then remain unpunished. Mahaffey's essay as a whole examines the way that *Ulysses* offers a revaluation of values, particularly as they are inflected by gender. Joyce writes against the grain of tradition, for instance, by offering a young male hero (Stephen Dedalus) who is not valorized as physical (who is cowardly even) and a mature female heroine who is (Molly). The common cultural and literary prescription of physical men and nonphysical women would "seem to preclude any meaningful heterosexual connection" (166). Joyce is also unique, Mahaffey points out, in his refusal to demonize female sexual power as evil or corrupt. Responding to earlier feminist complaints that "Joyce identifies women too completely with 'matter,'" Mahaffey poses some interesting questions:

> Which is the more misogynist stance, the one that celebrates the full experience of female flesh, or the one that censors even the mention of intimate articles of female clothing? In a culture in which thousands of anorectic young women are trying to melt the flesh off their bodies, amenorrheal from the attempt to eat nothing but "violets and roses,"

how can a representation of ample female flesh as something more beautiful than any work of art, something as vital as the earth itself, be considered misogynist?

Mahaffey goes on to argue that Molly emerges, of course, as much more than ample flesh when she finally in "Penelope" speaks for herself—"powerfully, lyrically, sometimes crudely, and without inhibition" (164–65). This essay speaks clearly not only to Joyceans but also to students: as a strong challenge to en-gendered assumptions (which many students will be familiar with), it is recommended reading.

Recent feminist examinations of *Ulysses* have turned to its representations of masculinities: one of the most thorough is found in Tracey Schwarze's *Joyce and the Victorians* (2002), a book that effectively combines feminist concerns with a thoroughgoing historicism, a backward look at the various Victorian discourses woven into Joyce's texts. In a chapter titled "The Discourse of Anxious Masculinity in *Ulysses*," Schwarze analyzes a wide range of male characters in the context of the Anglican minister Charles Kingsley's doctrine of "Christian manliness," Matthew Arnold's *Anarchy and Culture*, and homosexual figures such as Walt Whitman and Oscar Wilde. She persuasively argues that "Bloom's androgynous status as 'the new womanly man' ultimately owes as much to his conflicted position within competing currents of nineteenth-century masculinist discourse as it owes to the psychological emasculation he experiences over the impending infidelity of his wife" (72). The crucial discursive conflict in the second half of the nineteenth century arose between Kingsleyan advocacy of aggressive, stoic, competitive heterosexual virility and late Victorian aestheticism, with its homosocial and homosexual underpinnings. The former's doctrine of "muscular Christianity," directly alluded to in the "Hades" episode, was pitted against the latter's revival of Hellenism, which "attempted to reclaim the male body . . . in the name of beauty and sensuality" (76). This conflicting discursive backdrop enables Schwarze to produce a particularly nuanced reading of some of the en-gendered ambiguities surrounding Leopold Bloom (as well as other male figures). Bloom attempts to reimagine masculinity outside of the Kingsleyan parameters, but he is ultimately unable to avoid their influence in his self-assessments: "that he is a much 'softer' version of manhood than Victorian education aimed to produce causes him great consternation and prompts him to compensatory explanations—a revisionist history of his own masculinity—whenever possible" (79–80). Schwarze is particularly insightful about Bloom's clash with the Citizen in "Cyclops" and the ways the implications of this encounter are anxiously interrogated and revised as the day (and night) of June 16 move on.

Schwarze proceeds to examine the numerous self-subverting attempts throughout *Ulysses* to shore up masculinity, an always-precarious social construct. Blazes Boylan, for instance, emerges as not only the manly sexual stud but also as the exhibitionist Edwardian dandy, perpetually and theatrically on display. Eugene Sandow's exercises (which Bloom reminds himself to take up again) promise a hardened man through a hardened and muscular body; but they aestheticize that selfsame body and also specularize it, that is, transform it into an object to be gazed at (a usually feminine position). The Mulligan who proposed a fertilizing farm with himself as the primary phallic donor is also associated with Oscar Wilde and Hellenism. In "Cyclops," the dual fixations on feminine betrayal and the erection of Irish manhood/nationhood are symptomatic manifestations of a "masculinity attempting to disassociate itself from Ireland's own self-mythologization as a female figure, whether victim or warrior queen" (91). Schwarze, in short, demonstrates the unsuccessful nature of attempts to construct "proper" heterosexual masculinity by separating it from a racialized, feminized, or homosexual Other, external to the male subject: these are defensive political maneuvers (important for students to recognize as such) designed to create at least the illusion of masculine autonomy, but at the expense of denigrated alterity.

Part II

One future project for feminist criticism is to make *Ulysses* even more politically relevant to students by asking them to think about what the novel suggests about agency and choice as these related themes are connected to sex (male/female) and gender (masculine/feminine). Mr. Deasy introduces one such connection when he attributes predominantly female agency to a variety of historical disasters: Eve's introduction of sin into the world, Helen's causing of the Trojan War, a faithless wife and her lover (whom Deasy misidentifies) abetting the first Anglo-Norman invasion of Ireland, and Kitty O'Shea's supposed responsibility for the fall of Parnell (*U*, 2.389–95). Students are usually quick to notice that Mr. Deasy is paranoid in his fears of "intrigues" and "backstairs influence" (*U*, 2.343) and is also patently anti-Semitic: they can usually infer that his theories of historical agency are tinged with other biases. His discussion of negative female agency, which elides almost all male complicity in "sin" (a problematic term in itself), may be aligned with a fear of female power. Stephen later learns in "Aeolus" that Deasy's wife is indeed aggressive—an explanation for the headmaster's status as a grass widower—and infers personal experience as the specific source of the teacher's gynophobia. Theories of agency in "Nestor"—particularly ones that are both grandiose and facile—tell us more about the speaker than about history, and warn us that they should be regarded with a degree of skepticism.

In "Scylla and Charybdis," Stephen proceeds to construct another scenario of female agency in his theories about the relationship between Shakespeare's life and art. More so than Deasy, Stephen foregrounds the sexual dimension of female agency when he proposes that Ann Hathaway actively chose and seduced Shakespeare, and in doing so transgressed against traditional en-gendered positions that align "proper" femininity with passivity and "proper" masculinity with its opposite:

> [Shakespeare] chose badly? He was chosen, it seems to me. If others have their will Ann hath a way. By cock, she was to blame. She put the comether on him, sweet and twenty six. The greyeyed goddess who bends over the boy Adonis, stooping to conquer, as prologue to the swelling act, is a boldfaced Stratford wench who tumbles in a cornfield a lover younger than herself.

> And my turn? When? (*U*, 9.256–61)

As the last two internal questions that Stephen asks himself suggest, this theory (like Deasy's) is connected to personal fears and desires, with the difference that Stephen—in his loneliness and sense of himself as a sexual "loser" —welcomes and awaits female sexual agency in the form of being chosen by a woman. For Stephen goes on to argue that Ann Hathaway's sexual agency had profoundly ambiguous psychological effects on Shakespeare, insofar that it was unconsciously scarring and empowering at the same time. On the one hand, it left the artist in a state of sexual insecurity ("Belief in himself has been untimely killed" [*U*, 9.455–56]), a state he tries to cure—unsuccessfully—through promiscuity, through choosing multiple partners as a reaction-formation against being the chosen ("Assumed dongiovannism will not save him" [*U*, 9.458]). But on the other hand, the trauma becomes the wellspring of massive artistic creativity, as he relives both positions of the experience compulsively in his poems and plays: "Ravisher and ravished, what he would but would not, go with him from Lucrece's bluecircled ivory globes to Imogen's breast, bare, with its mole cinquespotted. He goes back, weary of the creation he has piled up to hide him from himself, an old dog licking an old sore" (*U*, 9.472–76). The violation of typical sex and gender alignments, wherein a man plays the feminine role of the seduced, and its aftereffects in Shakespeare's attempted "dongiovannism" become psychologically enabling insofar as these experiences allow him to feel what it is like to lack agency and to imagine having it (in excess) simultaneously: "In *Cymbeline*, in *Othello* he is bawd and cuckold. *He acts and is acted on.* . . . His unremitting intellect is the hornmad Iago ceaselessly willing that the moor in him shall suffer" (*U*, 9.1021–23; my emphasis). Shakespeare's perspective becomes labile, creatively flexible, contributing to the complexity of his art. In the end, however, the desire for agency wins out, according to Stephen, when Shakespeare punishes Ann Hathaway's sexual willfulness in his will, his final legal assertion of *his* will, by leaving her his second-best bed. Shakespeare's relationship with Ann is presented as a master-slave struggle, with the male artist finally gaining the position of control.

As the real creator of Stephen's speculations about Shakespeare's life and art, Joyce understood the ambiguities of agency: *Ulysses* shows through many examples that agency or mastery is usually desired, but that passivity —or, paradoxically, the choice of passivity—is psychologically complex and cannot simply be dismissed as "negative," as I hope to show later in my discussion of Bloom. Limited female agency and its consequences are probably most patently seen in the portrait of Gerty MacDowell in "Nausikaa." She is literally immobile through her half of the chapter, until she limps away, revealing what Bloom calls a "defect" (*U*, 13.774) and one cause of her lack of options. According to Don Gifford, marriage is an unlikely possibility (despite her efforts and vivid daydreams), given the high percentage of unmarried women in Ireland at the turn of the century (6); her lack of an education precludes the possibility of any genuine occupation aside from her dreary domestic routine. Her reliance on superstitions indicates an attempt to control her fate through coded rituals; her belief in "hope," "luck," and "chance" suggests an optimism that all too readily betrays its opposite. Because 1904 is a leap year, Gerty is technically permitted to propose marriage, but her "waiting, always waiting to be asked" (*U*, 13.208) makes her lack of agency apparent and seems the likelier passive position. Gerty's choices are limited to selecting brands of various commodities, which help explain her consumerist mentality. The choosing between various remedies for female ailments, styles of clothing, and beauty products also expresses a rigorous desire to control the body and its public appearance, a desperate agency that renders Gerty sympathetic (rather than pathetic) to many student readers. If one looks closely at the diction of "Nausikaa," one notices a heavy reliance on conditional verbs (such as *would* and *could*) and also an unusually high use of the words *if* and *because*. The former conveys Gerty's sense that her life is overloaded with contingencies over which she has little or no control ("she was just thinking would the day ever come when she could call herself his little wife to be" [*U*, 13.220]); the latter expresses a related obsession with causality ("She was wearing the blue for luck . . . because the green she wore that day brought grief because his father brought him in to study for the intermediate exhibition and because she thought perhaps he might be out because when she was dressing that morning she nearly slipped the old pair on her inside out" [*U*, 13.180–85]).

These verbal tics connect her to Stephen, her male counterpart or double in several ways. (For a more elaborate discussion of Gerty and Stephen, see Devlin, 79–81.) Stephen, of course, is traumatized by an event over which he acknowledges he has no control ("I could not save her," he thinks of his mother's death [*U* 381]); he remains haunted by her nonetheless because he did make a choice that preserved his integrity at the expense of *her* wishes—the choice of refusing to pray at her deathbed. The mixture of agency and its absence in this experience from his past—his simultaneous willfulness and helplessness—forces him to think, like Gerty, about causality, albeit in much more intellectual terms: "But can those have been possible seeing that they never were? Or was that only possible which came to pass? . . . It must be a movement then, an actuality of the possible as possible" (*U*, 2.50–67). Stephen's conclusion here implies that individuals—or at least fortunate ones—do have choices, that they can "move" toward one option rather than another. His internal monologue during his talk with Deasy reinforces his sense of agency: "The same room and hour, the same wisdom: and I the same. Three times now. Three nooses round me here. Well? I can break them in this instant if I will" (*U*, 2.233–35). When alone in "Proteus," Stephen articulates his dilemma as being trapped between a dangerous desire to control and an equally dangerous tendency to serve, as a telling resolution suggests: "You will not be master of others or their slave" (*U*, 3.295–96). In his hallucination of the maternal ghost in "Circe," however, he uses master-slave terminology to indicate that powerlessness is his deeper fear: "No! No! No! Break my spirit, all of you, if you can! I'll bring you all to heel!" (*U*, 15.4235–36). In the *Odyssey*, the position of the son is marked as one of lack of control: Telemachus is immobilized until Athene intervenes to set him in search of news of his father. Stephen has no goddess to help him in his struggles, and the figure cast as Athene/Pallas, disguised as Mentor, in the Linati and Gorman-Gilbert schemas—the old milkwoman in "Telemachus" (Ellmann 1972, appendix, n.p.)—does not even seem to notice him: "me she slights" (*U*, 1.419). (The Linati schema aligns through brackets Pallas Athene and Mentor as a single figure, as they are indeed in book 2 of the *Odyssey*. The Gorman-Gilbert schema makes Mentor's correspondence with the milkwoman explicit. See Ellmann, appendix.) The alignment of sonship with lack of agency may be one reason Stephen rejects Bloom's paternalistic hospitality, suspecting—not totally incorrectly—it might lead to unwanted obligations, phobically interpreted by the younger protagonist as restrictions.

Master-slave relationships, of course, in many ways organize the Blooms' marriage, as can be seen, most obviously, in the foregrounded issue of who has to serve the other breakfast in bed. The relationship is precariously balanced on alternations in activity and passivity from both parties. Curiously, however, both parties share a common feeling that they are the victims of restricted agency by the other. The end of "Ithaca" explains how Bloom's "complete corporal liberty of action [has] been circumscribed": "By various reiterated interrogation concerning the masculine destination whither, the place where, the time at which, the duration for which, the object with which in the case of temporary absences, projected or effected" (*U*, 17.2291–97). In "Penelope," Molly generalizes freedom of movement and of sexual choice as a male prerogative, along with the privilege of interrogating the opposite sex—the very complaint Bloom levels against her: "they can go and get whatever they like from anything at all with a skirt on it and were not to ask any questions but they want to know where were you where are you going" (*U*, 18.299). Later she reiterates the complaint and vows to resist any such restraints: "men again all over they can pick and choose what they please a married woman or a fast widow or a girl for their different tastes . . . but were to be always chained up theyre not going to be chaining me up no damn fear" (*U*, 18.1388–90). The validity of Bloom's complaint would seem to be supported by the "catechetical interrogation" Molly subjects him to in the wee hours of the morning of June 17; but since he introduces elaborate "modifications"—the text's euphemism for "falsehoods"—into his account of his day, and Molly knows this, how restricted is he in fact? On June 16, at least, as long as he has a cover story—unconvincing as it may be ("a pack of lies" is Molly's more accurate description)—Bloom has a relatively un-restricted "liberty of action." Bloom has indeed made a crucial choice on June 16—to stay away from home (a choice of implicit passivity I will dis-cuss below)—and in doing so has wandered all over Dublin. Molly's sense of restriction is also dubious, given the fact that she has managed to have an unconsummated affair with Lieutenant Stanley Gardner (which Bloom does not apparently know about) and given the fact that she is fairly well known by many other Dubliners, in a city that places a huge premium on musical talents. In "Hades," Bloom is even, in a sense, defined and identified through her—and only as a brief afterthought is she inserted into her private wifely role: when John Henry Menton asks, "Who is that chap behind with Tom Kernan," Ned Lambert replies, "Bloom . . . Madame Marion Tweedy that was, is, I mean the soprano. She's his wife" (*U*, 6.694). Molly's singing ca-reer—for which she has professionally maintained her maiden name—also certainly releases her from the confines of domesticity (she is going on a concert tour in the very near future without her spouse), and it also has all the hallmarks of success: after Bloom names a few of the "topnobbers" who are to perform on the upcoming singing tour, Mr. Power is quick to add, "And *madame*. . . . Last but not least" (*U*, 6.222)—an abbreviated reference to Madame Marion Tweedy.

I question, in short, Bonnie Kime Scott's claim, mentioned above, that Molly lacks accomplishment as a professional and also that she is "more act-ed upon than acting" (178). A close reading of an incident from the Blooms' courtship provides one clear example (among many others) of Molly's fe-male agency: I am referring, specifically, to her singing performance at Mat Dillon's party. In his recollection of their first meeting, Bloom vacillates be-tween two explanations for their pairing. Remembering the game of musical chairs where Bloom and Molly are left as the two final competitors, he thinks of this proleptic coupling as "Fate"—a situation determined by an indeter-minate mystical agency. Shortly afterwards, remembering her parlor perfor-mance of the song called "Waiting," during which he turned the pages of her music, he asks himself, "Why did she me? Fate" (*U*, 11.732). The sequence of thought is potentially contradictory, as the missing verb in the interrogative phrase is logically either "choose" or "ask"; and if Molly deliberately chose or asked Bloom to turn her pages, the operative force is not fate at all but instead her conscious selection of one of several male guests to be paired with her, center stage, so to speak. His invited proximity, of course, allows a closer inspection of her physical charms ("Bosom I saw, both full" [*U*, 11.732]) and a whiff of her perfume. The title of the song Molly chooses to sing may seem to imply a conventional feminine passivity: "Waiting" reappears later in "Nausikaa" when Gerty is described as "waiting, always waiting to be asked" (*U*, 13.208), as mentioned above. But the song's title belies its actual contents in several ways and gives no hint as to what the singer must do with her voice during the performance.

The song "Waiting" provides further proof of Molly's larger professionalism. Performed in her late teenage years, the song makes patent that Molly has a very impressive voice, given the vocal range and difficulty of the piece. Boylan's "Sea Side Girls," by way of contrast, sounds like a music-hall number that could be learned by an amateur. One can hear a rendition of "Waiting" on a tape called *The Joyce of Music* (performed by the New Hutchinson Family Singers), and its lyrics below are found in an accompanying booklet of the same title:

The stars shine on his pathway,
The trees bend back their leaves
To guide him to the meadow,
Among the golden sheaves,
Where stand I, longing, loving,
And list'ning as I wait
To the nightingale's wild singing,
Sweet singing to its mate.

The breeze comes sweet from heaven,
And the music in the air
Heralds my lover's coming,
And tells me he is there.
Come, for my arms are empty!
Come, for the day was long!
Turn the darkness into glory,
The sorrow into song.

I hear his footfall's music,
I feel his presence near,
All my soul responsive answers,
And tells me he is here.
O stars shine out your brightest!
O nightingale, sing sweet,
To guide him to me, waiting,
And speed his flying feet!

In the first verse, the singer announces her active desires perceived in the act of waiting ("longing, loving"), and at its conclusion she imitates the nightingale's song to its mate by producing a high soprano interlude of warbling with her voice (which you can hear clearly if you listen to the tape). In the second verse, the singer notes the proximity of the object of her desire and then imperiously commands him to "Come" for her ready embrace (with the repeated double entendre contained in the verb "come"). Verse three suggests the loved one's imminent presence and her longing impatience ("speed his flying feet"). Under the pretext of the socially acceptable party ritual of the parlor performance, Molly makes clear her attraction to Bloom. When one listens to the lyrics of the song she selects and its vocal execution—and I cannot believe she is deaf to either, given her Penelope-like wiliness—the operative force in the scenario is not "fate" but rather female agency and desire: Molly subverts the patriarchal censor that prohibits active expressions of female sexuality through careful musical choice. Later in the day, Bloom recalls what sounds like a conversation between him and Molly from some earlier point in their relationship together: "I always thought I'd marry a lord or a rich gentleman coming with a private yacht. . . . Why me? Because you were so foreign from the others" (*U*, 13.1207-10). Bloom's query ("Why me?") elides—in the present and perhaps in the past—both a verb as well as its agent, the full question, given the answer, probably being, "Why did you choose me?" As in the memory from "Sirens" (although in a different way), Bloom once again evades his status as the chosen, a status that is passive but honorific.

Like Shakespeare, Bloom is the "chosen"; Molly is the chooser—the secret agent, so to speak—but her monologue reveals that she does not feel she has chosen badly, that in contrast to other Dublin males, her spouse has many clear virtues, despite his many quirks: he is an abstemious drinker; he does not gamble or spend money recklessly; he is a caring father; he has a partial androgyny that allows him to identify with femininity ("I saw he understood or felt what a woman is" [*U*, 18.1578–79]); he has an occasional penchant for the poetic in his ability to understand and speak the "language of flowers"—eight poppies for a birthday on the eighth of September, a marriage proposal prefaced by a description of the beloved as a "flower of the mountain" (*U*, 18.1576); and—last but not least—he is not domineering ("I knew I could always get round him" [*U*, 18.1579–80]). Although one can say that this last trait means that Bloom is easily manipulated—a trait usually coded negatively due to its implicit lack of agency—Joyce gives us the option, I believe, of seeing his penchant for passivity as inseparable from his positively coded pacifism that we see in "Cyclops":

> —But it's no use, says he. Force, hatred, history, all that. That's not life for men and women, insult and hatred. And everybody know that it's the very opposite of that that is really life.
> —What? says Alf.
> —Love, says Bloom. I mean the opposite of hatred. (*U*, 12.1481–85)

In other words, in his creation of Bloom, I would argue, Joyce implies that passivity should not be unequivocally characterized as a weakness. Bloom's thoughts on Molly's impending affair with Boylan and Milly's blossoming adolescent sexuality provide support for this point because they can be interpreted, after all, in several ways: "A soft qualm, regret, flowed down his backbone, increasing. Will happen, yes. Prevent. Useless: can't move. Girl's sweet light lips. Will happen too. He felt the flowing qualm spread over him. Useless to move now. Lips kissed, kissing, kissed. Full gluey woman's lips" (*U*, 4.449–51). One could claim that Bloom here has a classic case of paralysis (a state that Joyce centrally critiqued in his early stories, *Dubliners*) or that these thoughts are early indications of the masochism that will be staged hyperbolically in "Circe." One could also suggest, however, that Bloom here is implicitly acknowledging the otherness of others, that he understands and accepts that others have desires of their own and that attempts at controlling others—even one's nearest and dearest—are indeed "Useless." Bloom experiences "regret" at this moment, hinting at his sense of some personal responsibility for the current state of his marriage, but he simultaneously faces the situation philosophically. It is possible to read, in short, his lack of intervention—the paradoxical choice of passivity—as a usually unrecognized virtue.

Finally, I think, Joyce dramatizes an alternative to the positions of "passive," stereotypically associated with "unmanliness," and "active," stereotypically associated with its opposite. He also makes it clear that "agency" can easily turn into a compulsive need to control and, even more dangerously, into outright aggression. For Joyce deliberately creates a hero who would find the ending of the *Odyssey* ludicrous, insane even: Odysseus's killing of 108 men who have made the mistake of courting his wife (even though he has been out of town for a mere twenty years) and of consuming his lavish supply of food and beverages—even his own son, who contributes to the final bloodbath, just until recently has participated in the ongoing party. The alternative to the categories "passive" and "active" is illustrated in what I consider to be the two most memorable scenes in *Ulysses*—Bloom and Molly's complementary but distinct memories of their lovemaking on Howth. In Bloom's imaginative re-creation of the scene in "Lestrygonians," the verb used most frequently is "lay"—it paradoxically conveys stillness in the midst of a very moving erotic connection:

> Coolsoft with ointments her hand touched me, caressed: her eyes upon me did not turn away. Ravished over her I lay, full lips full open, kissed her mouth. Yum. Softly she gave me in my mouth the seedcake warm and chewed. Mawkish pulp her mouth had mumbled sweetsour of her spittle. Joy: I ate it: joy. Young life, her lips that gave me pouting. Soft warm sticky gumjelly lips. Flowers her eyes were, take me, willing eyes. Pebbles fell. She lay still. A goat. No-one. High on Ben Howth rhododendrons a nannygoat walking surefooted, dropping currants. Screened under ferns she laughed warmfolded. Wildly I lay on her, kissed her: eyes, her lips, her stretched neck beating, woman's breasts full in her blouse of nun's veiling, fat nipples upright. Hot I tongued her. She kissed me. I was kissed. All yielding she tossed my hair. Kissed, she kissed me. (U, 8.904–16; my emphasis)

In Molly's recollection of the same scene, Bloom asks the question, but she makes it clear that she desires to be asked ("the day I got him to propose to me yes" [*U*, 18.1573–75]); she also visually insists that he propose to her twice ("then I asked him with my eyes to ask again yes" [*U*, 18.1605]). In Bloom's memory, he is the seduced ("Ravished") and the seducer, as the agents of the active verbs go back and forth between "I" and "she": there is no domination in this scene, nor acquiescent passivity, for both parties—like Shakespeare through his art—act and are acted on. In Joyce's lyric rendering of secular communion, the mutuality is all.

5

Ulysses and Queer Theory

A Continuing History

JOSEPH VALENTE

In order to trace the brief but desultory history of queer theory in Joyce studies and, in particular, the criticism of *Ulysses*, it is necessary first to specify what queer theory might be said to involve or entail, a question that comes trailing its own sometimes cloudy history. In a very real, if negative, sense, the origins of queer theory may be said to lie in late nineteenth-century legal and medical discourses that sought to define the homosexual as a disordered subspecies of the human community. For as Michel Foucault has remarked, instead of assailing these pathologizing typologies, the early gay-emancipationist movement sought to reappropriate and transvalue them, to demand legitimacy "using the same categories by which it was medically disqualified" (Foucault 101).

The gay liberation movement of the post-Stonewall era and its academic correlative, the gay studies paradigm, further developed this early emancipationist strategy. But whereas emphasis among the original emancipationists had been on the aim of what Judith Butler calls "resignification," on altering the social currency of the terms attached to homosexual desire and practice, the priority for the latter-day liberation agenda lay in the act of reappropriation itself, in making it clear that the gay population must and would "speak on its own behalf," and in resisting or discrediting continued attempts to obstruct such cultural enfranchisement by the heterosexual majority. As David Halperin delineates, this shift in emphasis caused significant ramifications in gay studies in the academy: "the aim is not to produce a . . . less tendentious form of expertise about homosexuality . . . the aim, rather, is to treat homosexuality as a position from which one *can* know, to treat it as a legitimated condition of knowledge" (60). What remained constant from the early emancipationist to the later liberation movement was the assertion of homosexuality as a distinct identity-formation.

But while gay studies adopted this sort of "minoritizing" perspective, its galvanizing "aim"—to translate homosexuality from an object of study to a site of cultural knowledge—carried the seeds of a dialectical reversal in which the self-coincidence of every sexual type or orientation would come into question. Homosexuality had emerged within both normalizing social discourse and the popular imagination as a merely supplementary reality, a fringe construct designed to consolidate "the cultural meaning of heterosexuality by encapsulating everything other than or different from heterosexuality" (Halperin 61). Asserting an identity thus defined "by opposition or negation" to dominant sexual standards was always, at some level, a self-marginalizing proposition. One could not affirm the virtue or legitimacy of same-sex desires without tacitly invoking their symbolic articulation as secondary and subservient to their heterosexual counterparts. For this reason, as Butler writes, "identity categories tend to be instruments of regulatory regimens," whatever politics they might claim (13). Having attained its hermeneutical objective, gay studies surpassed itself, and queer theory was born.

The advent of queer theory marks the point at which advocacy on behalf of a homosexual identity-formation passed into a homosexually inflected critique of the condition of identity per se. Rather than a determinate set of properties, practices, or perversions, "queer" has come to name the resistance or exorbitance of human sexuality to every classificatory regimen, hence the implication of each mode of desire or enjoyment in other erotic energies that they seem to exclude. Thus, "one of the things queer can refer to," on Eve Sedgwick's account, is "the open mesh of possibilities, gaps, overlaps, dissonances and resonances, lapses and excesses of meaning when the constituent elements of anyone's gender, of anyone's sexuality aren't made (or *can't* be made) to signify monolithically" (8). In this assault on the very possibility of a sexual norm, queer theory found its way back to one of those early medicalizing discourses that gay studies had largely repudiated. I refer, of course, to psychoanalysis, whose notion of an original state of "polymorphous perversity" has proven as congenial to the queer agenda as the notion of a cross-gendered oedipal complex was inimical.

But the rapprochement of queer theory with psychoanalysis has only served in some quarters to index its unhappy propensity for "despecifying" its own sexual content, for displacing the homoerotic from the center of its scholarly and political concerns. The consequence of such an erosion, Sedgwick argues, is "to dematerialize the possibility of queerness itself" (8). Her contention not only points up the exquisite proximity of the political strengths and liabilities of queer theory, both of which lie in its refusal to domesticate sexuality within definitional boundaries, but her contention also implies an uncanny relation between the vitality of queer theory and its "dematerialization." If queer theory responds, as D. A. Miller suggests, to a cultural tradition that suspends homosexuality in its definitional existence, amid a series of ambiguous and always deniable clues, it simultaneously threatens to suppress homosexuality in its definitional existence, relegating it to a series of outward and always reinterpretable traces. This self-negating impetus of queer theory greatly complicates the task of assessing its presence, let alone its imprint, in the study of *Ulysses*, where that same genealogy, marked by similar theoretical alliances, has played itself out in inverse order.

The First Wave

The queer exegesis of *Ulysses* began with Joyce's friend and confidante during the composition process, Frank Budgen. In *James Joyce and the Making of "Ulysses,"* he shrewdly remarks the homoerotic overtones of Bloom's evident desire to share his wife with other men, and his insight won immediate approval from Joyce himself: "You see an undercurrent of homosexuality in Bloom, and no doubt you're right" (146, 315). This perspective on the import of triangulated sexual desire strikingly anticipates Eve Sedgwick's well-known concept of "homosocial" mediation, which in crossing the hetero- and homoerotics made a decisive, if not inaugurating, advance in the development of queer theory. Yet despite the perspicacity of *Ulysses'* earliest readers, criticism of the novel soon lapsed into a settled heterocentrism; the most palpably "queer" aspect of the novel, the labile interplay it orchestrates between culturally polarized vectors of sexual desire, was regularly subject to, and may even have helped to facilitate, interpretation of the novel as a classic, heterosexual family-romance. Potential signs of homoerotic longing and satisfaction were decoded and situated otherwise, usually in terms of a broadly heterosexual deviance from respectable norms of sexual desire and practice. It was not until the mid-1990s that homoerotically engaged readings of *Ulysses* became current and queer theory, in its plenary sense, found application. Having said that, the celebratory emphasis in some of the earlier readings on Bloom's perverse sexuality, even within the "hetero" limits cited, arguably aligned them with or served to foreshadow some of the more "despecifying" variants of queer. So whereas in the theoretical arena, the concept of queer ultimately threatened to supersede the homosexually identified forms of analysis from which it evolved, its proleptic strains in certain treatments of *Ulysses* in the 1970s and 1980s threatened to preempt any identifiably homosexual object of analysis from the novel. In this sense, the time of queer theory in the study of *Ulysses* has been out of joint, with the aftermath of sexual identity politics preceding the politics themselves.

Until fairly recently, homosexuality rarely figured in the criticism of *Ulysses*, and only in its recognizably normative function as a *negative supplement*, consolidating the narrative centrality and enhancing the symbolic value of heterosexual romance in the novel. The first-wave readings of homosexuality in *Ulysses* can thus be seen as a kind of unregenerate counterpart to first-wave gay emancipationist discourse.[1] They too draw upon the pathologizing vision of "inversion" propounded in the sexual sciences of Joyce's day—in particular the Oedipus-centered Freudianism of the so-called American school. But far from resignifying the diagnostic categories used to disqualify same sex preferences, they tended to embrace them. Supported by the casual homophobia found in Joyce's letters and conversations,[2] these glosses typically find homosexuality to be the deviation of deviations in *Ulysses*, the one perversion represented not as a benign variation, an ersatz compensation for thwarted fulfillments, or a challenge to the dominant sexual regime, but as a peril to the development of the implicated characters.

Daniel Schwarz, for example, insists that "for Joyce homosexuality is an alternative to the fruitful intercourse with the world that Stephen requires, intercourse for which a passionate heterosexual relationship is a prerequisite" (76). He sees "the blatant homoeroticism" of the Martello scenes, by contrast, to carry "sterile" and "narcissistic overtones," judgments that recycle popular and scientific identification of homosexuality with immaturity, unripeness, even arrested development (76). A similar perplexity marks Jean Kimball's classic essay "Freud, Leonardo, and Joyce." Kimball identifies a "threat . . . made textually explicit in *Ulysses*, where it dominates Stephen's Bloomsday choices and is identified with his mother: the fear of homosexuality as a life pattern" (172). But the evidence she adduces of homosexual adherences on Dedalus's part never speaks to a "life pattern" and seems far less determinative, for her, than the fact that Stephen's ties to his dead mother fits the Freudian profile for the male homosexual, that is, excessively proximate and eroticized. Her reduction of homosexuality to "threat," on the other hand, exhibits a more widely derivative bias.

Ralph Rader's construction of *Ulysses*, finally, draws upon a popular narrative schema loosely aligned with sexual norms of the time: homoeroticism as a stage in heterosexual development that could become an impediment to its completion. Stephen's refusal to return to Martello Tower on the night of June 16, 1904, expresses his "fear and rejection" of Mulligan and the "loss of spiritual autonomy that homosexual attraction would seem to involve for him" (273). Moreover, it initiates a life-changing odyssey for Stephen—the "true" protagonist of *Ulysses* on this reading—from an immediately erotic mode of male-male intimacy to the female-mediated homosocial mode crystallized in Bloom's offer of his wife's "company." That Stephen refuses this offer, abruptly truncating the proposed narrative arc, does not daunt Rader as it should. He recalibrates the apparently broken *narrative* syntax of *Ulysses* in order to unveil the *allegorical* sentence it should have spoken: the saving, real-life passage of Joyce himself from a series of protohomosexual attachments—Byrne, Cosgrave, Gogarty—to a union with Nora. The aesthetic fecundity of the heterosexual bond, claims Rader, manifests itself in Joyce's attainment of an "androgynous art," evidenced and symbolized by the voice of Molly Bloom (274).

The shift (in every sense) to which Rader stoops clearly indicates the characteristic error of the first-wave readings, their over-reliance on received notions of homosexuality as interpretive templates. Guided too narrowly, perhaps, by Joyce's flip use of these notions in everyday correspondence, these critics tend to assume that contemporary sexual schemes and taxonomies, and the homophobic energies they galvanized, constitute a decisive structural impetus of his work, rather than, as with virtually every other ethico-political attitude that Joyce entertained, a focus of literary interrogation, negotiation, and reformulation.

The Second Wave

The second wave of sexual criticism of *Ulysses* was not primarily inspired by the gay liberation ethos or the gay studies methodology, both of which had only begun to gain a tenuous academic foothold during the period of its birth. It took its cue instead from the more widely influential discourse of poststructuralist theory. The American Freud of the first wave—the Freud of the normalizing renditions of the Oedipus complex—was supplemented, and even supplanted by the "French Freud" of Jacques Lacan and company, the Freud of "polymorphous perversity," a phrase that recurs with remarkable frequency in the critical literature of this vein. Whereas *Ulysses* had been seen to rewrite the unified, stable family-romance in multiple stylistic registers and across overlapping mythic frameworks, *Ulysses* is seen in this "second wave" as the writing of perversion, that is, the uncontrollable variability and waywardness of libidinal desire itself. Tony Tanner, for example, points out that in *Ulysses*, "there is no example of what might be called normal sexual intercourse and perversion is the usual mode of procedure" (13). Joseph Allen Boone provides a representative catalogue of perversion unfolded in "Circe" alone: "homosexuality, autoeroticism, masochism, fetishism, coprophilia, anality, transvestism" (197). The emphasis placed in these readings upon deviant sexuality in *Ulysses* serves, at least implicitly, to align the novel with the most advanced strains of queer theory, which trumpets the fundamental intractability of sexual desire to all preferential or practical norms and all self-consistent identity-formations—precisely the strain of queer theory that has proved open, as noted above, to a rapprochement with Lacanian psychoanalysis. It is also the species of queer theory that has incurred criticism for its despecifying of sexual content, its attenuation of the historical links between homoeroticism and queer sexual dissidence. The second-wave readings exhibit much the same tendency. Under this dispensation, homosexuality is no longer the troubling deviation of deviations in *Ulysses*, but neither is it the object of some more positive exceptionalism. It is but one in a considerable range of newly validated forms of perversity. Richard Brown speaks for this entire critical formation when having announced that Joyce's "writing and presentation of sexuality" may be regarded as "fundamentally perverse," he nonetheless insists, "Joyce did not apparently wish to make a special case for 'inversion' or homosexuality . . . in Joyce [it] is peripheral" (84). The tacitly homophobic reading of *Ulysses* in the first wave is thus countered by an explicitly heterocentric one in the second: Joyce proves less anxious about homoerotic possibilities than indifferent to them.

Owing in part to this assumption, and notwithstanding Richard Brown's broad survey of sexual discourse in Joyce's day, the readings in question shows little interest in the *historical* construction of the perversions they invoke. More attention to what Foucault has identified as a voluminous and generative discourse on sexual disorder at the fin-de-siécle would have inevitably led these readings to take up the particular question of male homosexuality, which in the wake of the Wilde scandal was the most prominent, the most densely coded and archived, and hence the most readily substantiated of the discursively fashioned "types" of deviation. The absence of a vigorously historicizing strategy in this criticism goes hand in hand with its despecifying of the sexual content of "queer."

Not entirely displaced by the new emphasis on perversity, the oedipal family-romance emerges, in this second wave, as its breeding ground. In "A Clown's Inquest into Paternity," Jean-Michael Rabaté anatomizes how for Stephen Dedalus the incestuous bond with his father, centered upon the womb of his recently deceased mother, manifests itself in an ambiguously eroticized estrangement of the two men, what Stephen himself translates as a universal and inviolable taboo on father-son incest as a result of the attendant "bodily shame" (*U*, 9.850). Stephen seeks not just a *symbolic* father with which to identify (that is, bearer of the phallic or master signifier) but a *surrogate* father, removed from the dueling conflicts of desire and identification animating the oedipal triangle. This same distance, however, can render the surrogate, in this case Bloom, the site of a certain easing if not lifting of erotic prohibition, a figure "combining incest and homosexuality." Thus, Mulligan's mocking admonition at the end of "Scylla"—"He looked upon you to lust after you. Oh Kinch, thou art in peril"—chimes with the end of "Eumaeus" (the most anally obsessed and homoerotically disposed of episodes), where Bloom and Stephen "walk towards the railway bridge, *to be married by Father Maher*" (*U*, 16.1887–88).

From the other side, Bloom's proscribed libidinal investment in his daughter, Milly, which Rabaté deems a key factor in Molly Bloom's adultery, undergoes a complicated form of transference in Bloom's psychic election of Stephen as, at once, a surrogate son, a surrogate paramour for his wife, and a prospective suitor for his daughter. The convoluted role Stephen might play in Bloom's family-romance is duly noted during their tête-à-tête in "Ithaca": "Why might these provisional contingencies between a guest and a hostess not necessarily preclude or be precluded by a permanent eventuality of reconciliatory union between a schoolfellow and a jew's daughter? / Because the way to daughter led through mother, the way to mother through daughter" (*U*, 17.940–44). Often glossed as the telos of *Ulysses*, the "atonement" of Stephen and Bloom would seem to involve the superimposition of two distinct oedipal triangles, leading on the one hand to the kind of symbolic displacement through which incestuous pressures supposedly find resolution and, on the other, to more perversely ramified and intertwined erotic affiliations. On Rabaté's account, Stephen and Bloom can only resist "unnatural" desires for incestuous objects by replicating them in synthetic forms, which he calls "figures of incestitude." His reading discovers in the law of "normal" sexual relations the impetus to perversion, a move that instances the core agenda of queer theory *avant la lettre*.

Colin MacCabe likewise judges perversion to be central, rather than threatening, to Joyce's aesthetic project in *Ulysses*, central not just to the representation of sexuality but to the sexual implications of Joyce's representational method. Unlike Rabaté, however, MacCabe does not understand perversion as a systemic effect of the Oedipus complex, in its several dimensions, but of the breakdown of the oedipal structure at its very foundation, the act of paternal identification. Stephen Dedalus's difficulty in *Ulysses* is "that he cannot find a figure that can occupy the place of the father," someone who can model, in a dialectic of rivalry and identification, an assured place for Stephen in the social order. The "real father's weakness" is redoubled in "the imaginary father of the nation . . . who lacks both a living language and political independence" (120). Neither one, in MacCabe's words, "can function as an origin secure enough to guarantee his present identity." Subjected to this overdetermined default of the paternal function, Stephen comes to experience the absence of any fixed reliable signified beneath the play of signifying differences as "the instability of [his own] sexual position" (123). His characteristically neurotic response is to deny the primacy of difference, semiotic or sexual, and to seek a transcendental ground of being. Exemplifying this quest, his poetic endeavor in "Proteus" aims first to arrest the endless "signatures" that have been vexing him ("Put a pin in that chap" [*U*, 3.399]), and second, to arrest the violent oscillation of sexual positions at work in his grief-ridden fantasies of encountering his undead mother.

But insofar as writing itself comprises a proliferation of possible meanings among "hitherto unnoticed receivers," it dissolves the "unitary subject" of Stephen's self-projective fantasies "in a play of voices," which is also to say a play of interpretive strategies and inferences contingent upon different libidinal investments in the text (123). Stephen's chosen medium of neurotic self-expression proves "throughout Joyce's work the very exemplar of perversion" (123), the psychic antipodes of neurosis, a submission rather than a resistance to the differential machinery of signification. The polyphonic stylistic experimentation of *Ulysses* progressively develops this identification of the written with a perverse dispersion of subjectivity, moving from a stream-of-consciousness technique, reflective of a stable ego, to systematic parodies, like "Cyclops," in which the signifying logic exceeds any sense of a controlling subjectivity.

The same paradox reasserts itself, for MacCabe, in the larger narrative scheme. Stephen's designated father-figure, Leopold Bloom, embodies not a solution to Stephen's dilemma, that is, a stable point of paternal identification, but a model for living his condition otherwise. The change in the dominant narrative focus from Stephen to Bloom is a move from neurosis as reactive fixation to perversion as transformative possibility. Submitting himself to the shifting patronymic signifier that mark his complex heritage as a "perverted Jew" (*U*, 12.1635), Bloom can acknowledge, *if only in fantasy*, the (sexual) differences constitutive of every subject position and to abandon on this basis all claims to phallic cohesion or transcendence. By MacCabe's lights, it is precisely this perverse willingness to vacate the illusory position of authority and self-possession that underwrites Bloom's status as modern Odysseus, a polytropic man for a polytropic novel.

Because the patriarchal definition of such a phallic position is so decisively gendered, MacCabe defines "the movement of writing, of perversion" that undermines it as "an insistent pressure of the feminine" (127). Bloom's perversion, accordingly, triumphantly asserts itself in what MacCabe calls "the bisexuality" of the "Circe" episode (128). "Circe" famously reshuffles the day's events according to a different textual calculus, so that each becomes something else while remaining vertiginously the same. That is, all the preceding textual motifs return in "Circe" "bearing different meanings and values" (128), but for that very reason bearing all the more plainly their underlying status as *written* signifiers whose immediate semiotic weight is always contingent upon their mode of articulation with one another. Such writing, MacCabe contends, "is experienced at its most corrosive as Bloom becomes a woman," which is to say as Bloom himself is rearticulated with the figure of Bella Cohen in a perverse "confusion of the notion of sexual identity" (128). Even as Bloom abandons, in his unconscious, the position of phallic security, the "Circe" episode, functioning as the text's unconscious, abandons secure gender disjunction in favor of geometrically multiplied sexual identities.

Two aspects of MacCabe's analysis have proven tremendously influential for later studies of sexuality in *Ulysses*, one in expanding the limits of queer Joyceanism, one in revealing and reinforcing them. The first, more obvious aspect is MacCabe's extension of the idea of perversion or non-normative sexuality beyond the psychological profiles and narrative performances of the novel's characters and to the writing of the novel conceived along post-structuralist lines. Pressing MacCabe's tack a bit further, well-known queer theorist Leo Bersani holds that Joyce divorces the sexual drives in *Ulysses* from any "affect," let alone psychology, the better to show their perverse inherence in "the arbitrary play and productiveness of the signifier" (176). In dissevering the drives from comprehensible motives and communicable emotions, *Ulysses* paradoxically demonstrates the irreducibility of these drives to the language that activates them: "the virtuousity of desire as linguistic effects is . . . meant to lead us to conclude that *language cannot represent desire*" (176). On Bersani's view, *Ulysses* queers sexuality not just by reference to symbolic norms but with respect to symbolic possibility.

Joseph Allen Boone also maintains that Joyce not only "valorizes" libidinous fluidity" in "Bloom's subconscious fantasies" but carries this "explosion of the polymorphously perverse" into the verbal texture of the "Circe" episode (195). Indeed, without asserting, *pace* Bersani, that language in *Ulysses* aims to *represent* desire, Boone does propose that the myriad intertextual references and allusions effectively register a sense of "sexual variation and unending capacities of erotic stimulation" (203). In other words, the carnivalesque writing of *Ulysses* is not just perverse in destroying the illusion of self-identical norms and normative subject-positions, but carries its own libidinal charge: "its excitations ripple across the surface of the entire artifact in multiple directions" (200). But for Boone this "textualizing of sexuality" is not "without affect" (Bersani 175); rather it bears the impress of authorial design and so exhibits the grain of authorial desire, evinces Joyce's own sexualized enjoyment-in-writing. On the odd, unsupported surmise that Joyce crafted his Circean tour de force entirely for the purpose of witnessing his literary omnipotence, Boone characterizes that enjoyment as one of "extreme exhibitionism . . . a pyrotechnic flexing of muscle equivalent to an act of masturbatory display" (201–2). The inscription of orgasmic fantasies in "Circe" is taken to be the inscription of Joyce's fantasies of "male prowess" recast as literary virtuosity. And while this mode of authorial *jouissance* is perverse on its face, a fetishistic substitution of pen for penis, Boone doubts whether Joyce's "signature punning and verbal bravado" (201), being a literary *parade virile*, represents the sort of *radical* perversion that challenges "identity, sexuality or narrativity as fixed categories" (202). In a critical catch-22, he doubts that the kaleidoscopically perverse representational method that gives "Circe" its protoqueer luster could have proceeded from anything but a hyperphallic motive that discredits that reputation in turn.

This brings us to the second major point of influence exerted by Mac-Cabe's analysis: the distinctive notion of "bisexuality" that he treats as the seal of achieved perversion in "Circe." MacCabe discovers this bisexuality in what he calls the "hall of mirrors" exchange of sexual roles between Bloom and Bella Cohen. On his understanding, it is this reciprocal sexual mobility that produces that "confusion . . . of sexual identity" fundamental to *Ulysses'* systemic perversion. But by the same token, precisely because the sexual mobility discerned by MacCabe unfolds reciprocally over time, it can entail profound gender dissidence—labeled androgyny by some critics, transsexualism by others—without violating the basic terms of compulsory heterosexuality. Instead of the oscillation between same-sex and cross-sex affections that bisexuality ordinarily signifies, MacCabe's version comprises a transgendering oscillation of position or standpoints *within* a cross-sexed encounter, hence a syncopation rather than a subversion of heterosexuality. Whereas Rabaté's protoqueer concept of perversion includes without foregrounding homosexuality, MacCabe's concept incorporates same-sex desire within an always already heterosexual frame.

The queer heterocentrism that MacCabe introduced to Joyce studies has become a relatively prominent approach, as I have discussed elsewhere. In her *James Joyce and the Politics of Desire*, Suzette Henke fuses psychoanalytic and deconstructive perspectives to offer an especially radical picture of Bloom's "deep-seated transsexual fantasies" (119–20). Henke's transsexual idea, however, does not encompass a truly polymorphous perversity, inasmuch as it presupposes a complementary transposition of masculine and feminine positions. Male homosexuality does figure in her analysis but only insofar as it is reputedly and explicitly identified with the adoption of a "feminine" or "womanly" position vis-à-vis some presumptively masculinized other. Henke in effect subscribes to the "inversion" model of homosexuality, which preserves the hegemonic force of the heterosexual norms within homosexual desire itself. As Christopher Craft has pointed out, "sexual inversion explains homosexual desire as a physiologically misplaced heterosexuality" (77). In reading Joyce's "verbal bravado" as the symptom of an essentially "male desire," Joseph Allen Boone takes the consolidation of the cross-gender grid to a still more comprehensive plane: *Ulysses* serves as staging ground for a sexuality whose irreparable errancy remains locked within the opposition, masculine/feminine.

If the first-wave readings of sexuality in *Ulysses* made too much of Joyce's acquiescence in the homophobic biases of his time, the second-wave readings made too little, eliding not only Joyce's express attitudes toward homosexuality but also the historical atmosphere in which they lived. In the process, it seems that the evidence of homosexuality in *Ulysses* has been muted. These are undoubtedly queer readings; they apotheosize *Ulysses* as the modern novel of universalized, even ramifying perversion, the seat of which they locate at or near the oedipalized heterosexual norm. But at the same time, the cross-gendered terms of that norm, the coupling of same and other, demarcated on a strictly gendered basis, is reproduced and then reinforced with each errant ramification, each new layer of perversion. Coming near the end of this wave, and undoubtedly influenced thereby, David Fuller's *James Joyce's "Ulysses"* translates this theoretical assimilation of same-sex and cross-sex perversion onto the narrative level of *Ulysses* as its basic erotic truth. "In *Ulysses*, homosexual feeling is a part of the experience of people who are predominantly heterosexual" (89).

The Third Wave

The challenge over the past decade for critics whose intellectual horizons have been informed by the transition from gay studies to queer theory, has been (*a*) to incorporate some of the analytical concerns and political incisiveness of the gay-studies approach without lapsing into the identity politics that queer theory has helped consign to obsolescence; and hence (*b*) to "re-signify" the queerness implicit in the second-wave readings by "respecifying" the homoerotic components necessary to an historically alert, exegetically complete, and politically meaningful valorization of perversion. Readings of the third wave are remarkably consistent in the dialectical strategy they employ to accomplish this delicate feat. Taking up the main omissions, limitations, and impasses to be found in their theoretically minded predecessors, they reflect them into the text of *Ulysses* and find them reflected upon there.

As noted, the obvious shortfall of this earlier criticism lay in its failure to delineate and engage the layered social construction of deviant, and specifically same-sex eroticism, and, correlatively, to trace the *divergent* impact of this definitional context on Joyce's attitudes and on his work. More recent, self-identified queer interpretations have located a primary focus for these questions of constructivism in Joyce's ambiguous invocations of the figure of Oscar Wilde, whose dual notoriety as convicted sodomite and aesthetic provocateur concentrated not just semiotic and sexual decadence, but the effective social attitudes toward them, in an especially germane fashion.

In "A Womb of His Own," David Weir summons the spectral presence of Oscar Wilde in Martello Tower and the National Library as an index of how the heightened collective phobia surrounding same-sex affection in the post fin-de-siécle period fuels the erotically charged conflicts between and within the aesthetic sensibilities of Buck Mulligan and Stephen Dedalus. Weir postulates that the copious Wildean motifs and allusions marking the boys of Sandycove serve to implicate them in a homosexual *ménage*. Far more interesting, however, is his suggestion that the characters' more direct forms of engagement with the legend of Wilde tend to confess their internalization of the homophobic sanctions of which he was a victim and is now a memoriam. The figure of Wilde proves, accordingly, at once magnetic and radioactive for Mulligan and Dedalus: he can be conjured as a genius only to be repudiated, repudiated as a pariah only at the risk of continued (sexual) identification. This ambivalent dynamic crystallizes in Buck Mulligan's declaration, "We have grown out of [outgrown, grown from] Wilde and paradoxes" (*U*, 1.554). In simultaneously avowing and disavowing a *kinship* of intellectual style with Wilde, Mulligan's words imply not just a divided attitude but a split identity. Weir discerns a strong erotic undercurrent to this self-division, which allows him to cast Mulligan in a more vulnerable light than his character usually enjoys. For Weir, Mulligan's brand of sartorial splendor, his celebration of the pose, and his "jocular" witticisms about homosexual pleasures combine to tag him as a "Wildean dandy," prone to "impulses," homoerotic impulses "that are genuine but which he cannot express directly, particularly in view of the fairly recent case of Wilde" (223).

Stephen's own conflicted reaction to Wilde's aesthetically rich but sexually abject legacy plays itself out in a predictably more cerebral vein, the crafting of his Shakespeare thesis. Weir notes that Stephen draws heavily for his theory of "aesthetic generation" on a long-established notion of "creative androgyny," which was typically framed as a man's spiritual incorporation of or fertilization by a feminine procreative energy. But of course androgyny was also during this period stereotypically attributed to another group of men, homosexuals, whom sexologists often classified as possessing "a woman's soul in a man's body." Given this dual association, Weir suggests, it is not surprising that homosexuals were also believed to be inherently prone to "aesthetic sensibility and perceptions" and even biologically called to the vocation of literature. With his flaunting of certain feminized styles and accessories, his notorious exultation of aesthetic value as the highest standard of experience, and his spectacular downfall, which made his name synonymous with homosexual degradation, Oscar Wilde stood at the intersection of these typologies as their joint exemplar. In his essay "Paring His Fingernails," Tim Dean posits that following Wilde's trials the "adjective artistic" became "one of the privileged codes for homosexuality" (1998, 251–52).

Now Shakespeare had garnered his own reputation for same-sex involvements, with which the library clique seems conversant, and his success on the London stage modeled in its way the sensation Wilde's social comedies caused in the early 1890s. Against this background, Stephen could readily have situated "the bard" as the great precursor to "the aesthete" in his dual role, the "androgynous angel" as early "Uranian." Instead, Stephen stakes Shakespeare's creative androgyny on his "thwarted heterosexuality," his emasculating seduction and adulterous betrayal by Anne Hathaway. Stephen steers clear of Shakespeare's more controversial relationship with William Herbert, to whom the Sonnets are dedicated. Wilde's fictional account of the homoerotic inspiration of the sonnets, "The Picture of Mr. W. H.," surfaces in the conversation to remind Stephen (and the reader) of his divergence. The reminder is sharpened by the striking formal and pragmatic similarities of Stephen's theory and that advanced in Wilde's story: both use aesthetically coherent, but woefully uncorroborated, even doctored accounts, openly disbelieved by their respective author-protagonists (Stephen and Cyril Graham). Weir links Stephen's disbelief to his "refusal or inability to fully incorporate the homoerotic implications of Shakespeare's life into his theory" (225), despite his acute sense of their importance, a disavowal echoed in this refusal to acknowledge the theoretical content of Wilde's theory even as he approximates its answerable narrative form. Implicit in Weir's argument is a representative precept of third-wave criticism: that Joyce works through some of his own homophobic feelings via transferential displacement onto his alter egos.

Buck and Stephen, Weir argues, are divided by their sexual attraction for one another and united in their socially enjoined determination to publicly disregard the very possibility. Their unconsciously evolved but exquisitely dialectical solution is to ventilate their self-protective antagonism toward one another in phobic references to same-sex love. Wilde appears in these comments, but only in his role as historical construct or caricature. When it comes to the fissured relationship that each has with his own sexuality, however, no such dialectical solution presents itself. Their inconclusive engagement with Oscar Wilde as a rounded historical personage represents an extended metaphor of this private dilemma, which weighs on their aesthetic aspirations.

Whereas Weir isolates the homoerotic affections of Dedalus and Mulligan, Garry Leonard, in exploring their respective strategies of disavowal, finds the "internalized homophobic reading" to be grossly reductive of the enormous historical complexity of their situation, that is, on the cusp of a dramatic shift in the structuring of male-male desire. In Leonard's view, an established nineteenth-century continuum of male-male desires—initiated, channeled and contained by various bourgeois institutions in the interests of advancing both patriarchal solidarity and class hegemony—gradually came into convergence, at about the time *Ulysses* represents, with a new, more rigorous disjunction of homo and heterosexuality. This cultural development reflected itself into individual development. Romantic friendships between men were cultivated within educational and social institutions as a means of cementing masculine privilege, but were to be discarded upon maturity in favor of the institution of marriage and the bioeconomic reproduction of elite rule. At Martello, Leonard argues, Stephen and Buck find themselves at the intersection of the individual and the cultural arc of change, entering upon professional life at a historical moment when that signified a "husbanding" of sexual affects. The break-up of the young men's friendship reflects their respective, ambivalent negotiations with social pressures to specify and not specify, sustain and not sustain their feelings for one another.

As Leonard sees it, Stephen has embarked on an "incessant search" for pretexts to end the friendship (16), of which Mulligan's famous "insult," whether to his mother or himself, is but the latest. "Frankly puzzled" at Stephen's extended grievance fest, Mulligan is actually no more in the dark than Stephen himself, whose sense of injury knows not its final cause: the indefinable social taboo on continuing a complexly motivated homosexual relation hitherto socially encouraged in its indefinability. Stephen acts as "an impossible person" (*U*, 1.222), in Mulligan's phrase, precisely because he has reached a stage at which Mulligan is himself an impossible person for Stephen to cathect appropriately. That Mulligan affects aestheticism and has attended Oxford—the cultural discourse and institution respectively identified most closely with the contested negotiations of masculine desire—lends a certain focus to Stephen's angst, as evidenced by his phobic vision of eroticized male hijinks at Magdalene College (*U*, 1.165–71). But these items also set the profound ambiguity of his relation to Mulligan in a wider cultural context. Buck's compliment that Stephen has "the real Oxford manner" (*U*, 1.54), for example, may or may not carry the sexual implication that Stephen chooses to place upon it ("Manner of Oxenford" [*U*, 9.1212]). Like many of the comments both Buck and Stephen make in and about the Tower, this one betokens an undecidedly nuanced affective possibility that can neither be reduced without violence to a univocally homoerotic signification nor be exempted, at this historical juncture, from such interpretive violence.

The context that Leonard provides for the workings of male same-sex desire in *Ulysses* helps to elucidate and redress another serious deficit in the "second-wave" readings we examined. The failure to distinguish homosexuality against the variegated background of perversion on display in *Ulysses* turns out to be a failure to historicize the gradual emergence of homosexuality as a discrete social category. During this transitional period, homoeroticism remained, if not indistinct, then profoundly imbricated with a range of other male homosocial desires that proved not inconsistent with what came to be known as a "heterosexual orientation." Representing precisely this period in *Ulysses*, Joyce preserves a sense of libidinal continuity from one object-relation to another, even as he registers the increasing social demand to fix and oppose homo and hetero passions.

Jennifer Levine's essay "James Joyce, Tattoo Artist" enlarges the framework of interconnections constitutive of homoeroticism in *Ulysses*. In the "Eumaeus" episode, her object text, the lateness of the hour, the mental fatigue of the characters, and the Homeric theme of enabling imposture become the occasion for Joyce to wage an assault on identity, individual, social, and semiotic, beginning with a slippery desultory prose that only comes to equipoise around the odd platitude, and culminating in the central figure, D. B. Murphy, who figures character as an open set of slippery ruses and desultory misrepresentation. Levine judges that "the reason for [this] indirection turns on homosexuality," the love that "dare not speak its name," except in coded allusion. Yet Levine professes no interest in discovering "the secret of *Ulysses*" in the repressed homosexuality of its characters or its author (102). To the contrary, the mystery of same-sex desire in *Ulysses* is aptly symbolized by the openly displayed, homoerotically suggestive, yet finally enigmatic tattoo on Murphy's chest (of the number 16 and the "Greek" Great Antonio): this desire hides, if at all, in plain sight.

Levine begins with the propositions that (*a*) desire is not a "particular emotion" but a "structure of relationships," and (*b*) it makes sense "to reinsert homosexual desire into the historically changeable structure of men's relationships with men" (102, 112). Like Leonard, in fact, she holds that the homoerotic and the homosocial exist in often disowned symbiosis, powerfully captured on the pages of *Ulysses*. "Eumaeus" itself "is underscored by a web of homoerotic allusions," each of which tends to fissure in secondary and tertiary layers of meaning with homosocial or heterosexual points of reference (112). At the center of the web stands Murphy, whose sexual itinerary seems divided between the "Greek" love of Antonio and the marital bed to which he is presently returning. What is most striking about this figure for Levine is his textual affiliation with Bloom. On the one hand, the men are symbolic mirrors of one another, doppelgangers in their mythic affiliations: both are versions of Odysseus, Shakespeare, Joyce himself. Both are cuckolds, wanderers, would-be fathers, and, above all, exiles whose outsider status is crowned by their imputed homosexuality: Bloom has been pronounced "Greeker than the Greeks" (*U*, 9.614–15), one of whom Murphy wears on his chest. On the other hand, it is Bloom who expresses the greatest suspicion of Murphy and evinces the greatest hostility toward him. In refusing to recognize his likeness or relatedness to his own double, Bloom reenacts in little the disavowed symbiosis of homosexuality and homosociality and reveals the social stakes involved. Within a patriarchal culture, homosociality is the condition of male belonging, for which the denizens of the masculinized space of the cab shelter are more than willing to compete, while homosexuality functions as a mark of the outcast. Having suffered exclusion all day as a Jew, a racial designation that brought his sexuality under aspersion as well, Bloom largely foists this status off on Murphy. His attempts to discredit the sailor to Stephen coincide with his efforts to impress upon the same audience the positive social contribution of the Jews ("though in reality I'm not one" [*U*, 16.1085]), thereby replaying his earlier dispute with the anti-Semitic Citizen in reverse order and to better advantage.

Bloom and Murphy not only mirror one another as outsiders but in the means whereby they seek to position themselves as insiders. Both circulate images of women for the purpose of simultaneously lubricating and safely mediating their relations with other men—Murphy, a South American post-card of "savage women in striped loincloths" (*U*, 16.476); Bloom, a photo of Molly in décolleté evening dress. In both cases, the men aim at promoting and participating in a sense of empowered masculine togetherness based upon a shared, prurient appropriation of a gendered other. Murphy's circulation of the postcard among the entire group, accompanied by his slanderous commentary, highlights the misogynistic aspect of this homosocial ritual. The postcard mobilizes an eroticized contempt for women that cements the men's fellowship while distancing them from the perceived taint of homosexual affection. In this sense, Levine demonstrates, homophobia and misogyny are inseparable as social pathologies. Conversely, Bloom's exhibition of Molly's photo to Stephen alone, accompanied by approving commentary, "underlines the special intimacy" that Bloom sought to establish with the young man. As Levine notes, however, the "mediating role" assigned Molly in this triangular scenario indicates that Bloom's gesture is not entirely free from a certain *structural* misogyny. "In a patriarchal society like Joyce's Dublin," she writes, "it is the bonds between men . . . that 'normally' take precedence" (115). If the erotic is a term reserved for the more intense bonds of desire—that is the more intense form of relationship—then this "precedence" alone would suggest that "the homosocial and the homosexual are not distinct as our culture tells us they must be." It is, in part, the staging of this imbrication and the tracing of its racial and gender implications that make *Ulysses* a recognizably "queer" document of high modernism.

In historicizing this intersection of homosocial and homosexual investments, both Leonard and Levine are able to identify a specific source of the profound erotic instability in *Ulysses*, its queer dimension, which earlier "second-wave" critics had consigned to the all-purpose category of perversion. In the same historicizing move, moreover, they are able to address an issue neglected by those earlier critics, the connection between this queer dimension and Joyce's own attitudes toward same-sex desire. Leonard finds the homosocial/homosexual nexus to occasion an inescapable sexual ambivalence in *Ulysses*, which might easily be taken to reflect the author's own experience. In this respect, Leonard's reading implicitly shows a way to peg, *without reducing*, Joyce's literary representation of male-male sexuality to the casual homophobia of his letters and conversation. Levine speculates that the considerable *anxiety* surrounding this nexus, for the characters, ultimately belongs to the author as well, and she opines that Joyce draws on his own homosexual "panic" to "speak to a more general ideological formation."

Colleen Lamos takes Levine's argument a step further in her essay "Signatures of the Invisible." She historicizes homosexual panic as a hermeneutic problem, one that involves, in different yet analogical ways, the author, reader, and protagonists of *Ulysses*. For Lamos, the observed tendency of (second-wave) Joyceans like Richard Brown and David Fuller to invoke homosexuality in *Ulysses* only to marginalize it continues a long tradition of "knowing ignorance" on this subject. From its "conceptual birth" in the late nineteenth century, the *ontological* status of homosexuality persisted in ambiguity, encompassing on one side a universal human propensity or susceptibility and restricted, on the other, to a highly pathologized minority. (Indeed, we might add that the turbulent symbiosis of the homosocial and the homoerotic hinges precisely on this ambiguity.) The social status of homosexuality, to be "shrouded in shame and confusion" (Lamos 1994, 338) has been more definitive but no less mystifying. As a result of this combined uncertainty, the "signs of homosexuality," are, Lamos argues, "neither verifiable nor deniable" (338). Each is radically interpretable. But operating under a cloud of stigma, these same signs provoke resistance in their prospective interpreters, who sense that any claim to interpretive competence in this regard might count on erotic complicity. As Lamos notes, "the signs of homosexuality are not only symptoms of an inner pathology, they are themselves tainting" (338).

On Lamos's reading, homosexuality functions, like many topoi in *Ulysses*, primarily as an object of contested semiotic awareness. What is unusual about homosexuality, however, is that social authority, respectability, and license accrue to significantly qualified, as opposed to plenary, displays of awareness. Lamos's contribution lies in showing us that queer knowledge in *Ulysses* is always a queered knowledge, an expertise that falters, a knowing without knowing. In "Scylla and Charybdis," the public credibility of Stephen's theory depends, in his own mind, on his knowing Shakespeare's life and time thoroughly and yet not knowing, actively resisting outward consciousness of the supposed homosexuality of the bard. His demurral, tellingly, takes the path of designating those who impugn Shakespeare's sexuality, Best and Mulligan, a "minion of pleasure" and a "catamite" respectively

(*U*, 9.1138, 735). That is to say, he translates their being (sexually) suspicious readers into their being (sexually) suspicious characters, "tainting" them with the signs of sodomy they have decoded. For his part, Mulligan stakes his claims to authority in the library scene on a mocking expertise about homosexual "pederasty" that, in Lamos's words, "scarcely conceals its own ignorance" or, if you like, ironically bares its own ignorance (346). Mulligan's not knowing what he knows on this subject creates an empowering distance from its "tainting" effects and thus preserves his status as a "manly man." For Lamos, the library debate on Shakespeare's homosexuality illuminates, from the inside out, the critical dialogue on the place of homosexuality in *Ulysses*, in that it reveals conceptual ambiguities and social motivations peculiar to this topic that may well affect, in different measures, our own readings.

Lamos expands on this argument in her subsequent essay, "The Double Life of 'Eumaeus.'" Like many critics before her, Lamos begins with the proposition that mistakes so pervade "Eumaeus" at every level that the episode must be regarded as thematizing error as a distinct mode of social interchange. But for her the key to error in "Eumaeus" is "fear and fascination with male same-sex desire, which "generates a systematic and unstable duplicity of sexual signs" (Lamos 1999, 252–53). That is to say, evidence concerning homosexuality is not misconstrued by the characters or the readers, nor is its significance misapprehended. Rather the nature and meaning of male same-sex desire is discursively produced as unconstruable and inapprehensible in any proper way. Thus the commission of error is everywhere flush with the circulation of data, all of which answers to the polarized affective responses that homosexuality seems to incite.

Fascination is nurtured inasmuch as the most patent show of homosexual involvement, being hollowed out by the structural equivocations of the signs themselves and the interpretive evasions they allow, retains "the allure of hidden knowledge" (253). Such is the case with Murphy and his "homosexual" tattoo for his audience in the cabman's shelter: even as he bares his "manly chest," Murphy and the sign etched thereupon both remain "provocatively mysterious." Such is the case as well, Lamos implies, with the space of "Eumaeus" itself, the cabman's shelter, for the readers of *Ulysses*, who experience a sense of its "dangers and thrills" only, or through the "erratic logic of guesswork" (253). On the other side, the fear of homosexuality, and in particular of being implicated therein, finds relief in the same structural errancy. The "mistakes and misjudgements" in Bloom's evaluation of Murphy allow for a prudent suspicion of the sailor that never passes into a clear apprehension of his avowed sexuality. This knowing ignorance of sexual perversion, in turn, allows Bloom to cultivate his special intimacy with Stephen and, in the end, to walk off arm in arm with him, "protected from homophobic retribution by their apparent ignorance" (248).

Thanks to the widespread presumption of a woman's sexual ignorance during this period, Lamos writes, the same psychic defense works especially well with respect to female homoeroticism, and while there is not a lot represented in *Ulysses*, Joyce does trade on the notorious invisibility of lesbian desire to create, in Molly Bloom, his ultimate example of the "ignorance is bliss" principle (Lamos 1994, 353). Molly's soliloquy enjoys a legendary reputation for unstinting sexual self-disclosure. Yet while she admits to a plainly homoerotic encounter with Hester Stanhope, she remains fully oblivious to its homoerotic quality and therefore freed of any anxiety about her own heterosexual credentials or, as it seems, any doubts of them on the part of her readers.

Molly's legendary sexual candor turns out to be a sign that Molly does not even have to labor at her enabling ignorance, unlike Joyce's other characters and, Lamos assures us, unlike Joyce himself. Like Levine, Lamos takes account of Joyce's own anxieties about same-sex desire in her assessment of his depiction of its social mythologies. Whereas Levine sees Joyce expressing and exorcising his own panic in the reactions of his characters, Lamos sees him expressing his own instinct of self-protection in the self-protective ignorance he exposes in them. These are two sides of the same "third-wave" perspective, in which Joyce dialectically engages the structural homophobia of his society as a means of offloading, if not overcoming, his own associations of homosexuality with personal shame and social abjection.

The Next Wave

It is precisely the linkage of queer sexuality with personal shame and social abjection that may serve to animate the next wave of sexual criticism on *Ulysses*. I would like to start with a premise directly opposed to all previous scholarship in this area, one that will lead us, in my view, to a more dialectical conception of queer ideology in *Ulysses*. Although inseparable in its own right from other strains of homosocial desire, homosexuality is a *socially* distinctive, tremendously important, and highly valued class of perversion for Joyce precisely *because* of the associated shame and stigma, of which Joyce's own occasional homophobia might be accounted a displaced form of sympathetic identification. That is to say, what critics have designated Joyce's homosexual anxiety or panic (as manifest in his alter egos) is in fact the psychic condition for Joyce's affirmative literary investment in same-sex desire, rather than his reason to elide or marginalize it. Conversely, Joyce's affirmative literary engagement with homoeroticism does not represent, *in any simple sense,* a suspension of or a victory over his homophobic shame or "othering." To understand this paradox, it is necessary first to appreciate the potent ethical value that shame held for Joyce, and why it plays such a role.

As distinct from guilt, a negative feeling about one's actions, shame goes to one's identity, personal and corporate. As Helen Lynd writes, "I feel guilty for what I have done, I feel shame for what I am" (22). For a native Irish Catholic like Joyce, shame was an inherited condition, at once racial and religious. On one side, the Augustinian worldview endemic to Irish Catholicism propounded the *essential* worthlessness of humanity; on the other, the type of Irishness that Catholicism marked, Celtic Irishness, was relegated in the ethnology of the early twentieth century to the lowest place among the dominant European races. James Joyce felt this overdetermined shame to be such an integral part of his identity that in later years he mocked it with a pun, calling himself "shame's voice" (Brivic 2001, 177), a title that implies a number of pertinent self-descriptions, the most pertinent one here being: Joyce's voice as a apologist for shame.

Because shame goes to one's very being, it is, "in specific terms, irreversible" (Lynd 50). All that can be done is to change the terms. In *The Trouble with Normal,* Michael Warner lays out two alternative methods for doing so. Typically, people attempt to rid themselves of shame by projecting it onto others who may be construed as socially inferior to themselves. The objects of this sort of projection, such as the community Warner denominates "queer," are compelled to bear a still more profound shame, a "tainted" identity (Warner 37). Within such stigmatized communities, in turn, the second, positive strategy emerges for confronting shame, one that is itself "queer" in challenging not just particular norms but the very idea of normativity as such. For Warner, this project necessitates learning to dispense with dignity, insofar as social virtue remains tied to hierarchical notions of honor and respectability (36). To be embraced instead is a more democratized style of dignity, which is capable of accommodating the potential for humiliation that is endemic to social, if not human existence. A commitment to this brand of dignity can serve, on Warner's account, to undermine the merit of respectability itself, thus giving the experience of shame or critical voice and authority (36–37).

Owing perhaps to his ambiguous social status as both a respectable middle-class paterfamilias and a perpetually mendicant Irish Catholic bohemian, Joyce adopted the remarkable strategy of employing both of these opposed methods in conjunction. The voicing of shame in Joyce's work targets, in the first instance, subdominant subjects and categories of social being. That is to say, Joyce's traffic in shame comprises a strong element of projection and othering. At the same time, however, the projection of shame in Joyce regularly possesses a kind of feedback mechanism, redounding upon its source and opening the possibility for a self-abasing partnership with the other. Through its deployment as an instrument and a currency of disaffiliation, shame is revealed to be a condition of a "queer" identification, an identification-in-abjection, outside the norms of respectability and entitlement. At the same time, it would also seem that lowliness in Joyce can only be suffered as a vehicle of belonging or solidarity if it is first inflicted upon or held against another. Thus, in "The Dead," a complacently bourgeois Gabriel must first register a certain disdain for the peasant Michael Furey, "a boy in the gas works," in order to see his own shame (literally) reflected back to him: "A shameful consciousness of his person assailed him. He saw himself as a ludicrous figure, acting as a pennyboy for his aunts . . . the pitiable fatuous fellow he had caught a glimpse of in the mirror . . . shame . . . burned upon his forehead" (1992, 221). While reflecting upon the muse of his villanelle, Stephen the misogynist takes stock of the "dark shame of her womanhood," the "strange humiliation of her nature," so that he might "with tender compassion," identify his sinful soul and hers (242). Just then, and only then, is he able to complete his poem. The narrative structure of *Giacomo Joyce* follows Joyce's own progress from degrading his young Jewish student—likening her to a series of animals—to identifying her now-liberated voice with his own. These examples, I believe, illuminate and help to resolve a long-standing, often implicit tension within Joyce studies.

As critics have taken up questions concerning Joyce and feminism, Joyce and Jewishness, Joyce and race, Joyce and colonialism, we have been sporadically troubled, I believe, by the felt necessity of squaring a literary project like *Ulysses*, which seems so impressively empathetic in its ethical and political implications, with the exposure in letters, his brother's Trieste diary, and reported conversations revealing a stubborn, residual misogyny and a certain proclivity for ethnic stereotyping. The solution, I would submit, is not to balance the two sides of the problem against one another, but to treat them as continuous in their opposition or antagonism. The distinctive curvature of Joyce's political ethos entails "othering," gendered and racial, as a *means* to identification-in-otherness, that is, in shamed exile from esteem or respectability.

If we apply the same formula to the *sexual* politics of *Ulysses*, we will see that the homophobic anxieties of the characters tell only half the story. Joyce designs certain narrative scenarios to reveal the psychic possibility and the ethical necessity of Bloom and Stephen converting their defensiveness toward a socially dishonored "type" of (sexual) difference into a recognition of their own ignoble *self-difference* as sexual beings, of the entanglement of their sexual desire and the varieties of desire they disown. I offer two examples, both of which, not coincidentally, concern decisive cruxes or turning points in the novel.

As I have explored elsewhere, Stephen actually delivers his Shakespeare theory twice in "Scylla and Charybdis," completing one version before the *entr'acte*, when Mulligan enters, and then beginning anew at that point (Valente 116–23). Playing the dandy, Mulligan introduces the issue of homoeroticism, which Stephen has managed to quarantine from his account to this point. With Richard Best's interest piqued, such exclusion is no longer possible, and Stephen must engage the question. At the same time, he redirects the "charge of pederasty brought against the bard" (*U*, 9.732), with whom he identifies, against Best, calling him "Tame essence of Wilde." Nevertheless, the discussion of perverse sexuality does provoke Stephen to articulate a crucial new element in his aesthetics theory, the idea of paternal incertitude. Applying only to male progeny, this signature tenet of Stephen's is patently crafted to immunize father-son identification from the taint of somatic or erotic connection. But the homosexual panic motivating this addition surges into the very texture of Stephen's language, undoing the careful repression of his Shakespeare narrative: "they are sundered by a bodily shame so steadfast that the criminal *a[n]nals* of the world . . . hardly record its *breach*" (*U*, 9.850–52). This "breach" of Stephen's defenses can occur, I would argue, only because Stephen's identification with Shakespeare encompasses that "bodily shame" to which "the charges of pederasty" still subject "the bard." His projection of Shakespeare's ignominy onto the "blood ephebe," Best, allows Stephen to share the "bodily shame," under color of denial, as a (homoeroticized) son. Just as his sharing of E—C—'s projected "shame" proves vital to finishing his villanelle, so his less-conscious participation in Best's projected debasement is key to bringing his Shakespeare theory to closure.

My final example is a frame of the masochistic encounter of Bloom and Bella. Amid the transgendering burlesque, a scene of plainly homosexual sodomy appears: "You were a nicelooking Miriam when you clipped your backgate hairs and lay swooning in the thing across the bed as Mrs Dandrade about to be violated by lieutenant Smythe-Smythe [etc.etc.]" (*U*, 15.2999–3008). The scene is crucial because in suspending the "reality" of gender transposition, however briefly, it permits us to see how this dramatic technique admits of other than *exclusively gendered* functions. This very scene, for example, confounds memory and fantasy, accusation and confession and so enacts a transfer of perspective, voice, even identity from Bloom to Bella and back. The gender switches throughout are meant in part to underline such transfers, to remind us that Bloom and Bella mutually ventriloquize or channel each other on a continual basis. This sort of radical mobility of subject position is not only what is most distinctive about the method of "Circe," it is what makes "Circe" the distinctive vehicle of Joyce's queer political ethos. For the episode's dreamscript enables a condensation of Joyce's characteristic double move of othering-identification into a seamless dialectical gesture. Bloom others the various roles he plays: the whore, the transvestite, the cuckold, the Jew, the queer; he impersonates them as wretched caricatures; but in so doing he immediately identifies with and *as* them. Conversely, he identifies with various subdominant subject positions, but only insofar as they have been othered, reduced to the lowest social denominator of social disrepute and humiliation. Bloom, that is, does not simply submit himself to abjection; he masochistically identifies with the abjection in the stereotyped others his fantasy conjures forth.

One way of understanding Joyce's achievement in the Bella encounter is to note that he takes us through the looking glass where the social construction of queer sexual arrangements passes into the queer sexual modeling of social arrangements. Joyce, in effect, rewrites his (and Bloom's) perverse mode of eros, masochism, in which an empowered (male) subject scripts his own abasement, as his preferred political ethos, in which a relatively disempowered subject or subject position serves as both medium (of projection) and telos (of identification). The masochistic contract becomes a blueprint for Joyce's dialectical social contract. Having said that, we should notice that the contract is not of the progressively liberalizing variety, nor is the dialectic a Hegelian one of progressive self-overcoming. What links queer sexuality and queer social ethics in *Ulysses* is an intense satisfaction that inheres neither in compliance with norms, nor in their eradication, but in the act of exceeding them; neither in social distinctions nor in their obsolescence, but in their compulsive erasure. It is, in short, a truly perverse form of satisfaction, dependent upon its antipathies, which is also to say it runs athwart of our more utopian ideas about queer sexuality, and about Joyce.

Notes

1. The critical "waves" do not succeed one another in lockstep; there is significant overlap. The order does reflect the vintage of their conceptual or theoretical instruments and assumptions, however.

2. Evidence of Joyce's condescending, sometimes disdainful, attitude toward homosexuality includes Joyce, *Selected Letters*, 74, 96, 136; Ellmann 1982, 438; and Power 71.

III

PRE- AND POST-PUBLICATION

6

Joycean Pop Culture

Fragments toward an Institutional History and Futurology

GREGORY M. DOWNING

I

It is clear from early in Joyce's career that he had ambitions to subsume into his literary work as much as he could of every kind of data forming the constituent detail of contemporary existence. By the time he completed *Ulysses* let alone *Finnegans Wake*, "as much as he could" ended up amounting to far more than is discernible in the literary work of his precursors and contemporaries. Given this ambition, he almost unavoidably included a great deal of not just elite but also popular culture. His efforts along these lines obviously inspired other modernists to find their own ways of deploying popular culture to narrative and thematic effect: recall Woolf's sky-written advertisement early in her own novelistic daybook *Mrs. Dalloway*, or Fitzgerald with his ominous ocular billboard in *The Great Gatsby*—both published just three years after *Ulysses*. However, Joyce's range of allusion to cultural environs is far broader than that of any of his epigones. It therefore only makes sense that the secondary literature on aspects of Joyce and his circumambient culture is far larger and wider-ranging than those devoted to other modernists. This essay examines one major aspect of that Joycean secondary literature: popular culture.

Nearly all of the twentieth century's myriad new conceptual frameworks and methodological innovations for professional analysis of literature were developed in part to account for the challenging breadth and innovation of Joyce's work. New Criticism, formalism, poststructuralism, postmodern analysis generally: all were pioneered and piloted partly to capture more of Joyce's work than prior exegetical methods had captured, or captured well. New Criticism and formalism aspired to convey less imperfectly the denser array of multiple patterns that readers were noticing in Joyce's work. Postmodern and poststructural modes often emphasized opposite or complementary issues, one of the most central being to critique aspects of a literary work that reveal and/or conceal problematic aspects of the society and culture that always encircle any text. As postmodern modes came to dominate professional and academic discourse about literature in the last quarter of the twentieth century, the Joycean secondary literature tended to open up intensive discussion of the problems and possibilities implicit in all areas of cultural reference in Joyce's work, including popular culture. It is important to situate these developments against their cultural-history backgrounds: an acknowledgment, in a way, of the New Historicist mode of cultural-history contextualization that postmodern analysis commonly recommends and enacts.

One of the most challenging parts of mapping an academic discipline or subspecialty is the contingency inevitably inherent in its history and its shapes. Had the entire field of intellectual endeavor been divided up at one moment in accordance with a single complete worldview, the resultant territories would present fewer hints of arbitrariness or puzzlement. But like anything else, intellectual endeavor has its historical aspects, as ideas are developed in some sort of succession. Cultural analysis from a European background reflects the understandable historical reality that its cultures first developed intellectual tools to explicate their own elite traditional religious and literary artifacts and other high-status phenomena. Only in the penultimate century of the second millennium CE did, for example, English studies emerge in service of the idea that modern literature deserved the same serious attention devoted to classical literature since ancient times, and likewise only then was social science created to serve the idea that society's structures—not only the esteemed but also the most informal and intellectually ignored—merited close analysis in search of insights into how society is shaped and might evolve in the future. Only in that same nineteenth century did folklore studies emerge to serve the idea that popular culture in general should be scanned carefully for what might be revealed about nonelite thinking, and likewise only then did ethnography and anthropology come into existence in pursuit of the sense that non-European cultural modes would also repay study.

Study of the popular-cultural aspects of literature is a more recent outgrowth of this same historical process of gradually expanding horizons. In the 1960s, a British cultural studies movement arose (not to be confused with another European definition of "cultural studies," in the sense of area studies, that is, studies of individual cultures as such, one at a time). This movement wanted to expand academic examination and interpretation via two new approaches: (1) analysis of popular culture (television programs, comics, advertising, etc.) along the kinds of lines formerly followed only in analyzing elite documents, and (2) placement of all cultural artifacts, including those such as serious literature that were already being examined by other disciplines via traditional elite modes, into the interpretive and evaluative contexts offered by antitraditional and anti-elite cultural and political analysis from a 1960s New Left perspective. The University of Birmingham became a locus for such analysis in 1964 with the founding of its Centre for Contemporary Cultural Studies, which brought together elements from the social sciences and sociology, close literary analysis, then-emerging communication or media studies, political theory, and historical methodologies. Already in 1957 cofounder Richard Hoggart's *The Uses of Literacy* had examined the British working-class culture he had grown up in from a perspective that mixed sociological, literary, and political analysis, all of it critical of the hierarchical assumptions characteristic of the traditional British class system.

Of course, long before cultural studies had even gotten established (let alone adopted by and adapted to North American academia), popular culture had already been forced on the exegetical attention of Joyce scholars simply by the fabric of Joycean textuality in itself. Several major specialties within Joyce studies predate the great influence, in the final third of the twentieth century, of cultural studies or popular-culture studies in something like the Birmingham mode as an acknowledged academic approach. For example, the study of music in Joyce's work had already come strongly to the fore in the 1950s, culminating in Hodgart and Worthington's 1959 *Song in the Works of James Joyce*, the first scholarly work to list allusions made to a single topic throughout the entire Joycean corpus, covered line by line.[1] While some of the music dealt with by *Song* is classical, a great deal of it is popular music in some sense or other, and Joyce's eclectic intermixing—or, perhaps more accurately, his programmatically synthesizing literary miscegenation—of elite and popular music only emphasized the status of the latter as a worthy topic for serious study, and thus more broadly as a significant cultural phenomenon in itself.

Zack Bowen, a student of Worthington, established his expertise in the field with a 1974 updating of her book.[2] He chronicled his ongoing interest in Joyce and music in 1995 when he brought out *Bloom's Old Sweet Song*, gathering items originally published from 1967 through 1992, and, three years later, published Jack Weaver's *Joyce's Music and Noise* in the University Press of Florida Joyce series that he edited. Meanwhile, Ruth Bauerle has focused her main energies on Joyce and music, often popular music, during a career that likewise spans from the late 1960s through the present. Her first book-length work, *The James Joyce Songbook* (1982), collected lyrics and music for nearly all of the two hundred songs Joyce was known to have alluded to several times or in several works; her 1993 *Picking Up Airs* volume collected work from several Joyceans, including Bowen, who had long been investigating the presence in Joyce's work of music, prominently including popular music. Then, in *Joyce's Grand Operoar* (1997), Bauerle edited and completed the accumulated decades of Hodgart's post-1959 work. Although opera may have a reputation now as elite culture, its status as vocal and dramatic made it in many ways popular entertainment in Joyce's day (recall the "When First I Saw" aria in "Sirens"), and therefore appropriate for treatment as popular culture by Joyceans. In that context, Timothy Martin's *Joyce and Wagner* (1991) and the 1999 volume *Bronze by Gold: The Music of Joyce* edited by Sebastian Knowles are actually, in some regards, as much a part of the history of popular culture in Joyce as the research on music-hall songs entered into in such impressive detail by the main stream of Joyce-and-music work from Hodgart and Worthington through Bowen and Bauerle.

Institutionally, it is interesting to note that the topic of (popular) music in Joyce's work has tooled along at a nice clip for nearly half a century now without having adopted the conceptual and terminological modes of cultural studies, which I will examine in more detail in a moment. The work of Bowen and Bauerle consists of textual explication and the identification of musical allusions in Joyce's work. In some measure, this might be regarded as a generational phenomenon; Bowen and Bauerle were trained and began publishing when formalism still reigned in the literature departments of American universities, and both of them have extended for decades the work of Worthington and Hodgart, whose methods derive from even deeper in the New Critical era of careful exegesis based on closely observed textual detail.

Cultural whigs, given their assumption that progress in the descriptive chronological sense equates to progress in the pregnant sense, often criticize or dismiss existing scholarly publications to the extent that they are linkable to prior (that is, "outdated") cultural modes and methodologies. We might instead note more neutrally that existing Joyce-and-popular-music spade-work offers information and possible insights that stick closely to the text and its actual cultural-history context. (In the case of popular music, this context consists of the lyrics, arrangements, themes, and implications of the popular music known to Joyce.) This has the advantage of making it poten-tially useful to future readers and scholars of any stripe—and one of the few things we can say with any certainty about the cultural future and the future of Joyce studies is that there will be lots of different stripes over time, and usually in fact at the same time. In that light, scholarly work that deals with the text in itself in some of its actual cultural context does a long-term service and hence, to borrow rather cheekily for application to academic libraries a term from supermarket language, possesses a longer potential shelf-life than scholarly products formulated to please the current cultural and political tastes of professional students of literature.

II

And this latter tendency is an important conceptual, rhetorical, and phatic factor in the process whereby cultural studies generally, and its popular-culture studies incarnation, have come to the fore in recent decades. Fused in the crucible of 1960s politics, cultural studies and cultural criticism resonate quite well with academics who were part of that era themselves or who have been trained by those who were touched by its main ideas. The central meth od is examination of literary texts and anything contained within them via a sociopolitical and cultural analysis that interprets any phenomenon with intensive attention to issues of material power: class, money, political and/or social power as wielded in any of its many overt or covert manifestations. Even when no advocacy, explicit or even especially strongly hinted at, ap-pears in the resultant analysis, the approach is usually—often, pervasively—critical of many elite or mainstream social arrangements, past and present. The pervasive if often indirect nature of the critique is reflected in the mul-tiple ways in which critique shows up in nearly every passage of a document generated using this approach. The sheer focus on aspects of popular culture already constitutes a critique of the narrowness of range of elite culture and elite literary study. And the substantive criticisms, implicit or explicit, always stick closely to a cohesive set of power-oriented sociopolitical and cultural criteria as they have evolved under the broad New Left ideological umbrella during the final third of the twentieth century and on into the still-new one: criteria and agendas that are extremely familiar in the written and oral discourse of every cohort within university humanities and social science departments, from current undergraduates to senior and emeritus faculty.

This is a significant conceptual and methodological transition. As we saw in our discussion of the history of Joyce-and-music scholarship, Joyce studies in general had developed, well prior to the ascent to prominence of academic cultural studies, a basically empirical, inferential, and contextualizing treatment of aspects of popular culture. Analysts of Joyce's work had noticed and been drawn to account for his popular-culture content in some basic fashion, without trying to advocate their own ideological preferences in any specific fashion. This had upsides and/or downsides, depending on the evaluative criteria one applies. But it certainly leaves future scholars with considerable latitude to move forward in whatever ways they wish, without having first to come to terms with all the details constitutive of the ideological advocacy of some prior scholarly era, overlain upon Joyce's work in the act of discussing it. One downside, though, is the deferral of the natural desire to come to specific conclusions concerning the overall implications of Joyce's work.

But whatever the potential positives and negatives of the basically data-gathering modes of pre-postmodern studies of Joyce and popular-culture topics such as music, in the decades following the rise to influence of post-modern cultural studies in Anglophone academia a second strand of often independent analysis of the presence of popular culture in Joyce emerged and over time attained prominence among Joyceans. Here in section 2 I will trace and analyze that quarter-century-long development, reserving evaluation and futurology for section 3.

The ground for this emergence within Joyce studies was seeded when European postmodern modes of literary analysis were applied to Joyce's work. Published scholarly analysis of the work of probably the most esteemed of Anglophone literary modernists was an understandably major factor in the rise of those modes to general hegemony in Anglophone humanities departments. The touchstone document in this process was Margot Norris's *The Decentered Universe of "Finnegans Wake": A Structuralist Analysis* (1976), which was actually a poststructural analysis, though neither term (that is, with or without the prefix) was well known in literature departments at the beginning of the final quarter of the twentieth century. Terminology aside,

Norris's first book marked a major shift in American scholarship. Meanwhile, R. B. (Brandon) Kershner's first articles, both on Joyce, appear in the same year, in the *James Joyce Quarterly* and *ELH*, and his third article, in 1977, is overtly popular-cultural in orientation: "Joyce as Historian: Popular Literature and Popular Consciousness."[3] Kershner will become the leading scholar on the topic of Joyce and popular culture in the 1990s, but from 1978 through 1986 he publishes little, and nothing on Joyce. So the potential marriage of Joyce studies and popular-culture studies in a postmodern fashion remains underexploited for some years, as other Joyce scholars work on exploring many of the other available postmodern avenues in the late 1970s and early 1980s.

It is therefore really Cheryl Herr whose early work first illustrates in great detail how some areas of postmodern analysis can be brought to bear upon the popular-culture aspects of Joyce studies. Her early publications on Joyce all deal with popular culture, and her 1986 book *Joyce's Anatomy of Culture* is the true mile-zero marker in the postmodern manifestation of this subfield. The book was epochal in its detailed examination of the relationship between Joyce's work and three areas of popular-culture discourse: newspapers with their articles, popular theater such as pantomime and music-hall performance, and the sermon—plus such related phenomena and typical objects of cultural-studies analysis as advertising (which both newspapers and theaters were involved with, not to mention the Catholic Church itself; see "advertisements" in Herr's index) and music (so central to the popular theatrical tradition). Rejecting as inadequate existing studies focused on style and voice, Herr views Joyce and the sociocultural context in and against which he operated as characterized by forms of language that enact and/or rebel against the attempted control of language and thought by which a society and its institutions (in Herr's book, press, stage, and church) seek either to enforce or resist controlling norms and hierarchies of value and power. Her preface and extensive introduction constitute a manifesto for critical cultural analysis carried out via examination of elements of popular culture literarily redeployed by Joyce's work.

In mapping out her theoretical position and affinities, Herr's introduction details her affiliations with an impressive array of postmodern authors and modes. Marxist theoreticians of literature and culture such as Jameson and Althusser, and such English Marxist literary scholars as Raymond Williams and Terry Eagleton, are cited as authorities for interpreting culture and literature in sociopolitical and socioeconomic context, with an emphasis on critically exposing and subverting the agendas in dominant ideological practices. The common educated-class mode of critiquing conventional society and its particular centers of power leads Herr to portray Joyce as a subverter of those discourses and a narrative critic of dominant social relations (class, gender, nation, religion, and so on). Methodologically, Herr's analysis of text and culture in pursuit of patterns of meaning is explicitly grounded in the semiotic (meaning-identifying) work of Umberto Eco, as well as in the *Ulysses*- and *Wake*-relevant concept of a "text of the culture," which Herr adopts from Cesare Segre, who had drawn in turn on the ideas of the Russian formalist Yuri Lotman. Yes, there is no specific mention of the term *cultural studies* yet—that will come in work that will arrive in Herr's wake. Nonetheless, *Joyce's Anatomy of Culture* represents a fully fledged critical semiotic analysis of ideological discourses present in some major popular-cultural aspects (journalistic, theatrical, homiletic) of Joyce's work, as well as in some of the sociocultural contexts of that work: a combination that reflects the cultural-studies mix of New Left social criticism with wide-ranging cultural analysis programmatically rivaling the sophisticated attention traditionally paid to elite culture. After all, the mix of modes that Birmingham-school cultural studies brought together in the 1960s was so central to the general educated-class ethos of the last third of the twentieth century that, even without primary Birmingham-school influence, the same mix ends up being replicated in a general fashion by Herr, who simply employs other theorists who in the mid-1980s phase of North American academic postmodernism seemed closer to hand and more fashionable than British scholars of the mid-1960s.

In the late 1980s and early 1990s, Herr continues along similar lines with publications that apply to Joyce and modernism such postmodern modes of cultural criticism as Marxism, feminism, postmodern psychoanalysis, and Foucauldian cultural-history analysis. Meanwhile, from the mid- through the late 1980s, Brandon Kershner returns to Joyce work and publishes several articles, culminating in his 1989 *Joyce, Bakhtin, and Popular Literature*. This is the second great pillar of Joycean popular-culture and cultural-studies analysis. Like Herr, he cites in his initial theoretical discussion the Western Marxists Jameson and Althusser (12–13) while adding the members of the Frankfurt school of Marxist cultural analysis (11) who are absent from *Anatomy*. Also like Herr, he deploys poststructuralist modes of literary and cultural analysis, citing names she too cites such as Kristeva and Culler

(19). However, the main theoretical underpinnings for Kershner's book come from a thinker not cited at all by Herr: the Russian formalist Bakhtin. This is diagnostic. Kershner's work certainly touches on the same general cluster of postmodern ideas for critically analyzing literature and culture as Herr's. However, where those ideas mandate a particular political or cultural stance, Kershner is a bit closer to the pre-postmodern mode in holding them at arm's length, treating them as useful concepts for explaining parts of some phenomena from some angles. This contrasts with Herr's mode of engaging, through the academic mediation of abstract terminology, in fairly unambiguous cultural politics, or political politics—at any rate, in criticism of various existing social arrangements accompanied by implicit or explicit advocacy of different ones.

Bakhtin, Kershner's major source and model, is well known for leaving his own particular politico-cultural position unclear, to the point where he has been portrayed as a covert advocate of anything from democratic humanism to orthodox Soviet Marxism, without any of those characterizations having been able to vanquish his therefore apparently programmatic ideological ambiguity, as Kershner himself rather approvingly mentions at the outset of his Bakhtin discussion (15). Kershner finds Bakhtin's flexibility and suggestiveness (15) appropriate not only to Joyce's work in itself but also to the inclusive, careful, flexible approach that Kershner wishes to take to Joyce. A methodology of subsumptive and open-minded analysis of the complexities of text and culture in their totalities grows out of such key Kershner-discussed Bakhtinian concepts as polyphony and heteroglossia (both express the idea that any text and any culture are constituted of multiple linguistically embodied perspectives), dialogism (Bakhtin's central concept that a text's and any sociocultural complex's multiple voices and worldviews jostle complexly with each other), and carnivalization (the crucial process whereby "monological" cultures and forms of discourse are critiqued and opened up to the possibility of greater acknowledgment of complexity by playful, boundary-violating, assumption-overturning linguistic and cultural modes, a process that Bakhtin emphasizes in his dissertation on Rabelais, and that Kershner in turn understandably views as highly germane to *Ulysses* and *Finnegans Wake* [17]). Hence, in the rest of his first chapter and in the body of his book, Kershner brings to bear a whole array of evidence concerning Joyce's actual familiarity with and deployment of what was viewed in Joyce's own cultural environment as popular literature and popular writing, while avoiding any cultural advocacy of his own, beyond a rather open-ended posi-tive valorization of textual and conceptual inclusion that seeks to promote improved awareness and better comprehension of the complexities—the dialogisms—inherent in Joyce's texts, in Joyce's ambient culture, and in the interface between those two phenomena, without overlaying the advocacy of any specific late twentieth-century political agenda.

Herr's 1986 and Kershner's 1989 books not only announce the onset but also form the two great monuments of cultural-studies analysis of Joyce ex-hibiting a popular-culture emphasis. Herr pilots the cultural-criticism mode and Kershner the cautious-and-careful-awareness-of-complexity mode. What naturally happens next is that other scholars also begin explicitly ap-proaching cultural issues in Joyce: for example, Mary Lowe-Evans's *Crimes Against Fecundity* (1989) examines Joycean attitudes toward sexual repro-duction. Her approach is much closer to Herr's than to Kershner's, whose work came out the same year as her own.[4] Meanwhile, other major new au-thors develop the cultural-studies and popular-culture approaches in differ-ent directions. Garry Leonard and Jennifer Wicke begin publishing related work in 1990–91, and eventually come to the fore as major specialists in the subfield.[5] In 1992, the February University of Miami Joyce conference is dedicated to "Popular Culture."

With the Herr and Kershner volumes in place as guidebooks and other scholars moving forward along similar lines, the ground is laid for 1993, the *annus mirabilis* of Joyce and popular-culture studies. First, the cultural-studies and popular-culture approaches are given the imprimatur, or more accurately the discatur (let-it-be-taught), of the Modern Language Asso-ciation when McCormick and Steinberg's *Approaches to Teaching Joyce's "Ulysses"* appears, containing essays about how to present *Ulysses* pedagogi-cally both through a popular-culture lens and with attention to the intersec-tion of cultural and political critique. The same year sees Kershner's edition of the text of *A Portrait*, accompanied by concise presentations of various postmodern analytical modes, with an essay-length application of each to *Portrait*. And other toilers in the popular-culture fields continue to harvest the results of their work. Beyond her essay in Kershner's *Portrait* volume and her coauthored essay "Political Contexts for *Ulysses*" in *Approaches*, Herr publishes more analysis of Joyce's deployment of sermons. Garry Leonard's first book-length study of Joyce appears, applying Lacanian postmodern psy-chocultural critical analysis to *Dubliners*.

But given the constant stream of new work on Joyce, it is easy for even the most assiduous scholar to miss, or fail to read immediately, important new publications. That makes all the more important the appearance in 1993 of not just a special issue but a double issue of perhaps the central document, from the early 1960s on, of Joyce studies, the *James Joyce Quarterly*. This issue (*JJQ* 30–31, nos. 4, 1 [Summer-Fall 1993]) consists of over a dozen often quite substantial essays, amounting to well over three hundred pages (that is, something comparable in verbal impact to Herr's or Kershner's work). The essays treat Joyce from a popular-culture angle, focusing specifically on the "Joyce and Advertising" subtopic on which Herr, following cultural studies and popular-culture studies, had placed some emphasis already in 1986. The issue opens with essays by Leonard and Wicke, the outside coeditors, followed immediately by one from Kershner, and then in turn from other figures who had either already published on Joyce from an angle connected to popular culture (such as Lowe-Evans) or else would become more prominent Joyce scholars later in the decade (for example, Mark Osteen, Kevin Dettmar, and Ellen Carol Jones, whose major book-length publications on Joyce would appear respectively in 1995, 1996, and 1998). The focus on advertising permits analysis of popular culture along the lines of the cultural criticism already traced by Herr: sociocultural critique based on economic issues with political implications. Look at the (in some cases, partial) titles and subtitles of the essays that appear earlier in the issue (the essays without wording like this in the title or subtitle are placed, with one exception, in the second half of the issue): "Advertising and Commodity Culture" (Leonard); "Modernity Must Advertise: Aura, Desire, and Decolonialization" (Herr); "Power, Pornography, and the Problem of Pleasure: The Semerotics of Desire and Commodity Culture" (Leonard); "Sex Credit: Consumer Capitalism in *Ulysses*" (Michael Tratner); "Bloom, Advertising, and the Domestic Economy" (Osteen); "Commodification, Exchange Value, and the Figure of Woman" (Stephen Watt); "Advertising Narcissism" (Peggy Ochoa); and "Selling *Ulysses*" (Dettmar). Meanwhile, it is interesting to note that Kershner's contribution, although it takes pride of place—understandably, given his 1989 monograph—right after the coeditors' own essays, is the only article in the issue's first half whose title and subtitle do not contain terminology of this kind. "The Strongest Man in the World: Joyce or Sandow?" foregoes the cues to political and economic criticism patent in the preceding list of title-wording, and even the question mark with which the title ends hints rhetorically at the perspective of complex ambiguity characteristic of Kershner's version of Joycean popular-culture work.

With its passport now boasting stamps of semi-official approval wielded from within the Joyce field by the *JJQ* as well as from the field's larger institutional context by the Modern Language Association, Joycean popular-cultural studies developed rapidly during the rest of the 1990s, now as a mainstream and even prestigious approach rather than an experimental or highly specialized one. Articles that the *MLA Bibliography* tags with the keyword *popular culture* continue to appear in *JJQ* from volume 32 (1994). The most prominent of the immediate after-echoes of 1993 is the following year's book-collection by Richard Pearce on the final episode of *Ulysses* from (as its subtitle explicitly notes) a cultural-studies standpoint, complete with essays from Herr, Leonard, and Wicke, as well as from Heininger, who had written the popular-culture essay for the MLA volume and McCormick, who had coedited it. The 1994 volume's roots are in the late 1980s, and the general approach is therefore closer to Herr's, whose essay immediately follows the editor's and who is listed by the index as mentioned in nearly twenty passages in the volume. Although "polylogue" in the volume's subtitle may seem to suggest Bakhtin or Kershner, this is actually only a postmodern-sounding way of saying that the volume is a book-collection. Kershner's name does not appear in the index, and his book is listed in the Works Cited list as only the very shortest item among the book's twelve essays.

But Kershner was working on his own book-collection. In 1996, as part of the then-new Joyce series at Florida, he does the same thing in book-collection format that the Leonard-Wicke *JJQ* double issue had done from within the bastion of the main Joycean periodical: compile a book-length series of essays illustrating and applying a popular-culture approach to many different areas of Joyce's work and its sociocultural context. Despite a somewhat smaller size, *Joyce and Popular Culture* ranges far more widely, in terms of both content and approach, than the *JJQ*'s "Advertising" issue. Though the volume does contain an essay from Leonard on advertising, such central Joyce-and-popular-culture figures as Herr and Wicke are absent. The collection instead displays popular-culture analysis by other scholars, as the approach becomes widely disseminated, comprehended, respected, and applied in an array of ways. There is material from newer Joyceans who had previously been working in related postmodern frameworks, for example, Vincent Cheng, who the prior year had published the first book on Joyce from a postcolonial-studies angle, and Derek Attridge, who with his "Theoretical Approaches to Popular Culture" contribution here ranges beyond the Joyce-and-postmodern-analysis-of-language specialty he had marked out for himself in the mid- and late 1980s. There is also work by Joyceans who have become interested in the popular-culture trend after engaging in decades of Joycean publication dating back to well before the advent of postmodern or cultural-studies analysis, for example, Zack Bowen, David Hayman, Michael Begnal, and Chester Anderson. There is work from scholars new to Joycean publication who, despite approaching Joyce's work from a not strictly postmodern theoretical angle, nonetheless deal with topics significant to cultural studies, for example, Donald Theall with his essay on Joyce, media, and communications technology. The essays range more widely as the popular-culture field gets more developed and the accumulation of existing publications opens up new possibilities while also closing off some topics as "already done": some *Joyce and Popular Culture* essays treat Joyce and late twentieth-century popular culture, as for example Adrian Peever writing on Joyce and film with special attention to the Irish actress and producer Fionnula Flanagan, and Helene Meyers discussing Amanda Cross's *James Joyce Murder* mystery novel.

So by 1996, "Joyce and popular culture" has become a large area of publication among all kinds of Joyce scholars with all kinds of approaches, with Herr and Kershner functioning not only as authors whose ongoing productivity continues to develop the subfield but also as scholarly models for, respectively, more politically advocatory and more complexly and ambiguously culture-analytical approaches to the study of the interface between Joyce and popular culture. We can only point to a few noticeable waves from this tide. More works on special topics that involve popular culture appear regularly in the late 1990s, not only from central figures such as Garry Leonard (whose *Advertising and Commodity Culture in Joyce* comes out in 1998) but also from an array of authors on an array of topics (aside from several mid/late-1990s items mentioned above, there is *Modernism's Body: Sex, Culture, and Joyce* by Christine Froula, 1996). More book-length essay-collections appear, such as Cheng, Devlin, and Norris's *Joycean Cultures/Culturing Joyce* and Brannigan, Ward, and Wolfrey's *Re: Joyce: Text, Culture, Politics* (both 1998). The February Miami Joyce conference in 2000 focuses on the topic "Joyce/Culture." More works like those by Booker, Gibson, and Schwarze are published. And in 2003 the trend seems as strong as ever, with Kershner editing yet another book-collection, but now with the other key term in his title: "Cultural Studies," in contrast to his 1996 volume's "Popular Culture." This volume and its ten essays make an excellent endpoint for our interim fragment toward a history of popular-culture studies among Joyceans. Besides being edited by Kershner with an analytical essay from him on the approach ("Contexts of Cultural Studies"), it also contains applications of the approach from such core figures as Herr, Leonard, and Kershner himself, as well as essays from such newer scholars as the author of *Joyce and the Victorians*, and also from other names encountered above, including, to close the circle where we began it, Norris.

III

Let me now move beyond the preceding chronicle's hints about where the "Joyce and popular culture" field should and/or will go as we penetrate further into the still-new century. The most important thing I can advocate, and that I think in fact I foresee, is still closer, more careful, and more widely ranging attention to the actual cultural contexts of Joyce's work. That is what is already most attractive about Herr's socioculturally contextualizing and even more so Kershner's Bakhtin-influenced approaches. Yes, Bakhtin's cultural-history status is odd: a 1920s analyst connected to Russian formalism who, owing to his somewhat fortuitous anticipation of several postmodern concerns, became fashionable among Anglophone academic literary analysts half a century after he began publishing, making his work a cultural anachronism before it was ever influential. Still, Bakhtin's interest in the complexity of texts and cultures and their interrelations makes him an appealing touchstone for careful analysis of Joyce's (or any) literary texts, within the entire vast and messy universe of cultural and conceptual contexts that in various ways helped generate Joyce's texts—and still environ them, when we think about how to interpret them effectively and with nuance. I would simply ask the rhetorical question: Why not just incorporate, as parts of a contextualizing but latitudinarian methodology of literary scholarship, some of the basic categories and strategies that Bakhtin and others touch upon through use of the idiosyncratic and hence in practice often rather hermetic personal terminologies that became more and more characteristic of twentieth-century literary analysis as the century progressed? Clear discussion of contextual issues in ordinary educated language would facilitate comprehension and broaden the audience for such work: careful contextualization, with openness to the complexities that constitute any text and any culture, avoiding or minimizing as much as possible any recourse to reductions or simplifications.

A famous and very diversely attributed modern proverb asserts that it is difficult to make predictions, especially about the future. However, for every proverb touching on part of the truth there is always another proverb encapsulating some complementary part of the truth: in this case, the proverb that says, "The best way to predict the future is to invent it," frequently encountered on the Internet because it is attributed to Alan Kay, creator of a technology that led to both the Macintosh and Windows operating systems. Joyce scholars are always already creating the cultural and scholarly future, and more careful contextualization is the key to ongoing progress along those lines.

One corner of Joyceworld that I am especially familiar with and can therefore talk about in closing is contextualization of Joyce's work against the background of ideas about language current when he was enculturated and when he was writing. Such central New Critical scholars as Hugh Kenner and such prominent postmodern scholars as Derek Attridge have paid solid attention to those contexts for several decades now. In recent years I have begun to contribute in this area, hoping to add something to the attempt to account for Joyce's sui generis but nonetheless contextualizable literary uses of language. (Sheldon Brivic deals with Joyce's language elsewhere in the present volume.) Certainly the study of Joyce-related linguistic issues in cultural-history context is significant not only because of the essentiality of language to any literary author's work but also with special intensity in the case of Joyce, the widest-ranging stylist in literary history. And study of Joyce's linguistic contexts is in fact popular-cultural study. Natural language and its structures are by definition the imperfect result of the aggregate conceptual activities of all the imperfect minds and partial perspectives that constitute human culture generally and any particular cultural context. More specifically, it is important to take into account that Joyce's cultural background and surroundings were pervasively affected by a stream of popularized and popularizing linguistic publications that appeared throughout the second half of the century and on into Joyce's maturity in the following century, based on the more strictly technical linguistic discoveries that were occurring so rapidly from early in the nineteenth century. Some of Joyce's background in linguistic discourse can be examined through genetic and archival study: study for example of the *Finnegans Wake* notebooks (such as Laurent Milesi has done for notebook entries drawn from the work of Richard Paget, and Dirk Van Hulle for those drawn from Fritz Mauthner), or the *Ulysses* notesheets (as Robert Janusko has done since the 1960s in identifying the "Oxen of the Sun" episode's formal sources in, mainly, popularizing anthologies of English prose style, sourcing work that I have begun to compile and supplement in recent years).[6] But Joyce would most likely have encountered the best-known popular-philology publications long before he began preserving the note-taking material that is known and currently available to scholars. Any Joycean employment of content from those basic popular-philology documents has therefore been discussed only as potential contexts, without definite documentation from Joyce's notes. (See, for example, several of my recent essays.) However, the recent discovery of long-lost Joycean working materials offers the possibility that the resultant National Library of Ireland acquisition—and other material yet to come to light?—may, when made accessible, help pin down Joyce's early popular-philology knowledge. In any case, it is clear that research on Joyce's extant notes often morphs into popular-culture contextualization, given that his notebook sources often prove to be newspapers and periodicals and other middlebrow publications.

But to the extent that the accumulating body of popular-culture work on Joyce, and in fact Joycean work in general, has constantly, continually, and carefully elicited for consideration more and more of the cultural and conceptual contexts of Joyce's extraordinary and ever more influential body of work, the positive trend is clear. As we have seen, the prominent and significant popular-culture component of Joyce's literary work already began to receive careful examination of its popular-music subarea nearly fifty years ago, in the New Critical era. Following the advent in the Anglophone world of postmodern theoretical frameworks for contextualizing and evaluating literature in sociopolitical and sociopsychological ways, Cheryl Herr begins in 1986 to apply some of them to such Joycean textual content and cultural context as pantomime and sermon, genres where important issues were discussed for broad audiences. In 1989, Kershner's monograph demonstrates how areas of Joyce's popular-cultural content can be explored effectively employing a more open-ended postmodern framework like that available from

Bakhtin. The work of these two scholars opens the way to two complementary and not infrequently intertwining approaches throughout the 1990s and on into the new century and millennium. Various forms of attention to various aspects of popular culture continue to pervade Joyce studies as it broadens and deepens, not only in terms of the ever-expanding areas of cultural content that scholars collect from Joyce's work and its cultural context (for example, his background in contemporary and often popularized ideas about language) but also in an expanding range of mutually complementary scholarly methods (for example, the recent rise of genetic studies, documenting Joyce's interest in what are often popularizing sources). With this sufficiently solid past as prologue, Joyceans interested in their field's futurology can support and contribute to the ongoing process of excavating his work and his contexts for aspects of the overall culture that in the first place clarify his thinking and hence reveal his relationship to his own cultural surroundings and backgrounds, and in the second place shed broader light on cultural issues of today, which descend of course from those with which he was dealing—and in fact whose trajectories, subsequent to Joyce, his own work has already affected and continues to affect.

Notes

1. Ruth Bauerle presents a thorough examination of the pre-1990 history of "Joyce and music" studies in her essay "Hodgart and Worthington: From Silence to *Song*," in Janet Egleson Dunleavy, ed., *Re-Viewing Classics of Joyce Criticism*, 200–215.

2. Before completing his degree, Bowen had already published "The Bronzegold Sirensong: A Musical Analysis of the 'Sirens' Episode in Joyce's *Ulysses*." Within a few years, Bowen covered the entire Joycean corpus prior to *Finnegans Wake* in his nearly four-hundred-page *Musical Allusions in the Works of James Joyce*.

3. Note that Kershner's publications appear under more than one version of his name in the *MLA Bibliography*, and at the time of this writing the multiple versions of his name still require separate electronic searches. In compiling the bibliography of Joycean popular-culture and cultural-studies work that I employed while preparing this essay, I received prompt assistance from Fritz Senn and Ruth Frehner of the Zürich Joyce Foundation, whose keyword-searchable index of the Foundation's research holdings identified quite a few relevant items not called up by an electronic search of the *MLA Bibliography*.

4. Kershner has been at the University of Florida since 1971, and Lowe-Evans, with a 1987 doctorate from Miami, is currently chair of English at West Florida.

5. In 1990–91, Leonard published two essays in the *James Joyce Quarterly*, one in the then-new *Joyce Studies Annual*, and two in other significant literary journals, all on postmodern themes and some with a popular-culture emphasis. See also Jennifer Wicke.

6. An installment of the referenced work from both Van Hulle and Milesi appears in Dirk van Hulle, ed., *James Joyce: The Study of Languages*. Janusko's sourcing work appears in his *Sources and Structures of James Joyce's "Oxen"* and in a series of subsequent articles.

7

Historicizing *Ulysses*

IRA B. NADEL

"Always historicize!" Frederic Jameson's exclamation has been zealously heeded by Joyceans for almost two decades, ever since Cheryl Herr's clarion call for a new approach to Joyce announced in the opening sentence of *Joyce's Anatomy of Culture* (1986): "In recent years, literary theorists have called for attention to the historical pressures that shape the composition of even the most aggressively reflexive work" (Jameson 1981, 9; Herr ix). Andrew Gibson's *Joyce's Revenge, History, Politics and Aesthetics in "Ulysses"* (2002) is only the latest in a series of works that have subjected *Ulysses* to matters of cultural identity, nationalism, politics, ethnicity, postcolonialism, history, race, advertising, and popular culture while the theater, the press, and the church have all become renewed sources for contextualizing the novel. Historicizing *Ulysses* as a critical practice is today inescapable, which the editors of *Joyce and the Subject of History* acknowledged in the opening sentence of their 1996 volume: "today's felt need to rethink historicity obligates and enables Joyce criticism as never before" (Wollaeger, Luftig, and Spoo 1).

But what has historicism brought to *Ulysses*? How has new historicism, cultural materialism, or the construction of social memory elaborated our understanding of the novel? And have source documents like the *Joyce Archive* contributed to this development? What, in short, is the impact of the historicist agenda on *Ulysses* and the survival of the text? How has the articulation of resistance and subversion in the text altered accepted readings of the novel? Has the critical project of historicizing significantly reconfigured Joyce's work?

More precisely, what does historicizing *Ulysses* mean? Again, Cheryl Herr: describing her 1986 study, she explains that she reads Joyce's work as a series of "cultural acts that expose the shaping operations and ideological practices characteristic of urban Ireland at the turn of the century" (ix). This *sedimented* reading—the term is Jameson's and implies "layers of previous interpretations"—means that the political, as well as social, environment of the novel becomes the focus of a historicized approach, marked by the intersection of Irish mass culture and Joyce's formal use of the popular media in the composition of the novel (Jameson 1981, 9; Herr 1986, ix). Andrew Gibson extends the historicizing practice of Herr in his reading of *Ulysses* as an act of "liberation from the colonial power [of England] and its culture." For him, *Ulysses* becomes "Joyce's revenge on the colonizer" (13, 15). To read Joyce in this fashion is to recognize the tension Stephen Greenblatt posited in "Resonance and Wonder": "certain aesthetic and political structures work to contain the subversive perceptions they generate . . . [but] they may be pried loose from the order with which they were bound up and may serve to fashion a new and radically different set of structures" (57). Historicizing *Ulysses* pries loose such bounded conditions and ideas.

Jameson defines "historicity" as "a perception of the present as history" (1994, 284). It represents neither the past nor the future but is a "relationship to the present which somehow defamiliarizes it" (284). Reification is its keynote, allowing us to draw back from the immediate and develop a sense of distance, an act Bloom repeatedly performs in *Ulysses*. To historicize a text is to recognize it as "embedded in a network of material practices" and to understand that the literary and nonliterary texts of an era are inseparable (Veeser xi). New Historicism's idea of "counterhistories" expands this approach, assaulting prevailing "modes of historical thought and methods of research" to extend a text's field of inquiry (Gallagher and Greenblatt 52). To oppose the received narratives of Joycean interpretation—his autobiographical novels deal with the rejection of Catholicism and Irish nationalism, while *Ulysses* is the expression of a sophisticated literary modernism that is fundamentally apolitical—is to explore the possibilities of new and unorthodox forms of historical knowledge incorporating unexpected sources. *Ulysses* is itself a counterhistory, positing the story of Bloom against that of Odysseus, or that of Bloom and his "outsider" status against those Dubliners he confronts as he journeys about the city. Just as Stephen offers a counterhistory to Mr. Deasy in "Nestor" concerning the state of the Jews in Ireland, Bloom offers a counterhistory to the Citizen and many others in the novel, while *Ulysses* offers a counterhistory to earlier forms of the novel in English.

But historicizing *Ulysses* is more than analyzing extraliterary sources like popular culture or advertising in Joyce's work; it is the ability to recognize how the text incorporates oppositional views, whether politically, culturally, or gender-based. The novel becomes a site of contested readings of the past transforming the work into a performative space that both mirrors the dominant cultural codes, as well as shapes and resists them. To historicize a text is, among other things, to identify its cultural contradictions.

For *Ulysses*, a series of new readings has resulted, outlining the subversive and marginal in the text. Race, empire, nationalism, and gender—to name but four topics—have now become essential avenues of exploration, giving form to Padraic Colum's remark that, for Joyce, "the blurred edges were as much a part of history as the clear text" (60). The suppressed, exploited, and abused overwrite the more traditional concerns of the novel with religion, politics, and historical identity.

Historicized readings of *Ulysses* begin with the problematized area of national and racial oppression. Studies like Enda Duffy's *The Subaltern "Ulysses"* (1994) or Emer Nolan's *James Joyce and Nationalism* (1995) reveal that the representation of otherness in the novel has an immediate bearing on the treatment of the Irish as objects of repression. One critical step is recognition that the novel's political and cultural engagements are equal in importance to its formal innovations. Articulation of Bloom's double marginalization as a Jew and a victim of English imperialism is the first of a series of new readings emanating from the historicizing agenda. In protest to the imperial order and historical oppression of the marginalized, Bloom declares, "No more patriotism of barspongers and dropsical imposters" (*U*, 15.98–99). Reading *Ulysses* in relation to race, ethnicity, imperialism, colonialism, nationalism, gender, and power is a liberating act for characters as well as critics.

Joyce understood the historicist method instinctively, alternating Irish notions of nationalism, for example, with a cosmopolitan modernism that has its roots in his multicultural life in Trieste, Zurich, and Paris. It is the difference between the Irishness of Professor MacHugh or Myles Crawford in "Aeolus," and Bloom's Hungarian/Oriental past.

Although topical texts, from newspaper and magazine articles to concepts of sovereignty, construct the fabric of *Ulysses*, "like early Irish literature, *Ulysses* poses ideological questions" that transcend the work itself (Tymoczko 135), questions identified with the suppressed or unofficial. The novel's engagement with disenfranchisement, displacement, and dispersal disrupts the supposed unity of history to expose the presence of the oppositional in the text. Historicizing *Ulysses* also unites fields normally separated into new combinations: ethnography, anthropology, art history, science, politics, and popular culture come together in unexpected ways. Encouraged by the boundary crossings of New Historicists, Joyceans have now readdressed questions of power, politics, gender, and economics. M. Keith Booker's *"Ulysses," Capitalism, and Colonialism* (2000) in many ways summarizes the new union.

Outlining the cultural politics of *Ulysses* against the problematic nature of Marxist readings and rejections of the text, while clarifying the postcolonial character of, in particular, Joyce's use of the Boer War, Booker corrects the recent emphasis on reading Joyce only within his Irish and often nationalist contexts. The Boer War becomes an occasion for a detailed critique of British imperialism in Booker's reading. Bloom, a member of the Irish colonial bourgeoisie, conducts a critique of British colonialism in Ireland, he further argues. To read Joyce today without such an awareness of political or historical issues is restrictive. Indeed, monastic readings of Joyce—those that focus on formal or technical features only—are now unique. The new practice replaces metaphor with history, ambiguity with politics, and discourse analysis with ideological critique to establish interlocking cultural constructions.

Earlier treatments of Joyce and history did not present such avenues, although to be fair they were not concerned with such a focus. Seamus Deane's "History as Fiction/Fiction as History" in *Joyce in Rome*, ed. by Giorgio Melchiori (1984), James Fairhall's *James Joyce and the Question of History* (1993), and Robert Spoo's *James Joyce and the Language of History* (1994) illustrate earlier concerns but also, by their neglect, reveal the tension between traditional discussions and those reflecting New Historicist principles subsumed in the totality of the expression "historicizing *Ulysses*." For example, the textuality of history as a discourse about the past is Spoo's interest, not the materiality of history as real events, the concern of New Historicists. History is a text for Spoo, contrary to Jameson's claim that history is not a text but "an absent cause" (1981, 35). Fairhall is more responsive to Joyce's use of real historical events, notably World War I, the Phoenix Park murders, and the legacy of British imperial domination of Ireland. Victor Luftig and Mark Wollaeger's "Why 'Joyce and History'? Why Now?" directly addresses the issue of what is history in Joyce, as well as the need for new approaches to what constitutes history, while rejecting a unitary view of the past. They also introduce such new topics—certainly for 1991—as nationalism, colonialism, race, and gender. Their collection *Joyce and the Subject of History* (1996) expresses the results of this new approach and deserves comment.

Acknowledging the reconception of Joyce and history, emanating partly out of competing and radically altered claims of anthropology, feminism, Marxism, deconstruction, and postcolonial theory, the eleven essays that make up *Joyce and the Subject of History* consolidate differences between history and theory in connection with Joyce. The collection addresses the problematized category of history that is both a threat and a challenge to Joyceans. And its net is wide, dealing with Joyce's entire oeuvre rather than *Ulysses* alone. However, the authors unite in their attention to the ephemeral, the postcolonial, and the marginal. What is fundamental to all of the contributions is the realization that history is not an "identifiable pattern of sequence and causality [but] a theatrical production that manufactures 'the past' while purporting to discover it" (Leonard 1996, 18). Citing de Certeau, Garry Leonard further notes that history "always seeks to produce a profitable form of the present by obscuring the possibility of multiple versions of the past" (18). Rather than suppress temporality, these critics celebrate it at the same time that they welcome and identify contrary versions of the past; the heterogeneous replaces the homogeneous. Solidifying the arguments and approaches in the essays is a twenty-eight-page bibliography titled "Criticism on Joyce and History" prepared by Spoo.

A closer look at empire, race, and gender in several separate studies will clarify the value of historicizing *Ulysses* and show how the novel can be read as a resourceful set of tensions that reconceive our notion of history and Joyce. Enda Duffy's *The Subaltern "Ulysses"* (1994), with its focus on Joyce writing against the Empire, using documents and photographs from the archives of empire to reveal the subversive character of the novel, is representative. He shows, for example, that Joyce's treatment of bigotry and injustice through Bloom displaces the issue of colonial oppression "onto the questions of the relationship of political power to the discourse of race" (127). He furthermore sees the 1904 setting as a "guerrilla text" in which the violence in Ireland while the novel was being written is complexly expressed by modernist textual strategies of estrangement. Forms of writing reflect forms of political fragmentation.

Vincent Cheng's *Joyce, Race, and Empire* (1995) expands Duffy's critique through detailed readings and references to Joyce's engagement with empire and race. Combining the resources of postcolonial theory, minority discourse, and cultural studies, Cheng emphasizes that Joyce wrote from the position of the colonial subject of an oppressive empire. The alternate narrative he constructs demonstrates that Joyce was definitely *not* apolitical. He convincingly shows that Joyce is anything but the "aestheticizing, privileged white male writer in the Great . . . Tradition" (3). The radical nature of his texts and their ideology demands, through the historicizing process, a de-centering and realignment of his work. The key motives of his work, Cheng argues, "were most frequently attempts to resist and defy the authorized cen-trality of canons, empires (especially England) and totalizing structures" (3). Cheng successfully defends this challenging thesis through a reading of the Joyce corpus based on the principle that Joyce's stylistic, linguistic, and liter-ary innovations are "grounded in his sense of ideological, ethnic, and colonial dispossession" (4). In short, his texts are "engagedly political and ideologically progressive" (4). Historicizing *Ulysses* reclaims the work from a moribund canonization by reestablishing its power and political force. Explorations of "racial difference within the discourse of power and empire"—this is the new vision of Joyce's fiction that Cheng proposes, removing the works from a sterile modernism (7).

In this reformulation, Joyce opposes anti-Semitism, racism, nationalism, male aggression, and imperialism; uncovering this other history in the novel redefines our conception of the writer. Joyce, Cheng emphasizes, "repeatedly gave voice in his works to those silenced and exiled to the margins of domi-nant cultures" (7). In this reading, Joyce becomes a writer of alternatives, alternatives to "the discursive and hegemonic constructions of a dominant culture" (7). Joyce not only depicts but critiques race in relation to impe-rialism's power (8). Importantly, reading Joyce in this manner transforms him into a voice of variant social discourses "within hegemony and resis-tance." His work is both an analysis and a critique of the racialization and colonization of the Irish. The cross- disciplinary approach Cheng employs revises conventional perceptions of Joyce's writing and demonstrates how the novel's representation of cultural hegemony shapes the fabric of everyday Irish life—often promoted by popular culture (170). Cheng shows that the novel is multivalent rather than binary, international rather than insular, and a sustained as well as incisive commentary on the ideologies of racial and im-perial politics in Joyce's Ireland. Deep in Joyce's works is a sustained critique of the discourses and issues of British imperialism and colonial resistance.

Issues of gender parallel those of empire, nationalism, and race in identi-fying the novel as a site of suppression that women, as well as other groups, in the text subvert. New Historicist readings of gender articulate the many ways the novel presents and overcomes female suppression. Feminist studies provided early probes of *Ulysses* and its link between gender and politics. *Women in Joyce*, edited by Suzette Henke and Elaine Unkeless (1982), was one of the first to approach the topic, soon followed by Bonnie Kime Scott's *Joyce and Feminism* (1984). In this work, Scott reveals Joyce's exposure to the assertive roles of Irish women and how the drive for Irish nationalism "became a liberating cause for young women." She also describes the importance and influence of what she calls "the female family of Joyce," namely Joyce's mother, sisters, aunt Josephine, Nora, and his daughter, Lucia (29, 54–84). Collectively, these early works revealed how the existence and representation of Irish women and Molly simultaneously exposed and critiqued the bipolar, sexist society that appeared to dominate the text.

The appearance of Brenda Maddox's *Nora* (1988), which reclaimed the importance of Nora for Joyce and his writing, assisted in the reconstruction of women in the novel, especially in Maddox's linking the habits of Nora to those of Molly. In her biography, Maddox also addressed vexing questions about the Joyce marriage, demonstrating Joyce's dependency on Nora and how she contributed to his writing through her sexuality and sense of humor.

Initially thematic in its orientation, feminist criticism soon investigated the performative elements of Joyce's women, arguing not only that Joyce makes his feminist arguments by having his female characters act rather than just talk, but that "Joyce's modernism [itself] is feminine" and his vernacular female (Wawrzycka and Corcoran 2, ix). Additionally, women labored behind the production of Joyce's modernist text (Nora Joyce, Jane Heap, Margaret Anderson, Harriet Shaw Weaver, and Sylvia Beach, to name the most obvious), confounding the singularity of male authorship. And underscoring the importance of women for his narrative, Joyce gives Molly, of course, the last word in the novel.

The textual construction of gender has now become identified as the primary way Joyce critiques the role of women in society. The presence of androgyny in the novel is another confirmation of the complex gender identities that coexist in the work. As New Historicists and others have shown, the link between gender, experimentation, and textual performance, foregrounded by Mina Purefoy, the ghost of Stephen's mother, and Bella Cohen, confirm Joyce's reinscription of the feminine. Molly, of course, embodies such rewriting, although her uncensored thoughts are culturally but not emotionally silenced. *Molly Blooms: A Polylogue on Penelope and Cultural Studies* (1994), edited by Richard Pearce, consolidates some of these new readings through studies of Molly and colonialism, reception, consumption, and sexuality. If "The Dead" dramatizes the oppression of women by art, marriage, and the Church, *Ulysses*, through Molly, shows how her conventional views actually contain elements of subversion that establish her individualism, power, and sexuality leading to an attenuated independence. The issue is not whether Molly "escapes from the narratives of gender, class, patriarchy, colonialism, and consumption" to offer a perspective on them, but how she "reproduces, negotiates and resists these narratives" (4).

Illustrating the intersection of colonial and racial discourses with gender is Andrew Gibson's account of popular women's magazines between 1880 and 1920 in *Joyce's Revenge*. Relating them to "Nausikaa," Gibson documents how Joyce's conception of Gerty MacDowell owes as much to the London-published popular women's magazines of the period as it does to conceptions of Irish popular romance. Gibson notes that a column in *The Princess's Novelettes* referred to in "Nausikaa" (13.110) had a gossip section entitled "All About People," dealing with life in the colonies, which included Ireland (129). *Lady's Pictorial*, cited in Joyce (13.151), provided columns of colonial anecdotes and issues plus an "Irish Letter" offering news of Irish fashion, namely the gentry, and their Irish balls, bazaars, and literary soirees.

The Princess's Novelettes included lists of such series as *The Empire Novels* and *The Boys of the Empire*, and the more feminine *Empire Bouquet Novels*. Frequently, stories in the *Novelettes* touched on colonial life: heroes had at least some experience in the colonies to make them glamorous. Even the advertisements in these popular magazines had a colonial flavor, whether for "Oriental Toothpaste" or "Imperial Curlers" (Gibson 130). Racism became a commodity whenever Indian women or Chinese or black faces appeared in advertisements as scenes of Empire entered every part of the home through such magazines and journals. Aligned with this depiction of the romantic colonies, women, in particular, were encouraged to settle in the colonies, a form of purposeful if sacrificial English cultural nationalism. Women became part of the civilizing mission guaranteeing the survival of a national heritage in alien environments. *The Lady's Pictorial* for June 18, 1904, contains a column, for example, encouraging the imagined "surplus" of women to go to the more flourishing colonies to marry British men who might be otherwise tempted to unite with native women (in Gibson 131).

Gibson further points out how Victorian and Edwardian domestic ideology influenced the content of these women's magazines, ranging from
hygienic concerns to physical fitness. Women's duties were also clear: domesticity, motherhood, self-sacrifice. Such responsibility, some columns
emphasized, was a duty to the race to perform instead of developing their
own intellects at the expense of reproduction. Yet there was also at the same
time a concern that the English race might be undergoing a deterioration as
a 1904 government document entitled "Report of the Physical Deterioration
Committee" outlined. Poverty, drink, and even squalor could be defeated
through the weaponry of a good housewife. An imperialist vocabulary urged
women to maintain their health as a moral duty owed to the race and Empire
(Gibson 131).

More specific connections between *The Lady's Pictorial* for June 11, 1904,
and *Ulysses* include an account of the Mirus bazaar and a full-page picture
of the Alake of Abeokuta (re *U*, 12.1514–33). A column in the issue entitled
"A Healthy Suggestion" also noted the deterioration of the English body
and that education in the gospel of health was necessary, especially for wom-
en. The ideology of national health and domestic knowledge went hand
in hand, as articles regularly repeated. Coordinated with this "message"
were the many stories, advertisements, and features that insisted that a girl's
destiny was romance, marriage, and a "snug and cosy little homely house"
(*U*, 13.239). These popular magazines—*Pearson's Weekly* is another cited in
"Nausikaa"—formed a matrix of colonial, racial, and domestic discourses
that established a norm of social signs, behavior, and appearances, producing
in the construction of Gerty, a "serviceable model of English and colonial
womanhood" (Gibson 133).

Gerty's desire to supply a man with hominess adopts the English ideology of domesticity, aided by improving her physical appeal, while physical
improvement becomes a matter of racial appeal. The emphasis of the magazines on a faultless body finds reflection in her desire to have alabaster hands,
a face of "ivorylike purity," and arms that "are white and soft" (*U*, 13.89, 88,
341). However, elements of racial subversion also appear in "Nausikaa," although they are subtle. The changeability of skin color, the imperfection of
the body (Gerty's limp, Edy's squint, Cissy's skinny legs), and fluidity if not
processes of the body—they flush, blush, dribble, ejaculate, menstruate, and
leak—contrast with the ideal of perfection. Cissy, in particular, undermines
the ideology of race and domesticity in the episode through an idiom that is

direct, improper, and rejects false English gentility (U, 13.57–62). The strain, rather than the ideal, of the domestic is an undercurrent throughout the section.

But the colonial is never far removed. The appearance early in the episode of two small boys in sailor suits embroidered with the name of a British naval vessel reminds readers of the invasion of the home and country by the English, as does the argument of the boys over whether or not their sandcastle should have a front door like the Martello Tower, reintroducing a symbol of British presence in Ireland that begins the novel (U, 13.44–45). As a prelude to Gerty and her reading, Bloom and his fantasies, and Cissy's parody of domesticity, colonial power appears and remains instrumental in the formation of young Irish minds. In this reading of "Nausikaa," Gibson demonstrates the importance and effectiveness of historicizing the text by identifying the linked discourses that inscribe political, domestic, sexual, and gender issues for Joyce.

Realigning the imperatives of gender by challenging received expectations of what readers anticipated from male and female characters is one of Joyce's goals in the novel that historicizing *Ulysses* has articulated. Critics have analyzed, through historicizing male/female identities, new resistances to imposed discourses and values. Contrary to showing women as weak, virginal, and innocent, Joyce represents them as strong, sexual, and experienced. This is not so much Gerty MacDowell versus Molly Bloom, but, rather, an attack by Joyce on the unreality of feminine ideals in general and a complaint against the fantasies engendered by popular culture that constructs such unreality. The irony is that Gerty relies on the very forms of the colonizer's culture that "Nausikaa" works to subvert (Gibson 139). Historicizing gender in the novel is the interrogation of conventional roles and their restrictions that govern males as well as females, in the process of which a subtext of a suppressed ideology emerges. But there is another point the study of gender uncovers, and Gibson states it clearly: part of Joyce's purpose is to show that Molly and others "are cheerfully at ease with contradiction" (Gibson 271). In terms of history as well as gender, there is at the end of *Ulysses* a relaxation of the cultural struggle between Ireland and England, gender and identity, self and other. Joyce "both sustains and relinquishes the terms of a ferocious, polar opposition" (Gibson 271). Historicizing the work makes such positions known.

Textualization has been another catalyst for historicizing the novel over the past two decades. Historicism, in fact, seems to have found grounding in textual and archival studies. This should not be a surprise given the impact of the *James Joyce Archive* (1977–79). The sixty-three-volume facsimile publication made available Joyce's manuscript materials whether notes, sketches, drafts, or fair copies for the first time in a uniform format and encouraged a reassessment of his textual practices. Hans Walter Gabler's edition of *Ulysses* (1984; corrected, 1986) was a major result, providing a manual of Joyce's textual procedures through its representation of the textual stages of the novel's composition. Via sigla that record all the variants in the manuscript documents, one has a physical and visual record of an unfolding, dynamic, historicized text. The establishment of this so-called continuous manuscript text, where all the stages of the novel's composition could be viewed at once, was both impressive and questionable. But despite challenges offered by John Kidd and others, the Gabler text has remained the most documented edition we have of the novel. Nevertheless, response to the temporary expiration of the *Ulysses* copyright in England in 1992 was the sudden appearance of three new texts.

A Penguin reprint of the 1960 Bodley Head edition with an introduction by Declan Kiberd was the first. Emphasizing the representation of history as the repudiation of the father, Kiberd notes that "in the colony that was Ireland," the rejection of the "genetic father in a colonial situation" meant a determination "to invent the self in conditions of cultural freedom" (Kiberd, lxx). Both Joyce and Yeats, Kiberd writes, attempted to "renovate a national consciousness on the basis of the occupier's set texts," a paradoxical but not impossible task (lxxiii). The uncreated conscience of Ireland called for a program of postcolonial liberation initially presented as a return to ancient traditions. But within the "ancient analogues Shakespeare, Cúchulainn, Odysseus—," there was space for radical innovation, which Joyce and Yeats pursued (lxxvi). Setting the novel within the Irish crisis of nationalism, identity, and history, Kiberd contextualizes the work outside of the hermetic modernism that earlier defined it.

Two other editions from the early 1990s similarly repositioned the text, the first a republication of an uncorrected first edition, the second a controversial, free-ranging revision of the novel offering a newly historicized version of the work. Jeri Johnson's 1993 Oxford World's Classics edition, a reprint of copy #785 of the first edition, errors included, made this important edition accessible to many. The extensive introduction, ancillary material, and explanatory notes revised the historicist character to the text, rationalizing its appearance as the form of publication "closest to Joyce in time" (Johnson ed., lvi). In 1997, a controversial countertext appeared: Danis Rose's "*Ulysses*": *A Reader's Edition*. In this edition, the contemporary contextualizing of the work resulted in a series of cavalier emendations, corrections, and alterations, seemingly done without regard to the integrity of the original motivated by exactly the opposite principles of the 1922 reprint. Where Johnson sought to preserve the originary character of the first edition, Rose sought its annihilation. The result is a text defined by its contemporary status, or, as the publisher proudly states, "completely redesigned and comprehensively edited . . . for our time" (jacket). "This is a people's *Ulysses* . . . a text which has been smuggled out of the ivory tower of the academics and put squarely in the marketplace." This is a liberated text, "liberated from the prison of its early publishing history" (publicity material). The goal, the editor explains, is "to maximize the pleasure of the reader" by "clarifying the sense and the sound of the individual sentences and freeing up the flow and the pace of the text as a whole." The result? What Rose calls "an integrated edition" (1997 Rose ed., vi).

Superseding this edition in June 2004 was "*Ulysses*": *A New Reader's Edition*, which offers yet additional textual changes by Rose including the elimination of apostrophes in Molly's section, which he had added amid much controversy to the 1997 version. The reversion back to the original punctuation occurred not for historical or textual reasons but legal, although he warns readers that in "some future time they may perhaps reappear like the virtual particles that they are: invisible but for all that, there" (2004 Rose ed., lxxii).

The textual reshaping of *Ulysses* represents a historicizing strand of the novel initiated by Sylvia Beach's statement in the first edition that errors in the text existed. But through a combination of New Historicist reconstructions of discourses, framing the novel by studying legal, religious, historical, and popular texts, joined with a concentration on establishing the social character of its textual construction (à la D. F. McKenzie and Jerome McGann), the contextualizing of *Ulysses* has been validated. Emanating from the publication of the *Joyce Archive* and then Gabler's multiplex (simultaneously screened) edition of 1984 and pursued by others such as Jeri Johnson and Danis Rose, the textual historicizing of the novel has widened, as it has reconstituted, the social and historical negotiations Joyce had to undertake to ensure publication of the novel.

As these and other historicist studies remind us, Joyce's presentation of the everyday through his "thick" descriptions of 1904 Dublin has taught us to understand "the social life of objects" paralleling what Walter Benjamin identified as "a change in the structure of . . . experience" (Richards 210; Benjamin 156). Furthermore, if Stephen Greenblatt is correct that "half-hidden cultural transactions" empower great works of art (1988, 4), then historicizing the novel has unveiled how Joyce employed these strategies through the "violation" of established social, political, and of course literary conventions. Such readings justify reclaiming *Ulysses* from the formalists. The source of historicizing the novel is the confluence of poststructural theorizing on the nature of history and historical narrative combining with the impact of material culture's interactive role with texts originating in the ideas of Jameson, de Certeau, Baudrillard, and others.

But if historicizing *Ulysses*—which has largely concentrated on a set of linked discourses (nationalism, empire, race, and gender) supported by readings of materialist culture—has been a catalyst for new readings of the novel, such an approach has also been incomplete. Various strands remain unexplored, one of them a mapping of the text not in the way Random House meant when they printed a map of Dublin on their sales poster literalizing the text by highlighting the location of the Round Tower, the Museum or the Library ("How to Enjoy James Joyce's . . . *Ulysses*"), nor as Michael Seidel in *Epic Geography* outlined in his tracing the mythical journey of Dublin's Odysseus—but in a New Historicist manner where a reading of Bloom's day becomes not where Bloom stopped but how he and the reader construct a social memory of Ireland through "the circulation of social energy" (Greenblatt 1988, 13).

Such an approach understands the social practice of space and time, the materialist reading of Bloom's journey reflecting his absorption and subversion of cultural codes as when he observes the behavior of his fellow Dubliners in "Lotus Eaters" or "Lestrygonians." Bloom and the reader gather information as they wander, becoming explorers and commentators (Irish flâneurs?), not tourists attuned to the social, historical, and even moral change related not to modes of perception or ideology but to the tactics and strategies of power. Observing forms of materialized culture becomes the primary act of such journeying. Bloom's sense of the cyclical hides and yet reveals his knowledge of the immediate as this well-known passage from "Lestrygonians" shows: "Cityful passing way, other cityful coming, passing away too: other coming on, passing on. Houses, lines of houses, streets, miles of pavements, piledup bricks, stones. Changing hands. This owner, that" (*U* 8.484–86). The reconstruction of discourses contemporary with Joyce, whether of politics, sexuality, or empire, is only the first stage of historicizing the text.

Historicism, however, has not been without its critics. Michael Gillespie, for example, in the introduction to *James Joyce and the Fabrication of an Irish Identity* (2001), cautions that historicism has become the new orthodoxy at the expense of other approaches. Patrick McGee, in *Joyce Beyond Marx* (2001), is even more skeptical, offering a sustained critique of the effort to restore political and social *bite* to Joyce's work, the term used by Myles Crawford in the offices of the *Freeman's Journal* when he encourages an article from Stephen Dedalus. Write something for me, he tells Stephen, "with a bite in it. You can do it. I see it in your face" (*U*, 7.616–17). McGee rightly points out that history always "speaks from the viewpoint of the dominant forces in a society," consolidating that viewpoint into an "official construction of a social reality" that blocks certain forms of human desire. Historical discourse, he warns, "tends to fall in love with its own image."

But history, according to McGee, also produces its own other, "an Echo that can subvert the dominant discourse through the subtle manipulation of its own words" (McGee 10–11). The adulation of historical criticism needs to be checked because he fears certain readings that try to pin Joyce down to certain historical meanings serve only the interests of specific social narratives (McGee 12, 169–70). McGee acknowledges, however, that Joyce's history expressed through words "constantly subverts itself through the manufacture of echoes" (12). Or as Benjamin asserts, "history decomposes into images, not narratives" (Benjamin in Buck-Morss 218).

But if historicism has overtaken Joyce criticism in the last two decades, it has also generated a reciprocal effect: that of historicizing history. Through the reappropriation and articulation of Joyce's political and historical contexts, history itself has been historicized. That is, revisions of Joyce's treatment of gender, politics, or nationalism have effected reconceptions of the sexual, political, and national in Irish studies. Complex associations between sex and politics in Irish history find a significant part of their impetus from recent work in Joyce studies. Ideas of Irish Catholic middle-class national identity are now being reevaluated in response, at least in part, to the historicizing of Joyce's writing.

Two examples of this reconsideration are *Gender and Sexuality in Modern Ireland*, edited by Anthony Bradley and Maryann Valiulis (1997), and *Sex, Nation, and Dissent in Irish Writing*, edited by Éibhear Walshe (1997). The editors of *Gender and Sexuality in Modern Ireland* recognize this exchange, acknowledging that if sexual identity and preference are more related "to culture than nature," and more fluid and nuanced then previously considered, "then one sees historical and fictional characters, their behaviour and relationships" in a different light. "The study of gender in Ireland has been suppressed" and only recently has been recognized, largely through the historicizing practices that have revised Ireland's nationalism and analyzed its postcolonial status (Bradley and Valiulis 2). Reciprocity has emerged between cultural studies applied to Joyce and a revised Joyce read against a redefined Irish studies in which a stabilized notion of Irish identity becomes nuanced and uncertain. Conversely, some of the new work on Joyce could not have occurred without the renegotiations of Irish authenticity and political identity taking place in the last two decades of Irish studies. The transnational, multicultural Joyce now validates as well as complements the multifaceted character of Irish culture.

The commanding presence of historicizing Ulysses may have resulted from the need to certify the novel as a vehicle of material history. By historicizing the work, we recuperate the form from the purely fictional and place it more centrally in the critical debate of how literature transforms the real. This parallels shifts in the theoretical paradigms that unite cultural materialism with literary movements seen in the current move to historicize modernism. Kevin Dettmar and Stephen Watt's collection, *Marketing Modernisms* (1996), Lawrence Rainey's *Institutions of Modernism* (1998), and Catherine Turner's *Marketing Modernism between the Two Wars* (2003) vividly demonstrate this approach to recontextualizing the term. In his chapter "Consuming Investments: Joyce's *Ulysses*," Rainey, in particular, situates the publication of the novel "within the context of a body of institutions, a corpus of collecting, marketing and discursive practices that constituted a composite social space" (44). Individual readers played a role secondary to that of dealers and speculators, he argues, transforming the individual common reader into groups of competing consumers.

George Bornstein's *Material Modernism* (2001) also extends the contextual approach to modernist texts by reexamining their original "site of production" and the physicality of their expression, supported by their "material forms of cultural transmission" (1). Crucial to his ideas and instructive for Joyceans is the idea that material textuality includes both physical features of the text and the multiple forms "in which the texts are physically created and distributed" (1). Bibliographic codes are important constituents of historical and political meanings. Bornstein's chapter on *Ulysses* (chap. 6) imaginatively uses Gabler's synoptic encodings of the text to study changing representation of the "Other" in the work: Jews, Africans, and Orientals. Historicizing *Ulysses* here uses textual construction to analyze cultural constructions like history and politics. Gabler's diacritical marks reinforce the conceptual idea that there is no single text, only a series of texts (138).

The effect of historicizing on our reading of *Ulysses*— understood not as a constellation of historical references and allusions, or a repository of historical moments but as the source of its own modernist self-construction—is to understand its engagement with, and subversion of, a set of cultural conditions. Historicizing *Ulysses* addresses these matters and provides a broader analysis and fuller evaluation of these concepts. But a paradox remains: fiction is imagined, and yet we strive to make it verifiable. Although it is unreliable because it is an imagined work of art, we nonetheless seek to give *Ulysses* a footing in the material world. Historicizing the text is the process for doing so. The literary depends on the external for the imagined. But we also face a danger: imposing on the novel the reconfiguration of our own cultural memory and historical consciousness without the sanction of the text. Yet, historicist theory argues that through the unmasking of the ideological and the historical, we can identify and absorb the cultural politics of the text, which, in all likelihood, may very well be a work of fiction. *Ulysses*, then, both reflects and refashions our understanding of the past through its uncovering the suppressed.

The circulation of symbolic capital in *Ulysses* has replaced the discourse on character, language, and theme, threatening, it must be said, those literary scholars more comfortable with aesthetics rather than social value. Historicizing *Ulysses* has shown that beyond the garden wall of the self-enclosed text is a teeming world of communal action that Joyce could not, and did not, avoid. In a passage from *Finnegans Wake*, he made this clear. It begins "yet to concentrate solely on the literal sense or even the psychological content of

any document to the sore neglect of the enveloping facts themselves circum-
stantiating it is . . . hurtful to sound sense" (*FW* 109.12–15). The working vocabulary of circulation, negotiation, and exchange replaces metaphor, irony,
or plot. The effacement of social circulation, class, and history has stopped.
Reframing *Ulysses* has become the process of identifying the politics of culture while resituating the demarcation between one discursive practice and
another to collapse the "working distinction between the aesthetic and the
real." However, the aesthetic is no longer an alternative to the real but its
intensification made clear through historicizing the text.

8

Before and After

The Manuscripts in Textual and Genetic Criticism of *Ulysses*

MICHAEL GRODEN

I wonder if any other novel got introduced to the reading world in the way *Ulysses* did. The 1920 New York court decision that declared *Ulysses* obscene while Joyce was still writing it led to its publication in France as a rare book, a cult object. Joyce wanted the book published in English-speaking countries, both as a recognition of its respectability and as a response to the pirated editions that appeared in the United States in the late 1920s, and one of his ways of aiding the process was to encourage friends and interested critics to write extended, learned studies of it. By the time Judge John M. Woolsey nullified the ban in 1933 and *Ulysses* appeared legally in the United States the next year, several articles and at least three books had been written about it. Just two weeks after Random House released *Ulysses*, it ran a two-page ad in the *Saturday Review of Literature* headed "How to Enjoy James Joyce's Great Novel *Ulysses*," urging potential readers to ignore the mass of criticism that had already built up around the book. A few months later, *Vanity Fair* published a parody—not of the book itself but of *Ulysses* criticism.[1] For better or worse, *Ulysses* has really never been available in English-speaking countries without an accompanying factory of critics, a labor force eventually dubbed the "Joyce industry."

The first Ph.D. dissertation to focus exclusively on Joyce, according to Tetsumaro Hayashi's census (10), appeared only three years after Joyce's death. It was Joseph Prescott's "James Joyce's *Ulysses* as Work in Progress," completed at Harvard University in 1944 and based largely on the proofs for *Ulysses* that Harvard had acquired in the 1930s. In the same year appeared the first posthumous publication of any Joyce work, Theodore Spencer's edition of the *Stephen Hero* manuscript (a manuscript also at Harvard). Spencer and Prescott must have spent a great deal of time in close proximity to each other in Harvard's library in 1942 and 1943, and they must have conferred with Harvard professor Harry Levin, whose book *James Joyce: A Critical Introduction*, published in the year of Joyce's death, was the first major book-length study of Joyce's works to be written by someone outside of his circle of acquaintances.

Aside from this temporary location of Harvard as the headquarters of the Joyce industry in the few years after Joyce's death, it is interesting that two of these three books were old-fashioned projects involving editing and manuscripts: Spencer's edition of a previously unpublished manuscript and Prescott's study of the proofs. (Thirty years later, Levin, too, became associated with Joyce's manuscripts when he wrote a critical introduction to the facsimile of the Rosenbach Manuscript.) If, as Peter Shillingsburg claims, the process of scholarly editing produces "editions that preserve or rescue a work of artistic, social, intellectual, or historical importance as an artifact" (3), then by the time Joyce died, his works had already entered the canon of works seen as worth preserving or rescuing. In a way, it didn't even take Joyce's death for *Ulysses* to achieve this status. Morris Ernst and Alexander Lindey, who argued the case for *Ulysses* before Judge Woolsey in 1933, proclaimed *Ulysses*—"in essence, an eleven-year-old text, never published in a trade edition," Kevin Dettmar reminds us as he quotes Ernst and Lindey—to be a "modern classic" or even simply a "classic" that had "stood the test of time."[2]

The Bloomsday centenary year of 2004 inspired a lot of backward-viewing in order to assess where we had gotten in the hundred years since Joyce's famous fictional day, and looking to the past naturally provokes attempts to look to the future. All literary research is historical in that it looks to a text produced in the past from some perspective in the present, producing its own version of Tom Kernan's "kind of retrospective arrangement" (*U*, 10:783). But we should not forget Bloom's thought in "Lestrygonians" when he sees A.E. walking ahead of him and realizes that he thought about him earlier: "Coming events cast their shadows before" (*U*, 8:526).

Even in noncentenary times, manuscript study is especially prone to before-and-after formulations. Scholars investigating literary manuscripts study documents from a work's own past, ones that precede the work that was eventually published—or sometimes was abandoned and left unpublished. There is always a past-and-future negotiation: we look to the past and try to re-create it (putting the manuscripts in the proper order, working out the sequence of composition and publication, comparing the text as it was written to the one that was published) but unavoidably from the perspective of a future in relation to those documents (publication, cessation of writing, the author's death, and so on). In other words, we look before but only from the position of the after—as Jean Bellemin-Noël has written (in words that are the provocation for my title), "We must never forget this paradox: what was written *before* and had, at first, no *after*, we meet only *after*, and this tempts us to supply a *before* in the sense of a priority, cause, or origin" (2005, 31; emphasis in original). We need to be aware, that is, of the "retrospective arrangement" we work with, since it is likely to be as much our own interpretive creation as historical fact.

In this essay, I want to look at two aspects of the uses of manuscripts—a term I will use to cover all the documents Joyce and the other people involved in putting *Ulysses* into print produced while he was writing *Ulysses*: notes, drafts, rough and clean manuscripts, typescripts (corrected and augmented by Joyce), and proofs (also corrected and augmented by Joyce)—in the study of *Ulysses*: first, textual criticism and scholarly editing, and second, manuscript study and genetic criticism. In both cases, I will isolate various dividing lines and look before and after each of these lines.

Textual Criticism and Scholarly Editing

These two interrelated activities constitute what for some people is the obvious place in which manuscripts get used in literary scholarship. In *Scholarly Editing in the Computer Age*, Peter Shillingsburg defines "scholarly editing" as work that produces "any sort of edition prepared by a person claiming to be a scholar" and as "editorial efforts designed to make available for scholarly use works not ordinarily available or available only in corrupt or inadequate forms" (2). Scholarly editing is also textual criticism, since the editor applies scholarship and critical judgment to produce a text of a work—as distinguished from, say, the kind of editing that helps to produce a work's first publication or the kind that attempts to correct a faulty text simply by looking for mistakes (as was done in several attempts to improve *Ulysses*). In their *Introduction to Bibliographical and Textual Studies*, William Proctor Williams and Craig S. Abbott define "textual criticism" as "the study of the transmission of texts and the application of this study to scholarly editing" (161), and crucial to this term and definition is the word *criticism*. D. C. Greetham defines "textual criticism" slightly differently as "that part of textual scholarship concerned with evaluating readings" (104); in other words, the textual critic confronts possible alternative words and/or punctuation for a particular place in a text and, using critical and scholarly skills, evaluates and assesses their claims to be in the text—and, if he or she is producing an edition, chooses one of the alternatives. These judgments are not made neutrally, since scholarly editing is based on a theoretical and critical approach to the writing and production process in general and to the specific processes for the particular work in question, a process that involves the manuscripts and their relations to each other. Sometimes this approach is merely implicit, but usually the editor spells out the approach and its underlying assumptions quite clearly.

I have isolated three dividing lines for textual criticism and scholarly editing.

1. The first dividing line occurred twenty years ago, in 1984, when Hans Walter Gabler published "*Ulysses*": *A Critical and Synoptic Edition*. This edition culminated over sixty years of concern about the text of *Ulysses*, makeshift attempts to correct the text, widespread assumptions that a scholarly edition was not possible, and an earlier, unfinished project by Jack P. Dalton to produce an accurate text.

Concern about the text began within the covers of *Ulysses* itself. A "Publisher's Note" in the 1922 first edition states: "The publisher asks the reader's indulgence for typographical errors unavoidable in the exceptional circumstances. S.B." (xi). This note, although accompanied by Sylvia Beach's initials, was actually written and revised by Joyce himself.[3] He expressed similar concern in at least three letters from late 1921 and early 1922: "I am extremely irritated by all those printer's errors. . . . Are these to be perpetuated in future editions? I hope not" (to Harriet Shaw Weaver, November 6, 1921; *Letters*, 1:176); "I hope it will be possible in that event to correct the numerous misprints" (to Harriet Shaw Weaver, February 8, 1922; *Letters*, 1:180; Joyce refers to Weaver's proposed English edition); "The edition you have is full of printers' errors. Please read it in this. I cut the pages. There is a list of mistakes at the end" (to Nora Barnacle Joyce, ca. January 5, 1924; *Letters*, 3:86; the more accurate edition that Joyce refers to is probably the fourth printing of January 1924).

The complex history of how *Ulysses* was written and how the printed editions relate to each other has often been told, but the outlines of the story bear repeating briefly.[4] Joyce wrote *Ulysses* episode by episode, and the process is almost entirely one of growth and expansion. For a few years after he started working on the book in 1914 he presumably hatched, discarded, and refined various plans; compiled notes; and produced some rough drafts. (Few documents survive as witnesses to this early work.) After Ezra Pound arranged for serial publication in the American journal *The Little Review* in early 1918, Joyce brought each episode to a temporary finish in a final working draft that he gave to a typist. (The manuscript of *Ulysses*, partly this final working draft and partly a fair copy that Joyce made of many of the pages, is called the Rosenbach Manuscript after the museum that ultimately acquired it.) Each episode was transcribed by a series of typists and printers, and some sections were set in proof as many as eight or nine times. Joyce often added to the text as he read and corrected the latest transcription, but as he corrected each typescript or proof page he seems not to have looked back to the original manuscript. Because an American court declared a serialized section of the book obscene, book publication in the United States or England became impossible, and Sylvia Beach, an American bookseller in Paris, offered to publish *Ulysses* there under an imprint named for her bookstore, Shakespeare and Company. As Joyce revised and corrected the proofs in 1921 for the book publication, he was often working on two or three episodes at the same time, reading proofs for early episodes, for example, at the same time as he was drafting the last two episodes, "Ithaca" and "Penelope." The French-speaking printers had to reset much type again and again because of Joyce's huge number of corrections, revisions, and additions, and they worked under very short deadlines as they approached the publication date that Joyce wanted—February 2, 1922, his fortieth birthday.

The first edition contained many errors, and Joyce prepared at least two errata lists. These errors were corrected in later Shakespeare and Company printings, but new ones were introduced at the same time. In 1932, the Odyssey Press of Hamburg published a new edition in which Joyce's friend Stuart Gilbert "specially revised" the text; Gilbert apparently compared the text to the first and to later Shakespeare and Company printings.[5] The Odyssey Press edition, in its fourth printing of 1939, is considered the most accurate of the unedited versions of *Ulysses* (see, for example, Ellmann 1982, 653). An American judge, John M. Woolsey, overturned the obscenity ban on *Ulysses* at the end of 1933, and Random House published the book in 1934, but—comically, tragically, melodramatically—someone at the press inadvertently picked up a copy of an error-riddled pirated American edition of the ninth Shakespeare and Company printing and, until the gaffe was discovered, this edition was used as the setting copy for the first American edition. The first English edition of 1936 was set from the more accurate Odyssey Press text, and revised and reset English and American editions appeared in 1960 and 1961, respectively. None of these editions was based on a comparison with anything other than earlier printed versions (none used Joyce's manuscripts or the corrected typescripts or proofs), and each edition introduced new errors as it corrected previous ones.

An astonishing array of materials for *Ulysses*—especially prepublication documents—has survived. They open up the process of Joyce's composition of the work for the purposes of scholarship and editing, but at the same time they leave tantalizing and important gaps. To edit *Ulysses*, Gabler went back to Joyce's writing process—to the extent that it can be re-created through Joyce's letters and accounts by other people involved and especially through the extant manuscripts—and both re-created and interpreted that process to produce one attempt at a text that was free of what the first edition called "all those printer's errors." Gabler's re-creation of the process, building on and expanding my account in *"Ulysses" in Progress*, is relatively straightforward, but his interpretation of that process is bold and original and has proven to be controversial.[6] He attempted to merge established Anglo-American methods of editing, in which the editor creates a new version of the work by choosing one text as copytext and emending the copytext with readings from other surviving documents, and German genetic editing, which is more concerned with documenting the stages the work went through during its composition. Rather than work with an existing version of *Ulysses* as copytext, Gabler assembled what he called a "continuous manuscript text" to serve that purpose. He reasoned that, in theory, Joyce's original manuscript (the Rosenbach Manuscript) plus all his additions on the many sets of typescripts and proofs should add up to the full *Ulysses*. In actuality, things were much more complicated: sometimes what Joyce wrote cannot be known conclusively because documents are missing; sometimes the printers set a different word from the one Joyce wrote and Joyce changed it to something else. The most complex uncertainty involves the Rosenbach Manuscript, only about half of which was the document that the typist used. For the rest of it, Gabler speculated that Joyce sent a manuscript to the typist and later recopied the text to provide a more attractive manuscript to send to John Quinn, a New York lawyer who purchased the manuscript-in-progress while Joyce was writing it. In several places, the text of the surviving Rosenbach Manuscript is fuller than the version that was typed, set by the printer, and published, containing words, phrases, and even sentences that were never typed or printed. Gabler worked with two guiding principles to deal with these differences. First, he accepted Joyce's written words rather than those in the typist's or printer's transcriptions unless the evidence convinced him to do the opposite, and he argued that all of Joyce's words, even if he wrote them onto a document that the typist and printer wouldn't see, were part of his revision process. Second, he followed what he called the "rule of the invariant context": if Joyce later worked on the text surrounding the problematic words, Gabler accepted the typed and printed version without the manuscript's words, but if the context was untouched, he admitted the manuscript's words into the text. This is how the edition's most famous and controversial "new" passage—Stephen Dedalus's thought during his discussion of Shakespeare in the National Library of Ireland, "Love, yes. Word known to all men" (*U*, 9:429–30)—entered the text.[7]

The edition was published to great fanfare on Bloomsday 1984. A few years later it was embroiled in controversy and attack. In the preface to the one-volume version of the edition that appeared in 1986, Richard Ellmann speculates that "few of the five thousand and more changes [Gabler] has introduced will excite great controversy" (x). How wrong he was, as were all of us who thought that the edition would simply be welcomed and gradually absorbed and understood. The words and phrases that were applied to the edition when it appeared—Garland Publishing and Random House called it "corrected" and "definitive" in their promotional brochures and ads; the *New York Times* carried a front-page story headlined "New Edition Fixes 5,000 Errors in *Ulysses*"—seemed uncontroversial. Like all editors, Gabler knew that no edition is or can be definitive or corrected or error-free, but he did not distance himself from these claims made on behalf of his edition, and they came back to haunt him.

When the edition was published, everyone knew that a clear dividing line had been crossed. At the time it was seen mistakenly as the difference between the faulty text that existed before and the fixed-up, correct one we had now. More properly, the fault line is this: before Gabler's edition, we had no text of *Ulysses* that had been put together by an editor who went back over the manuscripts using scholarly and critical skills (at best, earlier new editions were produced only by comparison with other printed texts), and after it we had one.

2. The second dividing line for editing and textual criticism, the so-called Joyce Wars, played out around the belief that faulty earlier texts of *Ulysses* were replaced by a fixed-up, correct one. Whatever was good or bad, useful or harmful, about the debate over Gabler's *Ulysses*, it eliminated forever any illusion about "corrected" or "definitive" editions. An edited text is a critical construct, not a "pure" or "true" version of the work.

The history of John Kidd's attack on Gabler's edition and the ensuing debate has often been told,[8] but I will summarize it briefly here. The debate began at the Society for Textual Scholarship conference in New York in April 1985, when Kidd delivered a paper called "Errors of Execution in the 1984 *Ulysses*," and Gabler, having seen a copy of Kidd's paper in advance, delivered a response immediately after it. Kidd went on to publish a blistering attack called "The Scandal of *Ulysses*" in the June 30, 1988, issue of the *New York Review of Books*, an issue that was published just as the 1988 International Joyce Symposium was beginning in Venice. (Hundreds of copies of the issue somehow found their way to Venice.) In the ensuing months, a flurry of letters to the editor in both the *New York Review* and the *TLS* (which had joined in the fray when a review of two new editions of Proust's *A la recherche du temps perdu* referred to Kidd's charges against the Gabler *Ulysses*) fueled the debate, and a couple of additional articles, including one by Charles Rossman in the *New York Review*, kept the controversy going. In his original article, Kidd promised that he would produce a full-scale article documenting his charges, but this got delayed, and it only appeared in *PBSA* (the *Papers of the Bibliographical Society of America*) in summer 1989. I responded to this two-hundred-page article in the *James Joyce Quarterly* in 1990, and Kidd countered my article in the pages immediately following. Gabler produced his own response to Kidd in *PBSA* in 1993.

Following a call in Kidd's original article for Random House, publishers of *Ulysses* in the United States, to withdraw the Gabler edition and return to selling its earlier text (one that had been on the market since 1961 but was withdrawn when the one-volume paperback version of the Gabler edition was issued in 1986), the publisher set up a committee to look into the matter, but the committee disbanded without ever reaching a recommendation. Random House restored its 1961 edition to print in 1991 and has sold both it and the Gabler edition since then. In the United Kingdom and the rest of the world, Penguin, which released the 1986 Gabler paperback, withdrew it in 1992 and replaced it with an annotated edition of the earlier Bodley Head edition (first released in 1960). Bodley Head, publisher of the hardcover Gabler text, released its own paperback in 1993, and it remains in print, although it is very hard to find.

Much of the "debate" consisted of name-calling and unproductive claims and assertions. I once described it as "a kind of World Wrestling Federation sideshow for the intellectual crowd" (1998–99, 235). People took sides without, in many cases, knowing much about editing theory and practice. Nevertheless, for the first time, the accuracy of the words that make up the text of this book—and, by extension, the words that make up the text of any book —was on everyone's mind. Textual criticism moved from the obscure side corridors of literary scholarship to the central arena. In many cases, disputes boiled down to a preference for an edition based on authorial intention or one based on the processes of production or on the inevitable compromises made in the real world and not on a consideration of Gabler's mixture of genetic development, authorial activity, and an "ideal" process of composition. Kidd claimed that Gabler had made many errors of his own, but only a few were ever demonstrated. What is absolutely clear, though, and what those of us supporting the Gabler edition failed to acknowledge or even recognize at the time, is that the Gabler edition is one possibility among many others. Editing *Ulysses* is a daunting task, to say the least, but there will always be room for alternative editions to Gabler's.[9]

Near the end of the "Joyce Wars," Vicki Mahaffey noted that "many of the most widely publicized attacks" on the Gabler edition were "based on premises about textual editing that the general reading public takes for granted, so that when a critic proves that Gabler has violated these guidelines, his editorial competence is implicitly or explicitly called into question. It takes a reasonably specialized reader to realize that the weakness of such arguments, which seem logically convincing on their own terms, is at the level of the premise, since Gabler does not share many of the premises on which the critique is based" (1991, 175). The debate hardly ever discussed the edition at the level of the premise, an odd gap when premise-based theory was so prominent in other areas of literary study. In a 1995 talk that was published in 1997, looking back at the controversy a decade after it began, Robert Spoo talked of "missed opportunities" in the discussion about and debate over Gabler's edition (108) and called for analyses of the edition written in the "spirit of high-minded debate" (118) that much of the earlier discourse lacked. We await a scholar, well-informed about both Joyce and textual criticism, uninvolved with the edition or with the participants in the original debate, who can revisit the debate and elevate it to the level Spoo desires.

Thus, before this second dividing line, there was a naively innocent assumption that editors can eradicate the errors in a text and produce a pure one. After it comes the more realistic recognition than an edition, like any act of criticism and scholarship, is an interpretation, prone to human error. The Gabler edition of *Ulysses* is such an interpretation—a bold one that challenges both Joyce scholars and textual critics and theorists—and the most useful purpose the debates might ultimately serve is to cement the realization that the edition is a work of interpretive criticism and scholarship—interpretation at the level of the text. It is a major achievement because of that, not despite it.

3. The final dividing line involving manuscripts and textual criticism involves editing theory itself. When Gabler began working on his edition in the mid-1970s, the dominant mode of editing was what is called "copytext editing."[10] Inaugurated by W. W. Greg in the late 1940s and refined by Fredson Bowers and then by many later textual critics and theorists, especially G. Thomas Tanselle, copytext editing involves choosing a state of the work (such as the first edition, the last edition produced in the author's lifetime, or a manuscript) as a copytext and then altering the copytext—emending it— based on readings from other authoritative documents. As Bowers defined it, the goal is to produce a text that comes as close as possible to the author's final intentions (Tanselle 1979, 310). The resulting text is called an "eclectic" text because it combines readings from different documents, and, by definition, it differs in small or large ways from any text that existed before.

Gabler's edition is a copytext edition, but it differs from the usual model in two major ways. First, his copytext is not a document that ever existed but a virtual one, the "continuous manuscript text," which consists of Joyce's handwritten words—as they can be found on the Rosenbach Manuscript and in the margins of the typescripts and proofs—stitched together to form a continuous text. This assembled copytext was then compared to other states of the text and emended. The second difference is that the edition attempts to reflect what Gabler described as "*Ulysses* as Joyce wrote it,"[11] with an emphasis on "wrote"—it aims to produce an ideal version of what Joyce actually wrote, not a text reflecting what Joyce might have intended by what he wrote. These two differences represent significant variations on mainstream copytext editing.

Almost simultaneously with Gabler's work on the edition, however, challenges to copytext editing were beginning to take hold. D. F. McKenzie argued that bibliography and textual criticism are "the study of the sociology of texts" (13) because they study "texts as recorded forms, and the processes of their transmission, including their production and reception" (12). Jerome McGann claimed that copytext editing, which privileges the author and denigrates all other contributors to the production of the work, ignores the fact that "literary works are fundamentally social rather than personal or psychological products" (1983, 43–44) and that they "are not produced without arrangements of some sort" (48). This approach, which has come to be known as the "social theory of editing," locates the author within a network of people who contributed to the production of the work, and an editor working along these lines will assess the relative importance of the different people involved before settling on an overall procedure and evaluating potential readings for a text. (Along these lines, McGann proposed an edition of *Ulysses* based on a "continuous production text" as an alternative to Gabler's "continuous manuscript text" [1985, 186].) It also pays attention to the work's reception, something that copytext editors, with their focus on the author, ignore.

McGann sums up the situation, one that still obtains and that applies to any work, in his article on Gabler's *Ulysses*:

> We must understand that Gabler did not have to proceed [as he did]. He could have aimed to produce a critically edited corrected edition of the original publication of 1922. . . . Were an editor to produce a fully and systematically corrected edition of 1922, . . . [t]hat text would differ from Gabler's text in many more than four thousand readings. . . . [S]uch an edition would represent a "correct" text of Ulysses. Would such a text mean that Gabler's text is "incorrect"?
>
> The answer is no, for the simple and obvious reason that we are dealing with two different conceptions of "the text of *Ulysses*". . . . A number of different *Ulysses* begin to occupy the space of critical possibility. . . . After Gabler I begin to imagine an entirely different genetic text of *Ulysses*, one which would represent the history of the work's initial *production* rather than its initial composition. (1985, 180–82; emphasis in original)

If there has been, as Robert Spoo indicates, a "paradigm shift in textual criticism" (1997, 118), Gabler's edition is both partly the cause of that shift, and also part of a shift away from the assumption that the kind of author-based edition his represents is the only way to proceed. Before this third dividing line, then, editions were often seen as approaching science, as quests for "truth"; after it, they came to be recognized as highly complex acts of criticism and interpretation.

Do we now need a new edition of *Ulysses*? Of course we do, in the same way that we need competing and conflicting interpretations and theories. Will we get one? Probably not for quite a while. John Kidd had a contract from W. W. Norton to produce a new edition, and his statements seemed to indicate that he would be oriented more toward production than toward composition, but he proved unable to complete his edition. The task is daunting, to say the least, and in addition to the amount of work involved, any new editing project would need the approval of the Estate of James Joyce, and such approval is not easily obtained.

My hope is that readers, and especially critics and scholars, will become more educated about what an edition consists of. Textual criticism and theory are not always easy to read, and editions are sometimes hard to follow, but they are hardly beyond the grasp of critics and scholars trained on complex theoretical texts. What a work says at any particular point in an edited text—its words, its punctuation—got there as a result of the editor's overarching view of the author's writing or the production; of the editor's more general theory of how texts get written, produced, and edited; and of his or her consistent but flexible way of proceeding to make decisions about particular readings. Readers who approach an edition—or who read the text in one—should have some informed sense of these aspects of editing.

Manuscript Study and Genetic Criticism

Study of Joyce's manuscripts for *Ulysses* for purposes other than editing the text long preceded their use for editing. There were some obvious reasons for this. For one thing, without an overview of how Joyce wrote *Ulysses* and how the manuscripts that became increasingly available for scholarly use in the 1940s and 1950s related to each other, it wasn't possible to think of editing the text. For another, many of the early *Ulysses* manuscript scholars (including me) were not trained in editing and textual criticism. From the start, then, the *Ulysses* manuscripts and editing were not automatically linked, even though "manuscript study" (the name often applied to this kind of work) was usually ghettoized as part of textual criticism.

I have isolated five dividing lines for manuscript study and genetic criticism.

1. The first dividing line is simple and clear: on February 2, 1922, *Ulysses* was published. Before this date, the manuscripts were papers that formed part of a work in progress. After this date, they were prepublication documents in relation to the work as it was presented to the public.

2. My second dividing line involves the appearance of my book *"Ulysses" in Progress* in 1977 and then the *James Joyce Archive* from 1977 to 1979. Before this, from the 1940s to the early 1970s, scholarly work on Joyce's manuscripts proceeded with an ad hoc, pragmatic approach to the manuscripts, with scholars working on the documents that were available to them: Joseph Prescott studied the first set of proofs (*placards*) at Harvard; A. Walton Litz used the notesheets at the British Museum (now the British Library) to offer, in *The Art of James Joyce*, a first account of Joyce's writing of *Ulysses*; Phillip Herring edited first the notesheets and then two notebooks and drafts for two episodes from the Poetry/Rare Books Collection at the University at Buffalo, State University of New York; and a series of dissertations at Columbia University studied Joyce's writing of individual episodes (Robert Hurley on "Proteus," Norman Silverstein on "Circe," Richard Madtes on "Ithaca," and James Card on "Penelope").

This work was possible because major library collections were established in the 1940s and 1950s, and scholarly catalogues for some of them appeared in the early 1960s. The major collections are at the British Library; the University at Buffalo, State University of New York; Cornell University; the National Library of Ireland; the University of Texas at Austin; and Yale University; with important documents also at Harvard, Princeton, and Southern Illinois Universities and at the Universities of Tulsa and Wisconsin at Milwaukee.[12] Peter Spielberg catalogued the Buffalo collection and Robert Scholes the one at Cornell.

This early manuscript work produced a great deal of valuable insight into Joyce's working methods and also preliminary (and, in some cases, lasting) transcriptions of some of the documents. Later work would not have been possible without these contributions. What the work did not produce was what many of the scholars probably hoped to find, a key to Joyce's works or access to their secret workings. As Litz wrote in the preface to *The Art of James Joyce*, "somehow the controlling design that I sought eluded me, and I have long since relinquished the comforting belief that access to an author's workshop provides insights of greater authority than those provided by other kinds of criticism" (v). In another essay, Litz suggests that every scholar approaching Joyce's manuscripts should be forced to read "The Figure in the Carpet," Henry James's short story about an obsessive and ultimately doomed quest for an authorially sanctioned key to a writer's works (1966, 103).

"Ulysses" in Progress presented the larger picture. It showed how the pieces fit together, how the notes related to the drafts (including what seemed to be the method behind Joyce's use of his visually dramatic colored crayons to cross out many of the notes), and it offered a stemma (family tree) depicting how Joyce progressed from his notes to his drafts, manuscripts, and corrected typescripts and proofs and on to the published work. If Joyce's writing still seemed like a puzzle, at least scholars now knew what the puzzle looked like.

At the same time, photo-reproductions of the manuscripts appeared in books, relieving scholars of the need to travel to the individual libraries or to work with microfilm copies if such copies were available. With the publication of the color facsimile of the Rosenbach Manuscript in two volumes in 1975 and then the black-and-white photo-reproductions of the other manuscripts in sixteen volumes of the *James Joyce Archive* from 1977 to 1979, anyone with access to a library that possessed these volumes could do at least preliminary work on the manuscripts.

In this second dividing line, before 1977–79, Joyce's writing processes were grasped only piecemeal, without a sense of the larger pattern, whereas after these years the outlines and major patterns were known, and photo-reproductions of the documents were available in book form for scholarly use as supplements to the original papers in the libraries.

3. Gabler's edition of *Ulysses* in 1984 is my third dividing line in this section because, after so many years of work on the manuscripts that was not directed toward establishing an accurate text of the book, the edition did precisely that. Because of the attention that was paid to the edition when it appeared, and the ensuing controversy that engulfed it, the manuscripts for several years were largely equated with editing. This coincided with the advent of the "age of theory," which, in North America at least, tended to reduce what little interest there was in manuscript study even further. Before this dividing line,

then, the manuscripts were used mainly for critical studies; after it, at least for a while, they were discussed, if at all, mostly in relation to editing.

4. My fourth dividing line is more complicated chronologically. By the mid- to late 1980s a new form of criticism, and a new approach to manuscripts, began to appear. Imported from France, "genetic criticism" (or *critique génétique*) combined detailed study of manuscripts with sophisticated theoretical perspectives. In its early years, many of its practitioners were contemporaries or students of Roland Barthes, Jacques Derrida, Julia Kristeva, and other leading Parisian theorists. In France, genetic criticism began in the late 1960s and developed in the 1970s, and so it was quite well established there in the 1970s and early 1980s, while North American manuscript studies remained resolutely untheoretical. It is my fourth dividing line here because it began to be known in North America mainly in the mid- and late 1980s.

The central concept in genetic criticism is the "avant-texte"—the critical gathering of a writer's notes, sketches, drafts, manuscripts, typescripts, proofs, etc.[13] The term was coined by Jean Bellemin-Noël in his 1972 book *Le texte et l'avant-texte: Les brouillons d'un poème de Milosz* [The text and the avant-texte: The rough drafts of a poem by Milosz]. Bellemin-Noël wanted to break with the notion of "variant," which implies *one* text with alternative formulations that can be studied independently of each other. To make a clean break, he used the neologism "avant-texte" to designate all the documents that precede a work when it is considered as a *text* and when both documents and text are considered as part of a system. Individual genetic critics use the term in somewhat different ways from each other, but it always carries the assumption that the material of textual genetics is not a given but rather a critical construction elaborated in relation to a postulated terminal state of the work.

Considered as text, the prepublication documents can be investigated in ways that parallel the approaches to published works, and genetic critics have investigated the avant-texte for many different works and authors using the conceptual resources of such different forms of literary study as narratology, linguistics, semiotics, psychoanalysis, sociocriticism, deconstruction, and gender theory. Earlier manuscript scholars tended to consider prepublication documents as valuable only in relation to the finished work. For genetic critics, on the other hand, instead of a fixed, finished object in relation to which all previous states are considered, a given text is—or texts are—contingent manifestations of diachronous plays of signifiers. "The writing," as Louis Hay puts it, "is not simply consummated in the written work. Perhaps we should consider the text as a *necessary possibility*, as one manifestation of a process which is always virtually present in the background, a kind of third dimension of the written work" (75; emphasis in original). For the editors of *Drafts*, a 1996 issue of *Yale French Studies* devoted to genetic criticism, "the work now stands out against a background, and a series, of potentialities" (Contat, Hollier, and Neefs 2). Process, potentialities: genetic criticism shifts the focus away from the text and toward the process of writing.

There has been a great deal of French and French-informed genetic criticism on Joyce. Much is on *Finnegans Wake*, but there is also quite a bit on *Ulysses*. Daniel Ferrer has been as active in this as anyone, with articles in both English and French ranging from "Reflections on a Discarded Set of Proofs," a consideration of Joyce's response to the printer setting an addition to "Circe" in the wrong place in the text, to "Paragraphs in Expansion" (coauthored with Jean-Michel Rabaté), a investigation of Joyce's writing that focuses on some of his revisions to his paragraphs in *Ulysses* and the *Wake*. To give just a couple of other examples, an issue of *European Joyce Studies*, called "Probes: Genetic Studies in Joyce" and edited by David Hayman and Sam Slote, deals mostly with *Finnegans Wake* but includes some important discussions of *Ulysses* (including Ferrer's article on the "Circe" proofs).[14] And, in "Wandering in the *Avant-texte*: Joyce's 'Cyclops' Copybook Revisited," I returned to a draft I had studied in detail in *"Ulysses" in Progress* and attempted to analyze it anew, especially with the aid of concepts from Bakhtin.

Before genetic criticism, "manuscript study" looked at prepublication documents in relation to a finished work. After it, the prepublication record, assembled by the critic as the avant-texte, becomes a text that can be studied in ways that parallel the study of published works, with writing in all its nuances and temporal complications as the main focus.

5. My final dividing line would have been impossible to imagine as recently as 2000. After forty years, the archive—the collection of extant manuscripts for *Ulysses*—has changed dramatically. This happened in three stages. First, in late 2000 a draft of "Circe" came to light; this was a draft that Joyce sent in 1921 to John Quinn, who was buying what is now known as the Rosenbach Manuscript, but that disappeared. Christie's in New York auctioned it in December 2000, and the National Library of Ireland bought it for $1.5 million. Then, in 2001, a draft of "Eumaeus," this time a completely unknown document, surfaced, and Sotheby's in London sold it at auction in July 2001 to an

anonymous private collector for £860,000 ($1.2 million).[15] Its whereabouts have not been disclosed. The surfacing of these two documents was tremendously exciting, but it turned out to be merely the tip of an iceberg.

In May 2002, the National Library of Ireland announced that it had spent £8 million ($11.7 million) to purchase about twenty-five manuscripts that Alexis Léon, son of Joyce's Paris friend Paul L. Léon, had offered in a private sale. The collection, which contains two early notebooks and some materials for *Finnegans Wake*, consists mostly of notes and early drafts for *Ulysses*. These documents will change the genetic record—and the avant-texte—of *Ulysses* in dramatic ways. Before this new collection, the extant notes for *Ulysses* included the notesheets for the last seven episodes at the British Library, two notebooks at Buffalo, and one notebook partially used for *Ulysses* at Cornell; now there are four more notebooks, including one that is probably from relatively early on in Joyce's work on the book. Before, pre–Rosenbach Manuscript drafts for seven episodes were extant ("Proteus," "Sirens," "Cyclops," "Nausikaa," "Oxen of the Sun," "Circe," and "Eumaeus"); now, there are drafts for ten episodes (they now exist for "Scylla and Charybdis," "Ithaca," and "Penelope" in addition to the seven from before), with additional drafts for "Proteus" (earlier than the one that at Buffalo), "Sirens" (also very early), "Circe" (two new drafts), and "Eumaeus." And previously incomplete drafts for "Sirens," "Cyclops," and "Oxen of the Sun" (two draft stages for "Oxen") are now complete. (I served as a consultant to the National Library of Ireland as it considered purchasing these manuscripts, and I have written three articles describing them in different ways. The Library has also released an online checklist of its collection.)

It is far too early to tell how these new manuscripts will affect Joyce scholarship and the picture that scholars will be able to create of Joyce at work. It is certain, however, that eventually they will have a major impact.

Genetic studies of Joyce have entered an exciting phase. Not only are the new manuscripts available, but as a field that has come to be called "textual studies" expands, interest in Joyce's manuscripts can be expected to grow. (Textual studies incorporates various material aspects of texts—their composition, production, and reception; their medium, whether orality, print, or digital; book history; as well as editing and textual criticism, bibliography, and genetic criticism. In their edited collection *Reimagining Textuality: Textual Studies in the Late Age of Print*, Elizabeth Bergmann Loizeaux and Neil Fraistat describe textual studies as "a broad umbrella for a host of subfields concerned with the production, distribution, reproduction, consumption, reception, archiving, editing, and sociology of texts" [5]). Hugh Kenner once wrote that "to read Joyce has always been somewhat to collaborate with him writing" (1980, 27), and Jean-Michel Rabaté has more recently expanded this idea in his call for an "ideal genetic reader" (or "genreader") of Joyce. Speaking primarily of *Finnegans Wake*, but in ways that apply to *Ulysses* as well, Rabaté argues that "texts have to be read in the context of an expanding archive" and that Joyce's texts "aim at giving birth to a new reader, a reader who has to approach the difficult and opaque language less with glosses and annotations than through the material evidence of the notebooks, drafts, corrected proofs reproduced by the *James Joyce Archive*" (2001, 196).

There is much work to be done both in editing and textual criticism and in manuscript study and genetic criticism. Joyce scholars have to respect copyright laws, and the manuscripts can be quoted only with the permission of the Estate of James Joyce. But there are many new opportunities, and the manuscripts will be an important part of *Ulysses* studies in Bloomsday's second century.

Notes

1. Riddell, "The People's Joyce." I learned about Riddell's parody in Kevin Dettmar's "James Joyce and the Great Books."

2. Dettmar, "James Joyce and the Great Books." Ernst and Lindey's statements are reproduced in Moscato and LeBlanc 243, 255–56.

3. See Slote, *"Ulysses" in the Plural*; Buffalo MSS V.D.1.a, p. 11 and V.D.1.b, p. 2; and Spielberg 89–90.

4. The rest of this paragraph adapts the description of Joyce's writing of *Ulysses* in my afterword to *Ulysses: The Gabler Edition*, 648–49. I have provided fuller accounts in *"Ulysses" in Progress* and in "A Textual and Publishing History."

5. For a much fuller account of the editions of *Ulysses*, see Slote, *"Ulysses" in the Plural*.

6. The rest of this paragraph adapts the description of Gabler's editing of *Ulysses* in my "Perplex in the Pen—and in the Pixels," 232–33. I have provided fuller accounts in the afterword to *"Ulysses": The Gabler Edition*, "Foostering Over Those Changes," and "A Response." For a list of writings on Gabler's edition and the subsequent controversy, see Rossman's bibliography.

7. The "Scylla and Charybdis" draft in the National Library of Ireland's new Joyce collection adds some complexity to Joyce's writing of this passage. The draft contains "Love, yes" as the answer to Stephen's question "Do you know what you are talking about?" but the text continues with the Latin *"Amor vero aliquid."* Joyce added

"Word known to all men" above "Love, yes." in the draft. For additional discussion of this passage in this draft, see my "'Proceeding Energetically from the Unknown to the Known.'"

8. See, for example, my "Perplex in the Pen—and in the Pixels," 234–39; Arnold, *The Scandal of "Ulysses"*; and Rossman's "Special Issue on Editing *Ulysses*."

9. A new edition of *Ulysses* did appear in 1997, this one edited by Danis Rose in Dublin and called *"Ulysses": A Reader's Edition*. Based on a re-creation of Joyce's writing of *Ulysses* from earliest drafts to final proofs, it also features what the editor calls "copyreading" (xvi), a series of corrections to Joyce's writing when the editor feels that different wording might serve the reader better. The Estate of James Joyce successfully prosecuted the edition for copyright infringement, and the edition is no longer in distribution. Rose published a revised edition, subtitled *A New Reader's Edition*, in June 2004.

10. There are many guides and introductions to editing and textual theory. See, for example, Greetham, "Textual Scholarship"; Shillingsburg, *Scholarly Editing in the Computer Age*; Williams and Abbott, *An Introduction to Bibliographical and Textual Studies*; and my "Contemporary Textual and Literary Theory."

11. The phrase "the work as he wrote it" is in Gabler's afterword to *Ulysses: A Critical and Synoptic Edition*, 3:1891, and "*Ulysses* as Joyce wrote it" is in his afterword to the 1986 *"Ulysses": The Corrected Text*, 649, and in his foreword to the 1993 *"Ulysses": The Gabler Edition*, xvii.

12. I offer a brief account of these collections in "Library Collections of Joyce Manuscripts" and a checklist, complete at the time of writing in 1980, in *James Joyce's Manuscripts: An Index*.

13. Attempts to render the term *avant-texte* in English have been extremely awkward—possibilities such as "pre-text" and "fore-text" are misleading and unattractive —and so, as Jed Deppman, Daniel Ferrer, and I did in our collection of translated French essays (*Genetic Criticism: Texts and Avant-textes*), I retain the French term here. The account of genetic criticism that follows adapts passages from our introduction to that book and from our entry on genetic criticism for the second edition of *The Johns Hopkins Guide to Literary Theory and Criticism*.

14. A second *European Joyce Studies* issue devoted to genetic studies of *Finnegans Wake* is "Genitricksling Joyce," edited by Sam Slote and Wim Van Mierlo; and Luca Crispi and Slote have edited the forthcoming *Genetic Guide to "Finnegans Wake."*

15. For more information on these two drafts, see Slote, "Preliminary Comments on Two Newly-Discovered *Ulysses* Manuscripts"; Goldman, "Two New *Ulysses* Working Drafts"; and also the two auction catalogs: Christie's, "James Joyce's *Ulysses*: The John Quinn Draft Manuscript of the 'Circe' Episode," and Selley, "The Lost 'Eumaeus' Notebook: James Joyce, Autograph Manuscript of the 'Eumaeus' Episode of *Ulysses*."

9

Ulysses

Bibliography Revisited

WILLIAM S. BROCKMAN

Bibliography is both a technique and a representative record, in both senses grounded in the evidence found in texts and documents. Its approaches to *Ulysses* have evolved over the course of James Joyce's life and the period following to encompass not only the physical history of manuscripts and printed books that constitute Joyce's personal legacy but also the scholarly history of Joyce's reception. Bibliography's techniques and styles of documentation have evolved equally, from printed checklists in literary journals and investigations in book collectors' periodicals to databases, digital images, and Web sites. Bibliography is itself a component of the reception of *Ulysses* and can function proleptically in anticipating research: it is both reflective and creative. Broadly speaking, bibliography is the sum of what *Ulysses* is: cumulative, influential in a way that parallels Eliot's assertion of the influence of writers of the past—"they are that which we know" (52). But bibliography is also a perspective rooted in physical evidence, fertilized by history, and despite its superficially systematic and rule-bound nature, subject to grow in numerous and unexpected directions.

The various branches of bibliography afford several methodological approaches to examining *Ulysses*. The field is commonly divided between analytical, historical, and descriptive bibliography—taken together, the study of texts as physical and cultural objects—and enumerative or systematic bibliography, the compilation and listing of citations. The former approaches are commonly applied to the study of the physical manifestations of an author's works and termed *primary bibliography*; the latter to arrangement and classification of writings about an author, generally referred to as "secondary bibliography." This essay will focus on the primary bibliography of *Ulysses*, with some comments related to matters of secondary bibliography.

We can consider the bibliography of *Ulysses* as being chronologically three-tiered. There are enumerations and studies of Joyce's sources, such as Gillespie's catalog of Joyce's early library, which attempt to set the stage for Joyce's works by examining their presumed influences. Bibliographies of editions of Joyce's works and of unpublished manuscripts offer details such as physical descriptions, locations, and histories of publication or ownership; still the standard resource for published works remains Slocum and Cahoon. Bibliographies of criticism account for the massive body of scholarship, biography, and other secondary work on *Ulysses*, the most comprehensive listing being the second edition of Deming.

The function of the bibliography of *Ulysses* has changed over time as critical perspectives have evolved, as unpublished materials have come to light, as the mass of knowledge about Joyce's life and the publication of his works has expanded. The treatment of Joyce's novel can serve as an example of ways in which the practice of bibliography for works of twentieth-century writers can be brought into accord with critical and historical considerations of recent years. The first bibliographic investigations of *Ulysses* developed from the interests of book collectors and dealers, concerned with the work both as a collectible and as a commodity. From its first publication in 1922, copies of *Ulysses* were often seen as precious objects, and, despite widespread trade publication beginning with Random House's edition of 1934, enough private and limited editions have continued to be issued to ensure its continued exotic status.

Initial publication of *Ulysses* was in issues of the New York literary magazine *The Little Review*, beginning in 1918 until court action in the United States (due to its alleged obscenity) ended the serialization in 1920 in the middle of the fourteenth episode. With *Ulysses* branded as obscene, Joyce had difficulty finding a publisher who would assume responsibility for such a substantial work whose publication might run the risk of prosecution. His fortunes turned when Sylvia Beach agreed to take on publication under the imprint of her bookstore in Paris, Shakespeare and Company. Her printer, Maurice Darantiere of Dijon, had already produced a number of limited editions of literary works, and he issued *Ulysses*, like other of his titles, in three variants, each on a different grade of paper. Joyce added substantial amounts of text to the proofs. The French typesetters' difficulties with integrating these handwritten notes into English text led to Beach's famous caveat in the opening pages: "The publisher asks the reader's indulgence for typographical errors unavoidable in the exceptional circumstances." The second and third impressions, under the imprint "for the Egoist Press, London by John Rodker, Paris," were intended for export. Darantiere's resetting of the 1926 edition corrected some of the earlier errors but generated a wholly new set that continued in successive impressions through 1930.

In 1926 and 1927, *Two Worlds Monthly* in New York ran a bowdlerized and unauthorized version of the first fourteen episodes of *Ulysses*. Its editor, Samuel Roth, went on to publish in 1929 a typographically imitated copy of the 1927 Paris impression, which, though unauthorized by Joyce and packed with textual errors, became the first American edition. Though these incidents infuriated Joyce, the complete text of *Ulysses* had never been registered under United States copyright regulations, and he had no legal recourse (Spoo 1999). In an attempt to set textual matters straight, the Odyssey Press, an ad hoc spin-off of the Albatross Press, enlisted Stuart Gilbert, Joyce's friend and collaborator in the French translation of *Ulysses*, to publish a 1932 edition whose text was touted as being "definitive."[1]

Extensive planning by New York publishers Bennett Cerf and Donald Klopfer intentionally brought *Ulysses* to trial in an attempt to give it a legal foothold in the United States. Their Random House edition, published in January 1934, followed quickly on federal judge John M. Woolscy's precedent setting decision of December 6, 1933, that the work was not obscene and could be imported into and published in the United States (Moscato and LeBlanc). In the haste to publish, however, Random House based its edition upon a copy of Roth's error-ridden pirated book and a hastily edited copy of the Odyssey Press edition, which promulgated and invented anew a hoard of textual errors that lived on for decades (McCleery, Brockman, and Gunn). Capitalizing on the "modern classic" status of *Ulysses*, the Limited Editions Club produced in the following year a deluxe version of 1,500 copies, illustrated by Henri Matisse (who, notoriously, never read the book and whose illustrations depict scenes from Homer's *Odyssey* [Goodwin]). The first English edition printed in England, a lavish run of 1,000 copies with binding designed by Eric Gill, appeared in 1936 under the imprint of John Lane The Bodley Head. With a text based on the Odyssey Press edition, this and a trade edition published the following year opened the door to publication in Great Britain and was the last distinct edition published during Joyce's lifetime.

For the most part, *Ulysses* was published for the next decades by Bodley Head and Penguin in British and commonwealth countries, and by the Modern Library and Random House in the United States. The Bodley Head published a slightly corrected edition in 1960, which Random House used as the basis for the 1961 edition. These, and texts derived from them, were assumed for the next two and a half decades to be the standard editions of *Ulysses* (though it has been widely acknowledged that both of these perpetuated and initiated hundreds of textual errors [Dalton]).

Publication in 1975 of a facsimile of the manuscript that Joyce sold to collector John Quinn in 1919 through 1921 and that Quinn then auctioned to collector A.S.W. Rosenbach signaled a growing interest in the origins of Joyce's work, and presaged Hans Walter Gabler's "critical and synoptic" edition of 1984. Gabler's edition employed the wealth of manuscript materials that had become available since the 1950s. His methodology was contentious; John Kidd generated much publicity in his attacks on the Gabler edition, culminating in an extended article in 1988; and the work was widely discussed at literary conferences (for example, Sandulescu and Hart). But Gabler's text has been acknowledged as the most reliable and is used by *James Joyce Quarterly* as its standard edition of *Ulysses*.

After initial publication by Garland in a three-volume edition, single-volume trade editions using the Gabler text appeared. The Book-of-the-Month Club, the Franklin Library, and other specialty presses offered illustrated or unusual editions through the 1970s and 1980s, the most notable of which was the Arion Press's elaborate hand-press production featuring etchings by Robert Motherwell.

As the 1922 edition of *Ulysses* moved into the public domain at the end of 1991 in the United States and the United Kingdom, several publishers took the opportunity to issue facsimile reprints. Throughout its history, as Gillespie and Gillespie have documented, the many published texts of *Ulysses* continue to confound the search for an authoritative text. Thus, from early on, the publishing history of *Ulysses* has been complex, with seemingly authoritative documentation subject to question.

Ulysses can be said to have spawned its own bibliography. Each of Darantiere's printings following the first included in the front matter a successive list of previous impressions, giving dates and places of publication. Like other paratextual materials that have been included to some degree in every edition of *Ulysses*—lists of errata, court decisions, and so on—this particular mini-bibliography of impressions established a venerability and a sense of lineage for the work. R. F. Roberts's seminal study of the first years of *Ulysses'* publication anticipated all further bibliographical endeavors by gathering the knowledge of the time. Published in the *Colophon*, a journal for bibliophiles, it shared space with articles on variant editions of Franklin D. Roosevelt's inaugural address and the publications of a late nineteenth-century private press. A bookseller himself, Roberts was actively involved in the collectors' market that was burgeoning in the 1930s.

Succeeding bibliographies in the 1940s by O'Hegarty and Parker built on Roberts's foundation but offered little in the way of additional information. From the present perspective, these are more interesting for their venues than their content. O'Hegarty, a book collector and dealer in Dublin and avid proponent of Irish culture, included a piece on Joyce's work among some two dozen bibliographies he contributed to the *Dublin Magazine* on then-contemporary Irish writers and political activists. Parker, an American librarian, published his bibliography of Joyce through a company that produced reference works such as indexes to monologues, plays, and fairy tales. With O'Hegarty, Joyce was being championed as an Irish writer; with Parker, he was relegated to the company of guides to the obscure.

Slocum and Cahoon's bibliography of 1953 remains the landmark in the field. Appearing within years of the first volume of Joyce's *Letters* and Ellmann's biography, it both represented and offered a stimulus to a rapidly growing academic interest in modernist literature as well as Joyce: Richard Kain's review noted that "it evidences Joyce's impact on the modern world . . . and, above all, it opens the way to future studies of considerable importance" (722). John Slocum, active as a collector of Joyce's work as early as the 1930s (Slocum), developed the idea for a bibliography in the 1940s as a collaboration with Roberts, who as a book dealer had steered Joyce materials in Slocum's direction. It was a natural affiliation—Roberts had the technical knowledge; Slocum was gathering an extensive collection of editions. But the project progressed little beyond planning when Roberts abruptly dropped out of the New York book world.[2]

Slocum found a new collaborator in Herbert Cahoon, a librarian at the New York Public Library. As one of the first publications in Rupert Hart-Davies's "Soho series," the Joyce bibliography established the "Soho recipe" for many succeeding bibliographies. It set up a format for description of books that emphasized first printings, and it grouped titles into sections by form—A, representing books; B, parts of books; C, contributions to periodicals; D, translations, and so on (Smith). Moreover, it was an example of a new conceptual approach to bibliographies: "The Soho planners recognized the need for the bibliographies to serve as essential tools, not only for librarians, collectors, and booksellers, but also for literary students and researchers with interests in textual scholarship, biography, or publishing history and practice as a social or economic phenomenon" (Laurence 12). Through the 1980s, similar compilations appeared in the Soho series for other modern writers, including Shaw, Lawrence, Mansfield, and Woolf.

Slocum and Cahoon established the bibliographical landscape of *Ulysses* as we have come to know it. Overall, the work remains reliable—though the devil is in the details. Their conflation of variants within entries—most notably the various Darantiere printings grouped within a single descriptive entry—fails to establish what should be an accurate chronological and textual relationship between distinct bibliographical entities.[3] Despite the assertion that "full bibliographic descriptions were made of all first editions . . . the compilers have considered an edition to be all copies printed from one setting of type" (v), Shakespeare and Company's "8th printing" of 1926, which was completely reset and hence constitutes a separate edition, is not given its own entry. Moreover, physical differences within variant states of the first printing are ignored.[4]

Though no comprehensive bibliography of Joyce's published works has appeared in the fifty years since Slocum and Cahoon's work, there has been vigorous scholarly activity. The perspectives of book history and textual studies have refreshed and expanded the concerns of bibliography in numerous studies focused on individual editions. Collector James Spoerri's report on the Odyssey Press edition detailed the binding variations and corrections to successive printings of this pivotal edition. Van Voorhis and Bloodgood brought the Collector's Edition, with its pages of ads for pornographic material (for example, *The Seduction of Suzy*), to the attention of readers of *James Joyce Quarterly*. Hettche and Melchior's investigation of the 1937 Bodley Head edition demonstrates how readily typographical errors are generated and carried from printing to printing. Ryder brought his background in book design to a survey of typographical features in various editions. Brockman compiled a comprehensive historical survey of Joycean bibliographies. Kugel offered a justification for Roth's supposedly unauthorized publication. Goodwin's article on the Limited Editions Club *Ulysses* revealed that the illustrations rejected for that edition, if used, would have provided a visual representation more closely in touch with Joyce's work than was Matisse's. Bishop (1994) offered an illustrated survey of book covers and jackets that pointed out how different the physical *Ulysses* has appeared to generations of readers. Nadel (1991) examined the range of post-Gabler editions published in the United States.

What might a future primary bibliography of *Ulysses* look like? Structure and presentation would vary significantly from Slocum and Cahoon's work. Expanded presentation of collational formulas—the components of bibliographical description that delineate the ways in which sheets of paper in a book are printed, folded, and gathered into signatures—could point out important variants within editions of *Ulysses* that might have been occasions for changes to plates during printing. A hierarchical numbering system could more accurately reflect the relations between titles, editions, and impressions than does Slocum and Cahoon's simple sequential numbering of editions. Photographic representation of title pages and other visually significant matter could replace the cumbersome appearance and typographic limitations of quasi-facsimile title-page transcriptions.[5] Such extensive visual representation might strain the bounds of a printed publication but could readily be accomplished through digital publication. Color photographs could represent colors of bindings (though of course variations between copies due to handling and exposure to light argue for a more codified description based upon a system such as Tanselle's). The fledgling *James Joyce Bibliography* project promises to incorporate these features into its online production (Barnes, Brockman, and Herbert).

A new bibliographical treatment of *Ulysses* would need to expand into the contexts of printing, book design, publishing, editing, reading, and reviewing as they have evolved since its first publication. Nadel makes a vigorous case for a new perspective in bibliography in calling for a practice that "reflects the theoretical shift to the social/historical dimension of a text's publication, stressing the text in the world rather than the world (bibliographically speaking) in the text" (1995, 245). Memoirs of publishers, such as Bennett Cerf's of his years at Random House, can provide an economic and cultural context that counters the idea of publishing as simply the printing and selling of a text from a manuscript. Textual studies, such as Michael Groden's *Ulysses in Progress*, can shed light on the compositional history of a work that provides a foundation for understanding the transmission of the text. Interpretive histories, such as Shari Benstock's *Women of the Left Bank*, can flesh out the modernist setting and illuminate early twentieth-century bookselling practices. Slocum and Cahoon were limited in the copies that could be examined to those in Slocum's own collection or those of a narrow circle of acquaintances with similar interests, such as Quentin Keynes or James Spoerri. The great Joyce library collections available to researchers at Buffalo, Texas, Tulsa, Southern Illinois, and Cornell—none of which was available to Slocum and Cahoon—contain previously unsuspected variants and a host of presentation copies that together can shed light on the text itself and the distribution of books.

D. F. McKenzie's concept of the "sociology of texts" argues that the literary work is inseparable from its physical manifestation. The book is not merely a vessel for a work—it is the work. For bibliography, this point of view diminishes the primacy of the first edition that has long been a mainstay of author bibliographies, and assigns an equal importance to successive editions that have undergone editorial treatment, or that have sold unusually well, or that have a physical design that interacts in a significant way with the text. Reception and readership as they are related to the physical manifestation of a work are elements that demand attention in a bibliography of today. For *Ulysses*, this perspective casts a wide net that captures all the editions and imprints enumerated at the end of this essay. The fat little Collectors Edition paperback with its ads for pornography expresses as much about the presumed audience for the novel as does the Franklin Library's staid volumes with gilt edges and elaborate binding. For *Ulysses* and other works whose many editions have spanned much of the twentieth century, we need a bibliography that, as Nadel says, sees the text in the world.

A most radical component of a bibliography, and a first for a modernist author, could be a census of copies of limited editions. Such a tool has been compiled for the first edition of *Ulysses* (Woolmer; Barnes). Similar censuses of the Egoist Press imprints and the limited numbers of the Odyssey Press and Bodley Head editions could offer valuable data regarding ownership and sale of copies, promote research on readership, and help resolve questions regarding intentional destruction of copies. Individual copies—no matter what their value—contain varying degrees of evidence as to their ownership and their use.

The concept of provenance, or the history of a book's ownership, has always been dear to collectors and rare book librarians. But to book historians too, the labels, annotations, signatures, covers, page cuts, mutilation, and normal marks of wear in mundane reading copies are just as important, for they reveal the use to which particular copies were put. And in the aggregate, such physical details can form incomparable evidence regarding the reception of a literary work and the broad regard for its author. Bishop pioneered this form of investigation in terms of *Ulysses* by reading the greasy smudges and biscuit crumbs he found in T. E. Lawrence's copy as evidence of its readership by the RAF servicemen to whom Lawrence loaned the book (1994, 27–28).

Doing this kind of research on an individual title requires examining a sizable number of copies—a process for which such a census would be invaluable. The greater number to which one has access, the more one can contextualize the physical evidence and make judgments about its meaning and relevance to critical and historical work. One can easily compare the extremely rare limited editions with the relatively common trade editions: both reveal evidence about production, sales, and readership.

Finally, a primary bibliography would need to account for the substantial number of translations of *Ulysses*. To date, *Ulysses* has been translated into some twenty-eight languages (of which Slocum and Cahoon accounted for eight), and in some cases, more than once in the same language.[6] Though Joyce had a hand in only one of these (the French of 1929), the complexities of the work make any translation an act of interpretation. The number of translations of *Ulysses* into non–Western European languages through the 1980s and 1990s parallels the dispersal of the critical literature and shows an increasing globalization of interest in Joyce's work.

Secondary bibliographies share with primary bibliographies issues of accuracy—but in the former, the issues relate to intellectual content rather than to physical factors. All bibliographers need to establish their relationship to an ideal of completeness, but whereas citation format and depth of description in a primary bibliography vary according to the importance of certain categories of materials (what Bowers terms the *digressive principle*), first publications of monographs and physical details of publication are generally of little importance in a secondary bibliography. Rather, identification of the work is the goal, and all citations tend to be given in a standardized brief format. The secondary bibliographer aims to scan a range of materials and to make judgment calls about the relevance of content to the subject matter at hand.

The secondary literature on *Ulysses* is enormous and diffuse, extending into many works on literary modernism and Irish literature. A variety of researchers may be seeking anything from a linguistic overview of the "Cyclops" episode to background material on contemporary Jewish culture in Dublin to a queer theory approach to the relationship between Leopold Bloom and Stephen Dedalus. Deming's bibliography of 1964 attempted a comprehensive listing of books, articles, and dissertations about Joyce and his work. Revised in 1974, it remains the summation of secondary work to its date. But as Herbert has shown in her dissertation on newspaper coverage of Joyce, Deming missed substantial portions of the contemporary media attention. And he categorically excluded book reviews and dissertations in the second edition, necessitating use of other sources for these important critical resources.

Any enumerative bibliography strikes a balance between breadth and focus. Printed bibliographies such as Deming's can arrange entries within a chronologically, author-, or subject-based scheme that allows a researcher to scan materials within a limited subject area. Other, more selective compilations such as *James Joyce in Spain: A Critical Bibliography (1972–2002)* aim to provide guidance and focus within a particular area. But in many ways the kind of enumeration and classification performed by subject bibliographies is much more effectively accomplished by digital databases, which may be cumulated, updated regularly, and searched in sophisticated ways. The extensive subject indexing of the *MLA International Bibliography* allows researchers to combine concepts via Boolean searching (for example, Deasy and anti-Semitism), or to identify treatments of comparisons with other writers or conceptual approaches (for example, Nabokov or parody). Yet the *MLA Bibliography*, despite its extensive international coverage, neglects a substantial amount of work on *Ulysses* in little magazines, specialist journals, and collections of essays. The *James Joyce Quarterly*'s "Current JJ Checklist" aims at comprehensive coverage but is frequently out of date and offers little subject access and no cumulative view. Though critical attention to *Ulysses* has always extended beyond the Anglo-American arena, the last couple of decades have seen substantial work being done in Japan, Hungary, Russia, Brazil, and Australia. While many readers are restricted to English-language materials, the critical writing being published in other languages represents, at the least, evidence of the reception of *Ulysses* in various countries and, in many cases, valuable original research, and deserves to be tracked bibliographically.

Fritz Senn proposed in 1978 an "international tentacular service" that could act as a clearinghouse to gather citations to the worldwide output of writing about Joyce. Such a service could operate like an electronic discussion group, open to contributions from all or, like the *MLA Bibliography*, accepting and vetting contributions from a finite body of specialists. Such a shared bibliography could be infinitely and immediately expandable, yet could allow users to create discrete subsets for specific purposes. This Joycean bibliographic utility would function most effectively in digital form, yet could be tailored to produce periodic snapshots of its contents. An editor could assign indexing terms to identify approaches or topics not immediately apparent in the title of a piece, and the database could be searched by categories particularly relevant to Joyce, such as episode numbers of *Ulysses*.[7]

One of the challenges of contemporary bibliography of *Ulysses* is to account for the rich collections of unpublished materials that have become available since the 1950s. An array of tools has been created to locate and describe extant letters and manuscripts. In the early 1960s appeared catalogs of the Cornell Joyce collection (early materials acquired from the widow of Joyce's brother Stanislaus [Scholes]) and of the collection at the University of Buffalo (later materials left behind in Paris by the Joyce family as they fled the German occupation [Spielberg]). Both catalogs provided tantalizing glimpses of possibilities for biographical and textual research—Scholes, by excerpting initial lines from previously unpublished letters, and Spielberg, by documenting and establishing a numbering system for the manuscripts, typescripts, and proofs for *Ulysses* held at Buffalo.

As research libraries acquired additional collections, other descriptive monographs appeared (for example, Lund). The sixty-three volumes of manuscript facsimiles in the *James Joyce Archive*, together with the finding lists in Groden's *Index*, gathered and made readily available holdings at Buffalo, Cornell, the British Library, Harvard, the University of Texas, and other locations to identify and relate the growing collections of notebooks, manuscripts, typescripts, and proofs. The unsealing of the Paul Léon collection at the National Library of Ireland in 1992 provided the opportunity for a compilation of a catalog of the professional correspondence and other materials gathered during the last two decades of Joyce's life (that is, Fahy).

Digitization and the Internet have afforded a previously unparalleled opportunity for the development of ready access to unpublished materials, though reproduction remains governed by copyright laws. Archivists have traditionally indexed manuscript collections with finding aids that detail the contents of boxes and folders. The ability to digitize these, to encode them in a markup language such as XML, and to make them available on the World Wide Web transforms the process of archival research. For one thing, digitized finding aids can be consulted anywhere in the world. For another, they can be searched electronically and can enable researchers to carry out finely detailed exploration. Examples of online resources that are particularly relevant to *Ulysses* are Harvard's description of the placards, Cornell's listing of early notes and drafts, and the National Library of Ireland's guide to its later notebooks, drafts, and related correspondence.

Often overlooked by researchers, but never forgotten by collectors, are exhibit, auction, and rare book dealers' catalogs. Though these frequently draw upon more formal bibliographies, their focus on individual items—with notes on provenance, markings, or divergences from standard bibliographies—transcends the scope of any individual bibliography, which must of necessity make generalizations about the titles and editions described.[8] The catalog of the Horowitz exhibit of signed first editions of *Ulysses* (Funke, Barnes, and Horowitz) shows the importance of association copies as evidence of individual printing variations and of distribution. More important, such evidence of the appearance of rare and unpublished items in the inflated market for modernist manuscripts shows the interplay of the published and unpublished in the reception and understanding of any literary figure throughout the twentieth century, essential to a bibliographic understanding of works such as *Ulysses*. The auction catalog for the Gilvarry collection (*Modern Literature. . .*) describes several important copies of *Ulysses* whose details expand upon the generalizations of Slocum and Cahoon. *Ulysses in Hand*, the catalog of the traveling exhibit of the Rosenbach Manuscript, illustrates and succinctly analyzes the relationships between that particular holograph and related typescripts and proofs, showing in detail how Joyce developed parts of the text into final published form (Barsanti).

A particularly important function of catalogs can be to act as surrogates for documents that are otherwise unavailable. The outstanding case, in terms of *Ulysses*, was the sale at Sotheby's in 2001 of a draft version of the "Eumaeus" episode, purchased by an unidentified private buyer. It remains unavailable for examination, and the only widely available evidence for its existence and content is the auction catalog, which provides substantial details regarding its physical aspects, but (presumably for copyright reasons) almost nothing regarding the text (*Lost "Eumaeus" Notebook*). The catalog and associated accounts in the media are all that the textual scholar has. Yet this is useful bibliographic evidence of Joyce's compositional practice regarding the episode. The example of the "Eumaeus" manuscript demonstrates the continuing relationship between collectors and bibliographers, at times supportive, at times contentious. Slocum's own collection formed the research library for his bibliography; and he credits numerous collectors and dealers—for example, Jacob Schwartz and Quentin Keynes—for their assistance. The astonishingly high prices in the rare book and manuscript market for copies of the first edition of *Ulysses* and of manuscripts that have come up for sale in the last few years guarantee the continuing involvement of collectors (whose interest in Joyce and ability to pay maintain high prices) with bibliographers and literary critics.[9]

Given the last decade's development of genetic approaches to *Ulysses* (succeeding more traditional textual studies) and interest in reception studies and history of the book, coupled with the increasing presence of computers in classrooms, the growing importance of digitization and Internet-based finding aids signals a change in the primary audience for bibliographic information that builds upon the influence of the Soho series. Scholars and teachers who might never have dreamed of employing manuscripts and studies of editions in their work now can find value in the examination of books and their underlying manuscripts. Those who choose to tackle *Ulysses* bibliographically will find that at least several questions remain unresolved. Some are specific, and further research may provide answers that most can rely on; others are ongoing, and will most likely never be resolved. Several examples follow.

The fate of the Egoist Press editions remains unclear. The lists of impressions in the Darantiere printings asserts the burning by New York postal authorities of 500 of the 2,000 copies of the 1922 Egoist edition and seizure by British customs authorities of 499 of the 500 copies of the Egoist 1923 edition. Slocum and Cahoon quote from a letter from Egoist Press publisher Harriet Shaw Weaver that more or less corroborates the burning of the 1922 copies (27). These claims have the apocalyptic ring of other Joycean tales of destruction (such as the Dublin publisher's purported burning of printed but unissued copies of *Dubliners*), and have been carried through Slocum and Cahoon's work (though with reservations) and repeated throughout much of the Joycean literature. Yet, as long ago as the 1940s, Joyce collectors, who came to develop a communal knowledge of Joyce's publications and learned to account for individual copies, came to doubt these bibliographical "facts."[10]

Clearly, if copies were indeed seized in the United States, they were not a sequential block of the numbered 1922 edition, as numbers from all ranges of the series are available in libraries.[11] The figure was Weaver's estimate of the total seized by governmental authorities from individuals attempting to import copies. A census of extant copies of the 1922 and 1923 editions might well supply evidence in support of an accurate explanation. Previously unexamined correspondence between, perhaps, Rodker and Beach might provide further details.

The question of the readership of the first edition of *Ulysses* remains contentious. Rainey has maintained that it was a "deluxe edition" marketed principally to dealers and speculators. Modernism, he maintained, required "not the individual reader but a new and uneasy amalgam of the investor, the collector, and the patron" (*Institutions* 56). His analysis is based upon archival research—the records of Shakespeare and Company—not upon the books themselves or their contemporaries. Bishop has pointed out that the 1922 *Ulysses* was more of a "reader's edition" than a collector's prize (1998, 16). And in fact *Ulysses* bears physical and stylistic similarities to a number of other of Darantiere's works during the same period: the three-tiered limited edition on various grades of handmade paper is not at all unusual.[12] Even a casual look at the 1922 *Ulysses* can show that this is not an elaborate production for bibliophiles (as Rainey maintains), but a fairly prosaic book. Though its cover design of white print on a blue background is bold, the cover is flimsy. The printing is far from outstanding: the typeface is small, and in many copies the inking is irregular. And Beach's warning about typographical errors would have undermined the status of a true deluxe edition. Through the 1920s, Darantiere's production of successive impressions of *Ulysses* deteriorates even further, with cramped page designs and cheap acidic paper that is now crumbling. Bibliographic examination can offer much regarding this edition's role relative to other contemporary publications.

What constitutes an "edition" of *Ulysses*? Slocum and Cahoon were criticized for inconsistent numbering of entries. Though definitions of the terms *edition*, *impression*, *issue*, and *state* are reasonably well-defined among bibliographers (Carter), the treatment of these in a particular instance needs to follow the logic of the publications at hand. For instance, the list of editions and important reprints of *Ulysses* that follows this essay separates out the 1926 resetting. This follows the definition of an edition as a single setting of type—as the 1922 and 1926 impressions were printed from different settings, they should be considered as distinct editions. Yet, as noted above, this contradicts Slocum and Cahoon's practice. Gabler set out in the appendix to his work what appears to be an orderly progress of editions, numbering each and identifying his as the eleventh (1855–56). Several years later, Kidd found much to criticize in this list, and asserted that Gabler missed seven settings, though he failed to identify these (*Inquiry* 509–14). Johnson identified as many as she could, though made no pretense of comprehensiveness (*Ulysses*, ed. Johnson 740–45). Kidd and Johnson both used the term *subedition* to elide between different instances without needing to specify the distinction between texts. Certainly, given the range of technologies used to print *Ulysses*, from the first edition's hand typesetting and letterpress printing on sheets to recent editions' digital composition and offset printing on rolls of paper, the application of a single terminology (such as in Bowers) to describe the situation and the results of the various processes is at best awkward. Yet, it is important to follow *Ulysses* through its numerous manifestations in some consistent fashion. For this situation there is no easy resolution—though it does serve as an example of the interpretive nature of bibliography.

Matters of copyright were a thorn in Joyce's side, and continue to this day to determine how and why *Ulysses* appears in print.[13] The piracy of the Roth edition of *Ulysses* left Joyce painfully aware of the troubles that he could face if his works were not properly registered. Such issues have, if anything, intensified. Spoo has argued that *Ulysses* was, due to its failure to be registered in the United States, almost never protected by copyright in the country. He asserts that the practice of "courtesy copyright" is all that has enabled Random House and its subsidiaries to dominate publication. The situation regarding later editions that include editorial changes ("derivative works") is unclear. Under the different laws of the United Kingdom, *Ulysses* had a several-years' hiatus from copyright from the end of 1991—fifty years after Joyce's death—until 1996, when that country implemented the European Union's terms extending copyright protection to seventy years following the author's death. Copyright issues were a significant factor in the planning of the Gabler edition and in negotiations with the Joyce estate (Spoo 1999, 55). The several facsimile reprints published in the 1990s and 2000s appeared when the 1922 edition was indisputably in the public domain. Yet, in 1997,

Danis Rose's heavily edited "reader's edition," published in London, engendered a lawsuit by the Joyce Estate that resulted in an injunction against sales of further copies. The estate won the suit on the basis of Rose's use of manuscript materials, themselves still under copyright protection in the United Kingdom. The laws of intellectual property as exerted by authors and their estates have much to do with what is published—and bibliographies must take into account at least the tip of the international legal iceberg in accounting for the appearance in print of their subjects' work.

Matters of book design frame the text of any work. Bibliographies have traditionally undervalued book jackets and covers, though in the case of *Ulysses* there has been a rich variety of designs. As a small recent example of their importance: Following publication of the Gabler edition of *Ulysses* in 1984, Random House replaced its Vintage paperback of the 1961 text with an edition of the Gabler text, labeled on the cover "The Corrected Text." But following controversy over Gabler's method, the sixth printing of that Vintage paperback issued several years later changed its blurb to "The Gabler Edition." Further, in 1990 Random House issued, in another Vintage imprint, the text of the 1961 edition, and continues to keep both the 1961 and the 1984 texts in print. These subtle changes in design and marketing pass unnoticed to most readers, but indicate the publisher's uncertainty about Gabler's work and exemplify greater issues of design that are essential factors in bibliographic work.

A text is never simply neutral. Examining the twentieth century through our twenty-first-century lens throws all into historical perspective. In 2002, Dover published a facsimile of the first 1922 *Ulysses*. A paperback, replete with the typographical errors that troubled Joyce, it nevertheless will sell many more copies than Sylvia Beach's limited edition. The work, *Ulysses*, has been represented by a number of texts in an array of physical embodiments. Bibliography, as the study of those texts and embodiments, is an essential tool for understanding the contributions that printers, publishers, editors, and readers have made to the novel. From the perspective of textual, analytical, and historical bibliography, and from enumerations of secondary work that provide a frame, the published and unpublished documents that constitute what we call *Ulysses* offer essential insight into the multifaceted social dimension of Joyce's work.

A Chronological Checklist of Editions, Imprints,
and Important Reissues of Ulysses in English[14]

1918–20. *Little Review* [New York]. Serial publication of 23 installments
from episode 1 through part of episode 14.

1919. *Egoist* [London]. Serial publication of 5 excerpts.

1922. Paris: Shakespeare and Company. Limited edition of 1,000: 100
copies on Dutch handmade paper, signed by Joyce; 150 copies on larger Vergé
d'Arches paper; and 750 copies on handmade paper. 4th to 7th impressions,
1924 to 1925.

1922. London: Published for the Egoist Press, London, by John Rodker,
Paris. Limited edition of 2,000. Reissued in 1923 (500 copies). 2nd and 3rd
impressions of the 1922 Paris edition.

1926. Paris: Shakespeare and Company. Identified in the front matter as
the "8th printing," but actually a resetting of the 1st edition. 2nd to 4th impressions, 1927–30.

1926–27. *Two Worlds Monthly* [New York]. Serial publication of episodes
1 through 14, with bowdlerized text.

1929. [New York: Samuel Roth]. Pirated edition, a reset copy of the 1927
2nd impression of the 1926 Paris edition.

1932. Hamburg, Paris, and Bologna: Odyssey Press. "Definitive standard
edition," revised by Stuart Gilbert. In three variations: single volume, double
volume, and double volume in limited issue of 35. 2nd to 4th impressions,
1933–39.

1934. New York: Random House. Set from the pirated Roth edition. Numerous impressions.

1935. New York: The Limited Editions Club. Introduction by Stuart Gilbert, illustrations by Henri Matisse. Limited edition of 1,500 copies signed
by Matisse, of which 250 were also signed by Joyce. Set from the Odyssey
Press edition.

1936. London: John Lane The Bodley Head. Limited edition of 1,000,
100 of which printed on mold-made paper, bound in vellum, and signed by
Joyce. Set from the Odyssey Press edition.

1937. London: John Lane The Bodley Head. Trade edition, slightly reduced facsimile, of 1936 edition. Numerous impressions.

1940. New York: Modern Library. Modern Library Giant series. Corrected reprint of 1934 Random House text. Numerous impressions.

1960. London: The Bodley Head. Resetting of the 1936 edition, with corrections to 1955 and 1958 impressions.

1960. Industry, Calif.: Collectors Publications. Unauthorized facsimile of the 1960 Bodley Head edition.

1961. New York: Random House. Corrected from the 1934 Random House. Also published in the same year in the Modern Library series and as a Vintage paperback.

1961. Garden City, N.Y.: International Collectors Library. Reset 1961. Random House text.

1968. Harmondsworth: Penguin Books. 1960 Bodley Head text.

1972. New York: Milestone Editions. 1940 Modern Library text.

1975. New York: Octagon Books, a division of Farrar, Straus, and Giroux in association with the Philip H. & A.S.W. Rosenbach Foundation, Philadelphia. 3 vols. "A facsimile of the manuscript," with critical introduction by Harry Levin and bibliographical preface by Clive Driver, and a facsimile reproduction of copy 766 of the 1922 first edition.

1976. Franklin Center, Pa.: Franklin Library. Illustrated by Alan E. Cober. 1961 Random House text.

1978. Franklin Center, Pa.: Franklin Library. Illustrated by Paul Hogarth. 1961 Random House text.

1979. Franklin Center, Pa.: Franklin Library. Illustrated by Kenneth Francis Dewey. 1961 Random House text.

1982. New York: Book-of-the-Month Club. Oxford Library of the World's Great Books. Foreword, Anthony Burgess; illustrations, Susan Stillmann. 1934 Random House text.

1983. New York: Oxford University Press; Franklin Center, Pa.: Franklin Library. Illustrated by Kenneth Francis Dewey. 1961 Random House text.

1984. New York and London: Garland Publishing. 3 vols. The "Critical and Synoptic Edition" edited by Hans Walter Gabler with Wolfhard Steppe and Claus Melchior. Reissued with corrections in 1986.

1986. New York: Random House. 1986 Gabler text.

1986. New York: Vintage. 1986 Gabler text.

1986. London: The Bodley Head. 1986 Gabler text.

1986. Harmondsworth: Penguin in association with Bodley Head. Penguin Modern Classics. 1986 Gabler text.

1988. San Francisco: Arion Press. "An edition of 150 copies for sale and 25 copies hors commerce, with 40 etchings by Robert Motherwell."

1989. Harmondsworth: Penguin. Penguin Modern Classics. Preface, Richard Unman. 1986 Gabler text.

1990. New York: Vintage Books–Random House. Vintage International. 1961 Random House text.

1992. London: David Campbell. Everyman's Library. Introduction, Craig Raine. 1960 Bodley Head text.

1992. New York: Modern Library. 1961 Random House text.

1992. London: Paladin, 1992. 1960 Bodley Head text.

1992. London: Octopus-Minerva. Introduction, Anthony Burgess. 1960 Bodley Head text.

1992. London: Penguin. Penguin Twentieth-Century Classics. Introduction, Declan Kiberd. Also released as an annotated student's edition. 1960 Bodley Head text.

1993. Oxford: Oxford University Press. The World's Classics series. Edited with an introduction by Jeri Johnson. Facsimile of copy 785 of the 1922 Paris edition.

1993. London: Bodley Head. Edited by Hans Walter Gabler with Wolfhard Steppe and Claus Melchior. Afterword by Michael Groden.

1993. New York: Vintage Books. Edited by Hans Walter Gabler with Wolfhard Steppe and Claus Melchior. Afterword by Michael Groden.

1994. London: Secker and Warburg. Introduction, Anthony Burgess. Reset 1960 Bodley Head text.

1994. London: Flamingo-Harper Collins. Flamingo Modern Classic. 1960 Bodley Head text.

1994. Shelton, Conn.: First Edition Library. Facsimile of 1922 Paris edition.

1996. Norwalk, Conn.: Easton Press. Facsimile of 1922 first edition, with facsimiles of Matisse illustrations from 1935 Limited Editions Club edition.

1997. Dublin: Lilliput. "Reader's Edition," edited by Danis Rose. Foreword, John Banville. Limited edition of 1,000, with 100 bound in goatskin and signed by Rose and Banville.

1997. London: Picador—Macmillan. Edited by Danis Rose.

1997. New York: Alfred A. Knopf. Introduction, Craig Raine. 1960 Bodley Head text

1998. London: Picador. Edited by Danis Rose.

1998. Washington, D.C.: Orchises Press. Facsimile of copy 784 of the 1922 first edition. Limited to 1,000 copies.

1998. London: Folio Society, 1998. Preface, Stephen James Joyce. Introduction, Jacques Aubert. Etchings, Mimmo Paladino. "Facsimile reproduction of the 1926 second edition, with badly broken characters corrected and blemishes deleted."

2002. Mineola, N.Y.: Dover Publications. Facsimile of 1922 Paris edition.

2002. New York: Random House. 1961 text, but with dust jacket reproducing the 1934 edition.

2003. Ann Arbor: Borders. Facsimile of 1922 Paris edition.

Notes

1. Though, as Gilbert himself admitted, the presumed supervision of the edition amounted to little more than a reading of proof (Dalton n.14).

2. Roberts's participation is documented in correspondence with Slocum in the James Joyce Collection, General Collection, Beinecke Rare Book and Manuscript Library, Folder 548.

3. Kain notes that sixty variants of *Ulysses* are cited under seven major headings.

4. The gatherings are not uniform throughout the first 1922 printing, as Slocum and Cahoon suggest. Their collation shows gatherings of eight leaves, whereas, in copy numbers 1–100 and 251–1000, signatures 27–38, 41, and 46 consist of signed gatherings of four leaves followed by unsigned gatherings of 4 leaves, and in numbers 101–250, signatures 2–46 consist of signed gatherings of four leaves followed by unsigned gatherings of four. These differences could signal changes within the printing of the edition, which in turn could suggest textual alterations.

5. For example, the title page of the 1935 edition would be rendered in quasi-facsimile form as follows: Ulysses [script] | by James Joyce | [ornament based on front cover design] | WITH AN INTRODUCTION BY STUART GILBERT AND ILLUSTRATIONS BY | Henri Matisse | THE LIMITED EDITIONS CLUB | *New York, 1935.*

6. These languages include Arabic, Catalan, Chinese, Croatian, Czech, Danish, Dutch, Finnish, French, Georgian, German, Hungarian, Irish, Italian, Japanese, Korean, Latvian, Macedonian, Norwegian, Polish, Portuguese, Romanian, Russian, Serbo-Croatian, Slovenian, Spanish, Swedish, and Turkish.

7. This proposal is adapted and technologically updated from that found in Brockman (135–36).

8. Bowers (113–23) set out precise standards for determining the "ideal copy." Though bibliographers might not adhere precisely to Bowers's standards, they must follow the basic concept.

9. A record was set for any Joyce book by the sale at Christie's New York of a signed first edition of *Ulysses* for $460,500 on October 11, 2002.

10. For instance, James Spoerri wrote to Quentin Keynes on June 10, 1949: "I think that if they renumbered the 500 copies of the third printing to correspond with the numbering of the 500 copies that were 'burned' by the U.S. Customs Authorities of New York, your deduction is correct that the 'burned' copies went unscathed through the fire and phoenix-like found their way into commerce. Your copy is 827. Mine is 877. Gotham has copies numbered, I believe, 814 and 864. Another fact which lays support to your theory is that the second printing is the one which, for many years, has been most plentiful upon the shelves of the booksellers and quite often it is found in pristine condition beautifully bound or boxed. What you should really do is put your hands on #827 of the second edition. This should clinch your contention." James Joyce Collection, General Collection, Beinecke Rare Book and Manuscript Library, Folder 552.

11. For instance, at the Harry Ransom Humanities Research Center of the University of Texas are 28 numbered copies of the Egoist's 1922 edition, which span the gamut of limitation numbers from #24 to #1984.

12. Darantiere had experience with limited editions and with English literature —including publications in the English language. In 1920 and 1921, he printed French translations of the religious and imagistic poems of the late nineteenth-century English writer Francis Thompson. These are indeed limited editions, but not spectacular: the one, *Une antienne de la terre*, in 1,025 copies on three varieties of paper; the other, *Le lévrier du ciel*, in only 50 copies on two varieties of paper. In 1921, he printed James Elroy Flecker's Orientalist-inspired *14 Poems* illustrated with lithographs in a folio edition of 500 copies on Vergé d'Arches paper—the same used for the middle range of *Ulysses*—and 50 copies on old Japanese vellum. These are precious productions, though not extravagant, and certainly formed the background for Darantiere's design of *Ulysses*.

13. This brief account of a complicated legal situation is derived from Spoo (1999).

14. The list is based upon personal examination of copies, and draws on comments and lists in Gabler, Johnson, Kidd, Nadel, Roberts, Slocum and Cahoon, and Slote, as well as bibliographic information from the OCLC *WorldCat* and *RLG Union Catalog* databases. To date, several digital copies of *Ulysses* have appeared informally on the World Wide Web or elsewhere, but none has been formally published. As the relation of editions is not logical and successive (and as the present essay points out, the very definition of edition is difficult to establish), there is no sense in numbering these, and the present list makes no attempt to do so.

Works Cited

Arnold, Bruce. *The Scandal of "Ulysses."* 1991. New York: St. Martin's, 1992. Rev. ed., Dublin: Liffey Press, 2004.

Attridge, Derek. *Peculiar Language: Literature as Difference from the Renaissance to James Joyce.* London: Methuen, 1988.

———. "Molly's Flow: The Writing of 'Penelope' and the Question of Women's Language." *Modern Fiction Studies* 35 (1989): 543–65.

———. *Joyce Effects: On Language, Theory, and History.* Cambridge: Cambridge University Press, 2000.

Aubert, Jacques, ed. *Joyce avec Lacan.* Paris: Navarin Editeur, 1987.

———. *The Aesthetics of James Joyce.* Baltimore and London: Johns Hopkins University Press, 1992.

Austin, J. L. *How to Do Things with Words.* 2nd ed. Edited by J. O. Urmson and Marina Sbisa. Cambridge: Harvard University Press, 1977.

Bakhtin, M. M. *The Dialogic Imagination.* Translated by Caryl Emerson and Michael Holquist. Austin: University of Texas Press, 1981.

Bal, Mieke. *Narratology: Introduction to the Theory of Narrative.* 2nd ed. Toronto: University of Toronto Press, 1997.

Banfield, Ann. *Unspeakable Sentences: Narration and Representation in the Language of Fiction.* Boston: Routledge and Kegan Paul, 1982.

Barnes, Laura. "Appendix." In *James Joyce: Books & Manuscripts,* by Jessy Randall and Glenn Horowitz, 109–34. New York: Glenn Horowitz Bookseller, 1996.

Barnes, Laura, William Brockman, and Stacey Herbert. *James Joyce Bibliography.* 2002. http://www.themodernword.com/jjb/index.html.

Barsanti, Michael. *"Ulysses" in Hand: The Rosenbach Manuscript.* Philadelphia: Rosenbach Museum and Library, 2000.

Barthes, Roland. *S/Z.* Translated by Richard Miller. New York: Hill and Wang, 1974.

———. "Introduction to the Structural Analysis of Narrative." In *Image-Music-Text,* edited and translated by Stephen Heath, 79–124. New York: Hill and Wang, 1977.

Bauerle, Ruth H. "Two Unnoted Musical Allusions." *James Joyce Quarterly* 9 (1971): 140–42.

———. *The James Joyce Songbook.* New York: Garland Press, 1982.

———, ed. *Picking Up Airs: Hearing the Music in Joyce's Text.* Urbana: University of Illinois Press, 1993.

————. "James Joyce and Opera: A Bibliography." *James Joyce Quarterly* 38, no. 1–2 (Fall 2000–Winter 2001): 157–81.

Beeretz, Sylvia. *"Tell Us in Plain Words": Narrative Strategies in James Joyce's Ulysses.* New York: Peter Lang. 1998.

Bellemin-Noël, Jean. *Le texte et l'avant-texte: Les brouillons d'un poème de Milosz.* Paris: Larousse, 1972.

————. "Psychoanalytic Reading and the Avant-texte." 1982. In *Genetic Criticism: Texts and Avant-textes,* edited and translated by Jed Deppman, Daniel Ferrer, and Michael Groden, 28–35. Philadelphia: University of Pennsylvania Press, 2005.

Beneveniste, Emile. *Problems in General Linguistics.* Translated by Mary Elizabeth Meek. Coral Gables, Fla.: University of Miami Press, 1971.

Benjamin, Walter. *Illuminations.* Edited by Hannah Arendt. Translated by Harry Zohn. New York: Schocken, 1969.

Benstock, Bernard. *Critical Essays on James Joyce's Ulysses.* Boston: G. K. Hall, 1989.

Benstock, Shari. *Women of the Left Bank: Paris, 1800–1940.* Austin: University of Texas Press, 1986.

Bersani, Leo. *The Culture of Redemption.* Cambridge: Harvard University Press, 1990.

Bishop, Edward L. "Re:Covering Ulysses." *Joyce Studies Annual* 5 (1994): 22–55.

————. "The 'Garbled History' of the First-Edition *Ulysses*." *Joyce Studies Annual* 9 (1998): 3–36.

Boheemen, Christine van. *The Novel as Family Romance: Language, Gender, and Authority from Fielding to Joyce.* Ithaca: Cornell University Press. 1987.

Booker, M. Keith. *"Ulysses," Capitalism, and Colonialism: Reading Joyce after the Cold War.* Westport, Conn.: Greenwood, Press, 2000.

Boone, Joseph Allan. "Staging Sexuality: Depression, Representation and Interior States in Ulysses." In *Joyce: The Return of the Repressed,* edited by Susan S. Friedman, 190–224. Ithaca: Cornell University Press, 1993.

Booth, Wayne C. *The Rhetoric of Fiction.* Chicago: University of Chicago Press, 1961.

Bornstein, George. *Material Modernism.* Cambridge: Cambridge University Press, 2001.

Boscagli, Maurizia, and Enda Duffy, "Joyce's Face." In *Marketing Modernisms,* edited by Kevin Dettmar and Stephen Watt, 133–60. Ann Arbor: University of Michigan Press, 1996.

Bowen, Zack. "The Bronzegold Sirensong: A Musical Analysis of the 'Sirens' Episode in Joyce's *Ulysses*." *Literary Monographs* 1 (1966): 247–98, 319–20.

————. *Musical Allusions in the Works of James Joyce: Early Poetry through "Ulysses."* Albany: State University of New York Press, 1975.

————. *Bloom's Old Sweet Song: Essays on Joyce and Music.* Gainesville: University Press of Florida, 1995.

Bowers, Fredson. *Principles of Bibliographical Description.* Princeton: Princeton University Press, 1949.

Bradley, Anthony, and Maryann Valiulis. Introduction to *Gender and Sexuality in Modern Ireland*, edited by Bradley and Valiulis. Amherst: University of Massachusetts Press, 1997.

Brannigan, John, Geoff Ward, and Julian Wolfreys, eds. *Re: Joyce: Text, Culture, Politics*. Basingstoke: Macmillan, 1998.

Brivic, Sheldon. "ii. Lacan on Joyce: A Catalogue." *James Joyce Quarterly* 29 (Fall 1991): 17–19.

———. *The Veil of Signs: Joyce, Lacan, and Perception*. Urbana: University of Illinois Press, 1991.

———. "Dealing in Shame: Gender in 'Circe.'" In *Masculinities in Joyce*, edited by C. Lamos and C. Van Boheeman, 177–96. Amsterdam: Rodopi, 2001.

Brockman, William S. "'Catalogue these books': Joycean Bibliographies, Catalogs, Checklists, and Desiderata." *Joyce Studies Annual* 4 (1993): 119–36.

Brooks, Cleanth. *The Well-Wrought Urn: Studies in the Structure of Poetry*. New York: Harcourt Brace, 1947.

Brown, Richard. *James Joyce and Sexuality*. Cambridge: Cambridge University Press, 1985.

Buck-Morss, Susan. *The Dialectics of Seeing: Walter Benjamin and the Arcades Project*. Cambridge: MIT Press, 1989.

Budgen, Frank. *James Joyce and the Making of "Ulysses."* Bloomington: University of Indiana Press, 1960.

Burke, Kenneth. "Fact, Inference, and Proof in the Analysis of Literary Symbolism." 1954. In *Terms for Order*, edited by Stanley Edgar Hyman, 145–72. Bloomington: Indiana University Press, 1964.

Butler, Judith. "Imitation and Gender in Subordination." In *Inside/Out: Lesbian Theories Gay Theories*, edited by Diana Fuss, 13–31. New York: Routledge, 1991.

Card, James Van Dyck. *An Anatomy of "Penelope."* Rutherford, N.J.: Fairleigh Dickinson University Press, 1984.

Carter, John. *ABC for Book Collectors*. 7th ed. New Castle: Oak Knoll Press, 1995.

Cerf, Bennett. *At Random: The Reminiscences of Bennett Cerf*. New York: Random House, 1977.

Chambers, Ross. *Room for Maneuver: Reading (the) Oppositional (in) Narrative*. Chicago: University of Chicago Press, 1991.

Chatman, Seymour. *Story and Discourse: Narrative Structure in Fiction and Film*. Ithaca: Cornell University Press, 1978.

Cheng, Vincent J. *Joyce, Race, and Empire*. New York: Cambridge, University Press, 1995.

Cheng, Vincent J., Kimberly Devlin, and Margot Norris, eds. *Joycean Cultures/Culturing Joyce*. Newark: University of Delaware Press/Associated University Presses, 1998.

Christie's. "James Joyce's *Ulysses*: The John Quinn Draft Manuscript of the 'Circe' Episode." Auction catalogue. Christie's New York, December 14, 2000.

Cohn, Alan M. "Current JJ Checklist." *James Joyce Quarterly* 14, no. 2 (Winter 1977): 191–97. Continues in each issue to present; compiled by William S. Brockman since vol. 28, no. 1 (Fall 1990).

Cohn, Alan M., and Richard M. Kain. "Supplemental JJ Checklist, 1962." *James Joyce Quarterly* 1, no. 2 (Winter 1964): 15–22.

Cohn, Dorrit. *Transparent Minds: Narrative Modes for Presenting Consciousness in Fiction*. Princeton: Princeton University Press, 1978.

Colum, Mary, and Padraic Colum. *Our Friend James Joyce*. Garden City, N.Y.: Doubleday, 1958.

Connolly, Thomas E. *The Personal Library of James Joyce: A Descriptive Bibliography*. University of Buffalo Studies 22, no. 1. Monographs in English. Vol. 6. Buffalo: University of Buffalo, 1955.

Contat, Michel, Denis Hollier, and Jacques Neefs, eds. Editors' preface. *Drafts*. Translated by Alyson Waters. *Yale French Studies* 89 (1996): 1–5.

Craft, Christopher. *Another Kind of Love*. Berkeley and Los Angeles: University of California Press, 1994.

Crispi, Luca, and Sam Slote, eds. *A Genetic Guide to "Finnegans Wake."* Madison: University of Wisconsin Press, forthcoming.

Dalton, Jack P. "The Text of *Ulysses*." In *New Light on Joyce from the Dublin Symposium*, edited by Fritz Senn, 99–119. Bloomington and London: Indiana University Press, 1972.

Dean, Tim. "Paring his Fingernails." In *Quare Joyce*, edited by Joseph Valente, 241–72. Ann Arbor: University of Michigan Press, 1998.

———. *Beyond Sexuality*. Chicago: University of Chicago Press, 2000.

de Man, Paul. "The Rhetoric of Temporality." In *Interpretation: Theory and Practice*, edited by Charles S. Singleton, 173–209. Baltimore: Johns Hopkins University Press, 1969.

Deming, Robert H. *A Bibliography of James Joyce Studies*. Univ. of Kansas Pubs., Lib. Series, 18. Lawrence: University of Kansas Libraries, 1964; 2nd ed. Boston: G. K. Hall, 1977.

Deppman, Jed, Daniel Ferrer, and Michael Groden. "Introduction: A Genesis of French Genetic Criticism." In *Genetic Criticism: Texts and Avant-textes*, edited and translated by Deppman, Ferrer, and Groden, 1–16. Philadelphia: University of Pennsylvania Press, 2004.

———. "Genetic Criticism." In *The Johns Hopkins Guide to Literary Theory and Criticism*, 2nd ed., edited by Michael Groden, Martin Kreiswirth, and Imre Szeman, 691–98. Baltimore: Johns Hopkins University Press, 2005.

Derrida, Jacques. "Two Words for Joyce." In *Post-Structuralist Joyce: Essays from the*

French, edited by Derek Attridge and Daniel Ferrer, 145–59. Cambridge: Cambridge University Press, 1984.

———. "Ulysses Gramophone: Hear say yes in Joyce." In *A Companion to James Joyce's "Ulysses,"* edited by Margot Norris, 69–90. Boston: Bedford Books, 1998.

Dettmar, Kevin. *The Illicit Joyce of Postmodernism: Reading against the Grain*. Madison: University of Wisconsin Press, 1996.

———. "James Joyce and the Great Books." *The Common Reader* 2, no. 1 (n.d.). http://www.greatbooks.org/tcr/dettmar21.shtml.

Devlin, Kimberly J. *James Joyce's Fraudstuff*. Gainesville: University Press of Florida, 2002.

Division of Rare and Manuscript Collections, Cornell University Library. *Guide to the James Joyce Collection*. 1893[?]-1941. 2003. http://rmc.library.cornell.edu/EAD/htmldocs/RMM04609.html.

Downing, Gregory M. "Richard Chenevix Trench and Joyce's Historical Study of Words." *Joyce Studies Annual* 9 (1998): 37–68.

———."Sunny Jim: Joyce and Max Müller's Comparative Religion." *James Joyce Quarterly* 39, no. 1 (Fall 2001): 101–12.

Duffy, Enda. *The Subaltern Ulysses*. Minneapolis: University of Minnesota Press, 1994.

Dunleavy, Janet Egleson. *Re-Viewing Classics of Joyce Criticism*. Urbana and Chicago: University of Illinois Press, 1991.

Eco, Umberto. *Opera Aperta*. Milan: Gruppo Editoriale Fabbri, 1962. Portions available in English in two volumes: *The Open Work*. Translated by Anna Cancogni. Cambridge: Harvard University Press, 1989.

———. *The Aesthetics of Chaosmos: The Middle Ages of James Joyce*. Translated by Ellen Esrock. 1982; reprint, Cambridge: Harvard University Press, 1989.

Eliot, T. S. "Tradition and the Individual Talent." In *The Sacred Wood: Essays on Poetry and Criticism*, 2nd ed., 42–59. London: Methuen, 1928.

Ellmann, Richard. *James Joyce*. 1959. Rev. ed., New York: Oxford University Press, 1982.

———. *"Ulysses" on the Liffey*. New York: Oxford University Press, 1972.

———. Preface to *"Ulysses": The Corrected Text*, edited by Hans Walter Gabler, ix–xiv. New York: Random House, 1986.

Erdman, David V., ed. *The Poetry and Prose of William Blake*. Garden City, N.Y.: Doubleday, 1965.

Erzgräber, Willi. *James Joyce: Oral and Written Discourse as Mirrored in Experimental Narrative Art*. Translated by Amy Cole. Frankfurt am Main: Peter Lang, 2002.

Fahy, Catherine. *The James Joyce—Paul Léon Papers in the National Library of Ireland: A Catalogue*. Dublin: National Library of Ireland, 1992.

Ferrer, Daniel. "Reflections on a Discarded Set of Proofs." In "Probes: Genetic Studies in Joyce," special issue, *European Joyce Studies* 5 (1995): 49–63.

Ferrer, Daniel, and Jean-Michel Rabaté. "Paragraphs in Expansion (James Joyce)." 1989. In *Genetic Criticism: Texts and Avant-textes*, edited and translated by Jed Deppman, Daniel Ferrer, and Michael Groden, 132–51. Philadelphia: University of Pennsylvania Press, 2004.

Fish, Stanley. *Is There a Text in This Class?: The Authority of Interpretive Communities*. Cambridge: Harvard University Press, 1980.

Fitch, Noel Riley. *Sylvia Beach and the Lost Generation: A History of Literary Paris in the Twenties and Thirties*. New York and London: W. W. Norton, 1983.

Fludernik, Monika. "The Genderization of Narrative." *GRAAT*, no. 21 (1997): 153–73.

———. "Narrative and its Development in Ulysses." *Journal of Narrative Technique* 6, no. 1 (Winter 1986): 15–40.

Foucault, Michel. *The Order of Things: An Archeology of the Human Sciences*. New York: Random House, 1970.

Frank, Joseph. "Spatial Form in Modern Literature." In *The Idea of Spatial Form*, by Frank, 3–66. New Brunswick, N.J., and London: Rutgers University Press, 1991.

French, Marilyn. "On Danis Rose's Edition," *James Joyce Quarterly* 35, no. 4 (1998): 830–34.

Froula, Christine. *Modernism's Body: Sex, Culture and Joyce*. New York: Columbia University Press, 1996.

Fuller, David. *James Joyce's "Ulysses."* New York: St. Martin's, 1992.

Funke, Sarah, Laura Barnes, and Glenn Horowitz. *James Joyce: "Ulysses": An Exhibition of Twenty-four Inscribed Copies of the First Edition*. New York: Glenn Horowitz Bookseller, 1998.

Gabler, Hans Walter. "A Response to John Kidd, 'Errors of Execution in the 1984 *Ulysses*.'" *Studies in the Novel* 22 (1990): 250–55.

———. "What *Ulysses* Requires." *PBSA* 87 (1993): 187–248.

Gallagher, Catherine, and Stephen Greenblatt. *Practicing New Historicism*. Chicago: University of Chicago Press, 2000.

Genette, Gérard. *Narrative Discourse: An Essay in Method*. Translated by Jane E. Lewin. Foreword by Jonathan Culler. Ithaca: Cornell University Press, 1980.

Gibson, Andrew. *Joyce's Revenge: History, Politics, Aesthetics in "Ulysses."* Oxford: Oxford University Press, 2002.

Gifford, Don. *"Ulysses" Annotated: Notes for James Joyce's "Ulysses."* Revised and expanded. Berkeley and Los Angeles: University of California Press, 1988.

Gilbert, Stuart. *James Joyce's "Ulysses": A Study*. New York: Vintage, 1955.

Gillespie, Michael Patrick. *Reading the Book of Himself: Narrative Strategies in the Works of James Joyce*. Columbus: Ohio State University Press, 1989.

———, ed. "James Joyce and the Fabrication of an Irish Identity." *European Joyce Studies* 11. Amsterdam and Atlanta: Editions Rodopi b.v., 2001.

Gillespie, Michael Patrick, and Paula F. Gillespie. "The Search for an Edition." In *Recent*

Criticism of James Joyce's Ulysses: An Analytical Review, 106–26. Studies in English and American Literature, Linguistics, and Culture: Literary Criticism in Perspective. Rochester: Camden House, 2000.

Gillespie, Michael Patrick, with the assistance of Eric Bradford Stocker. *James Joyce's Trieste Library: A Catalogue of Materials at the Harry Ransom Humanities Research Center, The University of Texas at Austin*. Austin: Harry Ransom Humanities Research Center, University of Texas at Austin, 1986.

Goldberg, S. L. *The Classical Temper: A Study of James Joyce's "Ulysses."* London: Chatto and Windus, 1961.

Goldman, Arnold. *The Joyce Paradox: Form and Freedom in his Fiction*. Evanston: Northwest University Press, 1966.

———. "Two New *Ulysses* Working Drafts." *Joyce Studies Annual* 12 (2001): 3–9.

Goodwin, Willard. "'A Very Pretty Picture M. Matisse But You Must Not Call It Joyce': The Making of the Limited Editions Club *Ulysses*. With Lewis Daniel's Unpublished *Ulysses* Illustrations." *Joyce Studies Annual* 10 (1999): 85–103.

Greenblatt, Stephen. *Shakespearean Negotiations*. Berkeley and Los Angeles: University of California Press, 1988.

———. "Resonance and Wonder." In *New Historicism and Cultural Materialism, A Reader*, edited by Kiernan Ryan, 55–60. London: Arnold, 1996.

———. "The Circulation of Social Energy." In *Modern Criticism and Theory*, 2nd. ed., edited by David Lodge with Nigel Wood, 494–528. London: Longman, 2000.

Greetham, D. C. "Textual Scholarship." In *Introduction to Scholarship in Modern Languages and Literatures*, 2nd ed., edited by Joseph Gibaldi, 103–37. New York: Modern Language Association of America, 1992.

Grice, Paul. *Studies in the Way of Words*. Cambridge: Harvard University Press, 1989.

Groden, Michael. *"Ulysses" in Progress*. Princeton: Princeton University Press, 1977.

———. *James Joyce's Manuscripts: An Index*. Garland Reference Library of the Humanities. Vol. 186. New York and London: Garland Publishing, 1980.

———. "Library Collections of Joyce Manuscripts." In *A Companion to Joyce Studies*, edited by Zack Bowen and James F. Carens, 783–85. Westport, Conn.: Greenwood, 1984.

———. "A Textual and Publishing History." In *A Companion to Joyce Studies*, edited by Zack Bowen and James F. Carens, 71–128. Westport, Conn.: Greenwood, 1984.

———. "Foostering Over Those Changes: The New *Ulysses*." *James Joyce Quarterly* 22 (1985): 137–59.

———. "A Response to John Kidd's 'An Inquiry into *Ulysses*: The Corrected Text.'" *James Joyce Quarterly* 28 (1990): 81–110.

———. "Contemporary Textual and Literary Theory." In *Representing Modernist Texts: Editing as Interpretation*, edited by George Bornstein, 259–86. Ann Arbor: University of Michigan Press, 1991.

————. Afterword to *"Ulysses": The Gabler Edition*, edited by Hans Walter Gabler. New York: Vintage, 1993.

————. "Wandering in the Avant-texte: Joyce's 'Cyclops' Copybook Revisited." In *The Future of Modernism*, edited by Hugh Witemeyer, 181–99. Ann Arbor: University of Michigan Press, 1997.

————. "Perplex in the Pen —and in the Pixels: Reflections on the *James Joyce Archive*, Hans Walter Gabler's *Ulysses*, and 'James Joyce's *Ulysses* in Hypermedia.'" *Journal of Modern Literature* 22 (1998–99): 225–44.

————. "The National Library of Ireland's New Joyce Manuscripts: A Statement and Document Descriptions." *James Joyce Quarterly* 39 (2001): 29–51.

————. "The National Library of Ireland's New Joyce Manuscripts: A Narrative and Document Summaries." *Journal of Modern Literature* 26, no. 1 (Fall 2002): 1–16.

————. "The National Library of Ireland's New Joyce Manuscripts: An Outline and Archive Comparisons." *Joyce Studies Annual* (2003): 5–17.

————. "'Proceeding Energetically From the Unknown to the Known': Looking Again at the Genetic Texts and Documents for Joyce's *Ulysses*." *Variants*. Forthcoming.

Gunn, Ian, and Alistair McCleery. *"Ulysses" Pagefinder*. Edinburgh: Split Pea Press, 1988. Updated by *Ulysses Tables*. http://www.harenet.demon.co.uk/splitpea/utables.pdf.

Halperin, David. *Saint Foucault*. New York: Oxford University Press, 1995.

Harari, Roberto. *How James Joyce Made His Name: A Reading of the Final Lacan*. Translated by Luke Thurston. New York: Other Press, 2002.

Hart, Clive, and David Hayman. *"Ulysses": Critical Essays*. Berkeley and London: University of California Press, 1974.

Hay, Louis. "Does 'Text' Exist?" 1985. Translated by Matthew Jocelyn and Hans Walter Gabler. *Studies in Bibliography* 41 (1988): 64–76.

Hayashi, Tetsumaro. *James Joyce: Research Opportunities and Dissertation Abstracts*. Jefferson, N.C.: McFarland, 1985.

Hayman, David. *"Ulysses": The Mechanics of Meaning*. Englewood Cliffs, N.J.: Prentice-Hall, 1970.

Hayman, David, and Sam Slote, eds. "Probes: Genetic Studies in Joyce." Special issue, *European Joyce Studies* 5 (1995).

Heaney, Seamus. *Opened Ground: Selected Poems 1966–1996*. New York: Farrar, Straus, and Giroux, 1998.

Heinzelman, Kurt, ed. *Make It New: The Rise of Modernism*. Austin: Harry Ransom Humanities Research Center, University of Texas, Austin, 2003.

Henke, Suzette. *James Joyce and the Politics of Desire*. New York: Routledge, 1990.

Henke, Suzette, and Elaine Unkeless, eds. *Women in Joyce*. Urbana: University of Illinois Press, 1982.

Herbert, Stacey. *Reporting on the Artist as a Modernist: The Press and the Making of James Joyce, 1917–1924*. Ph.D. diss., State University of New York at Buffalo, 2002.

———. "A Draft for '*Ulysses* in Print: The Family Tree,' an Installation for the Exhibition 'James Joyce and *Ulysses* at the National Library of Ireland.'" *Genetic Joyce Studies* 4 (Spring 2004). http:www.antwerpjamesjoycecenter.com/GJS/.

Herr, Cheryl. *Joyce's Anatomy of Culture*. Urbana and Chicago: University of Illinois Press, 1986.

———. "Art and Life, Nature and Culture, *Ulysses*." In *Joyce's "Ulysses": The Larger Perspective*, edited by Robert D. Newman and Weldon Thornton, 19–38. Newark: University of Delaware Press, 1987.

———. "Joyce and Marxism: Prefatory Note." In *James Joyce: The Augmented Ninth*, edited by Bernard Benstock, 309–11. Syracuse: Syracuse University Press, 1988.

———. "Fathers, Daughters, Anxiety, and Fiction." In *Discontented Discourses: Feminism/Textual Intervention/Psychoanalysis*, edited by Marleen S. Barr and Richard Feldstein, 173–207. Urbana: University of Illinois Press, 1989.

———. "'The Strange Reward of All That Discipline': Yeats and Foucault." In *Yeats and Postmodernism*, edited by Leonard Orr, 146–66. Syracuse: Syracuse University Press, 1991.

———. "The Sermon as Massproduct: 'Grace' and *A Portrait*." In *James Joyce: A Collection of Critical Essays*, edited by Mary T. Reynolds, 81–95. Englewood Cliffs, N.J.: Prentice Hall, 1993.

Herring, Phillip F. *Joyce's Uncertainty Principle*. Princeton: Princeton University Press, 1987.

Hettche, Walter, and Claus Melchior. "A Famous Fighter and Mairy's Drawers: Joyce's Corrections for the 1936 John Lane Edition of *Ulysses*." *James Joyce Quarterly* 21, no. 2 (Winter 1984): 165–69.

Hodgart, Matthew, and Ruth Bauerle, *Joyce's Grand Operoar: Opera in "Finnegans Wake."* Urbana: University of Illinois Press, 1997.

Hoggart, Richard. *The Uses of Literacy: Aspects of Working-Class Life with Special References to Publications and Entertainments*. London: Chatto and Windus, 1957.

Holland, Norman N. *The Dynamics of Literary Response*. New York: Oxford University Press, 1968.

Homer. *The Odyssey*. Translated by Samuel Butler. Roslyn, N.Y: Walter J. Black, 1944.

Houghton Library, Harvard University. *Joyce, James, 1882–1941. Ulysses Placards. Guide*. 1999. http://oasis.harvard.edu/html/hou00053.html.

"How to Enjoy James Joyce's Great Novel *Ulysses*." *Saturday Review of Literature*, February 10, 1934, 474–75.

Hurley, Robert Edward. "The 'Proteus' Episode of James Joyce's *Ulysses*." Ph.D. diss., Columbia University, 1963.

Iser, Wolfgang. *The Implied Reader: Patterns of Communication in Prose Fiction from Bunyan to Beckett*. Baltimore: Johns Hopkins University Press, 1974.

————. *The Act of Reading: A Theory of Aesthetic Response*. Baltimore: Johns Hopkins University Press, 1978.

Jakobson, Roman. *Roman Jakobson: Echoes of His Scholarship*. Edited by Daniel Armstrong and Cornelis H. van Schooneveld. Lisse: Peter de Ridder Press, 1977.

Jameson, Fredric. *The Political Unconscious*. Ithaca: Cornell University Press, 1981.

————. *Postmodernism or, The Cultural Logic of Late Capitalism*. Durham: Duke University Press, 1994.

Janusko, Robert. *Sources and Structures of James Joyce's "Oxen."* Ann Arbor: UMI Research Press, 1983

Jauss, Hans Robert. *Toward an Aesthetic of Reception*. Translated by Timothy Bahti. Minneapolis: University of Minnesota Press, 1982.

Jones, Ellen Carol, ed. *Joyce: Feminism/Post/Colonialism*. Amsterdam: Rodopi, 1998.

Jordan-Smith, Paul. *A Key to the "Ulysses" of James Joyce*. Chicago: Covici, 1934.

Joyce, James. *Ulysses*. Paris: Shakespeare and Company, 1922.

————. *Ulysse*. Translated by M. Auguste Morel, assisted by Stuart Gilbert. Paris: La Maison des Amis des Livres, Adrienne Monnier, 1929.

————. *Finnegans Wake*. 1939. New York: Viking, 1982.

————. *Stephen Hero: A Part of the First Draft of "A Portrait of the Artist as a Young Man."* Edited by Theodore Spencer. New York: New Directions, 1944. Rev. ed., with additional pages edited by John J. Slocum and Herbert Cahoon, 1955, 1963.

————. *Letters*. Vol. 1, edited by Stuart Gilbert. New York: Viking, 1957, 1966. Vols. 2–3, edited by Richard Ellmann. New York: Viking, 1966.

————. *The Critical Writings of James Joyce*. Edited by Ellsworth Mason and Richard Ellmann. New York: Viking Press, 1959.

————. *Dubliners*. Edited by Robert Scholes. New York: Viking Press, 1967.

————. *A Portrait of the Artist as a Young Man*. Edited by Chester Anderson. Viking Critical Edition. New York: Penguin, 1968.

————. *Joyce's "Ulysses" Notesheets in the British Museum*. Edited by Phillip F. Herring. Charlottesville: University Press of Virginia, 1972.

————. *Selected Letters*. Edited by Richard Ellmann. New York: Viking, 1975.

————. *"Ulysses": A Facsimile of the Manuscript*. Edited by Clive Driver. 2 vols. New York: Octagon; Philadelphia: Philip H. and A.S.W. Rosenbach Foundation, 1975.

————. *Joyce's Notes and Early Drafts for "Ulysses": Selections from the Buffalo Collection*. Edited by Phillip F. Herring. Charlottesville: University Press of Virginia, 1977.

————. *James Joyce Archive*. 63 vols. Edited by Michael Groden et al. New York: Garland, 1977–79.

————. *"Ulysses": A Critical and Synoptic Edition*. Edited by Hans Walter Gabler with Wolfhard Steppe and Claus Melchior. 3 vols. New York: Garland, 1984.

————. *A Portrait of the Artist as a Young Man*. Edited by Seamus Deane. London: Penguin, 1992.

———. *Ulysses*. Edited by Jeri Johnson. Oxford: Oxford World's Classics, 1993.

———. *"Ulysses": The Corrected Text*. New York: Random House/Vintage; London: Penguin, 1986; *"Ulysses": The Gabler Edition*. New York: Vintage; London: Bodley Head, 1993.

———. *The "Finnegans Wake" Notebooks at Buffalo*. 5 vols. Edited by Vincent Deane, Daniel Ferrer, Geert Lernout. Turnhout, Belgium: Brepols Publishers, 2001.

———. *"Ulysses": A Reader's Edition*. Edited by Danis Rose. London: Picador, 1997. *"Ulysses": A New Reader's Edition*. Cornwall: Houyhnhnm, 2004.

Kain, Richard M. Review of *A Bibliography of James Joyce, 1882–1941*, by John J. Slocum and Herbert Cahoon. *Sewanee Review* 61, no. 4 (Autumn 1953): 717–22.

Kearns, Michael. *Rhetorical Narratology*. Lincoln: University of Nebraska Press, 1999.

Keats, John. *The Selected Letters of John Keats*. Edited by Lionel Trilling. Garden City, N.Y.: Doubleday Anchor, 1956.

Kelly, Joseph. "A Defense of Danis Rose." *James Joyce Quarterly* 35, no. 4 (1998): 811–24.

Kenner, Hugh. *Joyce's Voices*. Berkeley and Los Angeles: University of California Press, 1978.

———. "An Insane Assault on Chaos." Review of the *James Joyce Archive*. *New York Times Book Review*, June 22, 1980, 7, 26–27.

———. *Ulysses*. 1980; rev. ed., Baltimore: Johns Hopkins University Press, 1987.

Kershner, R. B. "Joyce as Historian: Popular Literature and Popular Consciousness." *Eire* 19 (1977): 104–12.

———. *Joyce, Bakhtin, and Popular Literature: Chronicles of Disorder*. Chapel Hill: University of North Carolina Press, 1989.

———, ed. *James Joyce: "A Portrait of the Artist as a Young Man."* Boston: Bedford–St. Martin's Press, 1993.

———, ed. *Joyce and Popular Culture*. Gainesville: University Press of Florida, 1996.

———, ed. *Cultural Studies of James Joyce*. Amsterdam: Rodopi, 2003.

Kiberd, Declan. Introduction to *"Ulysses": Annotated Students' Edition*, by James Joyce. London: Penguin, 1992.

Kidd, John. "An Inquiry into *Ulysses*: The Corrected Text." *PBSA* 82 (1988): 411–584.

———. "The Scandal of *Ulysses*." *New York Review of Books*, June 30, 1988, 32–39.

———. "Errors of Execution in the 1984 *Ulysses*." *Studies in the Novel* 22 (1990): 243–49.

———. "Gabler's Errors in Context: A Reply to Michael Groden on Editing *Ulysses*." *James Joyce Quarterly* 28 (1990): 111–51.

———. "Making the Wrong Joyce." *New York Review of Books*, September 25, 1997.

Killham, John. "'Ineluctable Modality' in Joyce's *Ulysses*." *University of Toronto Quarterly* 34 (1965): 269–89.

Kimball, Jean. "Freud, Leonardo, and Joyce: The Dimensions of a Childhood Memory." *James Joyce Quarterly* 17 (Winter 1980): 165–82.

Knowles, Sebastian D. G. *Bronze by Gold: The Music of Joyce*. New York: Garland Publishing, 1999.

Kugel, Adelaide. "'Wroth Wrackt Joyce': Samuel Roth and the 'Not Quite Unauthorized' Edition of *Ulysses*." *Joyce Studies Annual* 3 (1992): 242–48.

Lacan, Jacques. "Le sinthome: Jacques Lacan's Seminar XXIII, 1975–76." Edited by Jacques-Alain Miller. Translated by Luke Thurston. Unpublished.

Lamos, Colleen. "Signatures of the Invisible: Homosexual Knowledge and Secrecy in Ulysses." *James Joyce Quarterly* 31 (Spring 1994): 337–55.

———. "The Double Life of 'Eumaeus.'" In *"Ulysses": En-Gendered Perspectives*, edited by K. Devlin and M. Reizbaum, 242–53. Columbia: University of South Carolina Press, 1999.

Lanser, Susan Sniader. *Fictions of Authority: Women Writers and Narrative Voice*. Ithaca: Cornell University Press, 1992.

Laurence, Dan. *A Portrait of the Author as a Bibliography*. Washington, D.C.: Library of Congress, 1983.

Lawrence, Karen. *The Odyssey of Style in "Ulysses."* Princeton: Princeton University Press, 1981.

———. "Joyce and Feminism." In *The Cambridge Companion to James Joyce*, edited by Derek Attridge, 237–58. New York: Cambridge University Press, 1990.

Lázaro, Alberto, and Antonio Raúl de Toro. *James Joyce in Spain: A Critical Bibliography (1972–2002)*. Coruña: Universidade da Coruña, Servicio de Publicacións; Asociación Española James Joyce, 2002.

Leonard, Garry. *Advertising and Commodity Culture in Joyce*. Gainesville: University Press of Florida, 1998.

———. "Joyce and Lacan: 'The Woman' as a Symptom of 'Masculinity' in 'The Dead.'" *James Joyce Quarterly* 28 (1991): 451–72.

———. "The Virgin Mary and the Urge in Gerty: The Packaging of Desire in the 'Nausicaa' Chapter of *Ulysses*." *University of Hartford Studies in Literature* 23 (1991): 3–23.

———. "Women on the Market: Commodity Culture, 'Femininity,' and 'Those Lovely Seaside Girls' in Joyce's *Ulysses*." *Joyce Studies Annual* 2 (1991): 27–68.

———. *Reading "Dubliners" Again: A Lacanian Perspective*. Syracuse: Syracuse University Press, 1993.

———. "The History of Now: Commodity Culture and Everyday Life in Joyce." In *Joyce and the Subject of History*, edited by Mark A. Wollaeger, Victor Luftig, and Robert Spoo, 13–26. Ann Arbor: University of Michigan Press, 1996.

———. "A Little Trouble about Those White Corpuscles: Styles of Masculinity in

'Telemachus.'" In *"Ulysses": En-Gendered Perspectives*, edited by K. Devlin and M. Reizbaum, 1–19. Columbia: University of South Carolina Press, 1999.

Levin, Harry. *James Joyce: A Critical Introduction*. New York: New Directions, 1941. Rev. ed., 1960.

———. Introduction to *"Ulysses": A Facsimile of the Manuscript*. 2 vols. New York: Octagon; Philadelphia: Philip H. and A.S.W. Rosenbach Foundation, 1975.

Levine, Jennifer. "James Joyce, Tattoo Artist: Tracing the Outlines of Homosocial Desire." In *Quare Joyce*, edited by Joseph Valente, 101–29. Ann Arbor: University of Michigan Press, 1998.

Lévi-Strauss, Claude. *Structural Anthropology*. Translated by Claire Jacobson and Brooke Schoepf. New York: Basic Books, 1963.

Lidderdale, Jane, and Mary Nicholson. *Dear Miss Weaver: Harriet Shaw Weaver 1876–1961*. New York: Viking Press, 1970.

Litz, A. Walton. *The Art of James Joyce: Method and Design in "Ulysses" and "Finnegans Wake."* New York: Oxford University Press, 1961.

———. "Uses of the *Finnegans Wake* Manuscripts." In *Twelve and a Tilly: Essays on the Occasion of the 25th Anniversary of "Finnegans Wake,"* edited by Jack P. Dalton and Clive Hart, 99–106. Evanston: Northwestern University Press, 1966.

Lloyd, David. *Anomalous States: Irish Writing and the Post-colonial Moment*. Durham, N.C.: Duke University Press, 1993.

Loizeaux, Elizabeth Bergmann, and Neil Fraistat, eds. *Reimagining Textuality: Textual Studies in the Late Age of Print*. Madison: University of Wisconsin Press, 2002.

The Lost "Eumaeus" Notebook: James Joyce, Autograph Manuscript of the "Eumaeus" Episode of Ulysses: Lot 197 in the Sale of English Literature, History, Children's and Illustrated Books and Drawings. London: Sotheby's, 2001.

Lowe-Evans, Mary. *Crimes Against Fecundity: Joyce and Population Control*. Syracuse: Syracuse University Press, 1989.

Luftig, Victor, and Mark Wollaeger. "Why 'Joyce and History'? Why Now?" *James Joyce Quarterly*, 28, no. 4 (Summer 1991): 841–51.

Lund, Steven. *James Joyce: Letters, Manuscripts, and Photographs at Southern Illinois University*. Troy, N.Y.: Whitston Publishing Company, 1983.

Lyall, Sarah. "A New Edition Purges What May Have Been Joyce's Errors and Enrages Critics." *New York Times*, June 23, 1997.

Lynd, Helen. *Shame and the Search for Identity*. New York: Harcourt Brace, 1958.

MacCabe, Colin. *James Joyce and the Revolution of the Word*. 2nd ed. New York: Palgrave Macmillan, 2003.

Maddox, Brenda. *Nora: The Real Life of Molly Bloom*. Boston: Houghton Mifflin, 1988.

Madtes, Richard E. *The "Ithaca" Chapter of James Joyce's "Ulysses."* Ann Arbor: UMI Research Press, 1983.

Mahaffey, Vicki. "Intentional Error: The Paradox of Editing Joyce's Ulysses." In *Representing Modernist Texts: Editing as Interpretation*, edited by George Bornstein, 171–91. Ann Arbor: University of Michigan Press, 1991.

———. "*Ulysses* and the End of Gender." In *A Companion to James Joyce's "Ulysses,"* edited by Margot Norris, 151–68. Boston: Bedford Books, 1998.

Manganiello, Dominic. *Joyce's Politics*. London: Routledge and Kegan Paul, 1980.

Margolin, Uri. "Story Modalised, or the Grammar of Virtuality." *GRAAT*, no. 21 (1996): 49–61.

Martin, Timothy. *Joyce and Wagner: A Study of Influence*. Cambridge: Cambridge University Press, 1991.

Martin, Wallace. *Recent Theories of Narrative*. Ithaca: Cornell University Press, 1986.

McCleery, Alistair, William S. Brockman, and Ian Gunn. "The Text of the Random House 1934 Edition of *Ulysses*." Forthcoming.

McCormick, Kathleen, and Erwin R. Steinberg, eds. *Approaches to Teaching Joyce's "Ulysses."* New York: Modern Language Association, 1993.

McCourt, John. *The Years of Bloom*. Dublin: Lilliput Press, 2000.

McDowell, Edwin. "New Edition Fixes 5,000 Errors in Ulysses." *New York Times*, June 7, 1984.

McGann, Jerome J. *A Critique of Modern Textual Criticism*. 1983. Reprint, Charlottesville: University Press of Virginia, 1992.

———. "*Ulysses* as a Postmodern Work." 1985. In *Social Values and Poetic Acts: The Historical Judgment of Literary Work*, 173–94. Cambridge: Harvard University Press, 1988.

McGee, Patrick. *Joyce Beyond Marx*. Gainesville: University Press of Florida, 2001.

McKenzie, D. F. "Bibliography and the Sociology of Texts." In *Bibliography and the Sociology of Texts*, 7–76. Cambridge: Cambridge University Press, 1999.

Melchiori, Giorgio, ed. *Joyce in Rome*. Rome: Bulzoni, 1984.

Merritt, Stephen. "The Death of Ferdinand de Saussure." In *The Magnetic Fields, 69 Love Songs*. Merge Records, 1999.

Milesi, Laurent, ed. *James Joyce and the Difference of Language*. Cambridge: Cambridge University Press, 2003.

Miller, J. Hillis. *Fiction and Repetition: Seven English Novels*. Cambridge: Harvard University Press, 1982.

———. *Reading Narrative Discourse*. Norman: University of Oklahoma Press, 1998.

———. *Speech Acts in Literature*. Stanford: Stanford University Press, 2001.

Modern Literature from the Library of James Gilvarry: Friday, February 7, 1986. New York: Christie Manson and Woods, 1986.

Moscato, Michael, and Leslie LeBlanc, eds. *The United States of America v. One Book Entitled "Ulysses" by James Joyce: Documents and Commentary: A 50-Year Retrospective*. Frederick, Md.: University Publications of America, 1984.

Mulvey, Laura. "Visual Pleasure and Narrative Cinema." In *Visual and Other Pleasures*, 198–209. Bloomington: Indiana University Press, 1989.

Nadel, Ira B. "The American *Ulysses*: 'A Lasting Bloom.'" *James Joyce Quarterly* 28, no. 4 (Summer 1991): 967–81.

———. "'Forget-Me-Not': Joycean Bibliography." *James Joyce Quarterly* 32, no. 2 (Winter 1995): 243–59.

National Library of Ireland. "The James Joyce Manuscripts Purchased from Mr. and Mrs. Alexis Léon, May 2002." http:// www.nli.ie/pdfs/joycelist.pdf.

———. *The Joyce Papers 2002*. 2002. http://www.nli.ie/pdfs/joyce02.pdf.

———. "Collection List No. 689–The Joyce Papers 2002 (MS 36,639)." Comp. Peter Kenny. http://www.nli.ie/pdfs/mss lists/joyce02.pdf.

Nolan, Emer. *James Joyce and Nationalism*. London: Routledge, 1995.

Norris, Margot. *The Decentered Universe of "Finnegans Wake": A Structuralist Analysis*. Baltimore: Johns Hopkins University Press, 1976.

———. *Joyce's Web*. Austin: University of Texas Press, 1992.

O'Hegarty, P. S. "A Bibliography of James Joyce." *Dublin Magazine*, n.s., 21 (January-March 1946): 38–47.

O'Neill, Christine. *Too Fine a Point: A Stylistic Analysis of the Eumaeus Episode in James Joyce's "Ulysses."* Trier, Germany: Wissenschaftlicher Verlag Trier, 1996.

Osteen, Mark. *The Economy of "Ulysses": Making Both Ends Meet*. Syracuse: Syracuse University Press, 1995.

Parker, Alan. *James Joyce: A Bibliography of His Writings, Critical Material, and Miscellanea*. Useful Reference Series, 76. Boston: F. W. Faxon, 1948.

Pascal, Roy. *The Dual Voice: Free Indirect Speech and Its Functioning in the Nineteenth-Century European Novel*. Totowa, N.J.: Rowan and Littlefield, 1977.

Pearce, Richard. *The Politics of Narration: James Joyce, William Faulkner, and Virginia Woolf*. New Brunswick, N.J.: Rutgers University Press, 1991.

———, ed. *Molly Blooms: A Polylogue on "Penelope" and Cultural Studies*. Madison: University of Wisconsin Press, 1994

Power, Arthur. *Conversations with James Joyce*. New York: Barnes and Noble, 1974.

Prescott, Joseph. *Exploring James Joyce*. Carbondale: Southern Illinois University Press, 1964.

Prince, Gerald. *Narratology: The Form and Functioning of Narrative*. Berlin: Mouton, 1982.

Propp, Vladimir. *The Morphology of the Folktale*. Translated by Laurence Scott. Austin: University of Texas Press, 1968.

Rabaté, Jean-Michel. "A Clown's Inquest into Paternity." In *The Fictional Father*, edited Robert Con Davis, 73–114. Amherst: University of Massachusetts Press, 1981.

———. *James Joyce and the Politics of Egoism*. Cambridge: Cambridge University Press, 2001.

Rader, Ralph. "Mulligan and Molly: The Beginning and the End." In *Joyce in the Hibernian Metropolis*, edited by M. Beja and D. Norris, 270–78. Columbus: Ohio State University Press, 1996.

Rainey, Lawrence. "How Molly Bloom Got Her Apostrophes," *James Joyce Quarterly* 35 (1998): 588–96.

———. *Institutions of Modernism: Literary Elites and Public Culture*. New Haven and London: Yale University Press, 1998.

Read, Forrest, ed. *Pound/Joyce: The Letters of Ezra Pound to James Joyce with Pound's Essays on Joyce*. New York: New Directions, 1967.

Rice, Thomas Jackson. *James Joyce: A Guide to Research*. New York and London: Garland Publishing, 1982.

Richards, Thomas. *The Commodity Culture of Victorian England*. Stanford: Stanford University Press, 1990.

Riddell, John. "The People's Joyce." *Vanity Fair* 42 (June 1934): 57, 72b.

Rimmon-Kenan, Shlomith. *Narrative Fiction: Contemporary Poetics*. London: Methuen, 1983.

Riquelme, John Paul. *Teller and Tale in Joyce's Fiction: Oscillating Perspectives*. Baltimore: Johns Hopkins University Press, 1983.

———. "*Stephen Hero* and *A Portrait of the Artist as a Young Man*: Transforming the Nightmare of History." In *The Cambridge Companion to James Joyce*, 2nd ed., edited by Derek Attridge, 103–21. Cambridge: Cambridge University Press, 2004.

Rossman, Charles. "The New *Ulysses*: The Hidden Controversy." *New York Review of Books*, December 8, 1988, 53–58.

———. "A Bibliography of the 'Gabler *Ulysses*.'" *Studies in the Novel* 22 (1990): 257–69.

———, ed. "A Special Issue on Editing *Ulysses*." Special issue, *Studies in the Novel* 22, no.2 (Summer 1990).

Ryan, Marie-Laure. *Possible Worlds, Artificial Intelligence, and Narrative Theory*. Bloomington: Indiana University Press, 1991.

Ryder, John. "Editing *Ulysses* Typographically." *Scholarly Publishing* 18, no. 2 (1987): 108–24.

Sandulescu, C. George, and Clive Hart, eds. *Assessing the 1984 "Ulysses."* Princess Grace Irish Library, 1. Gerrards Cross, Buckinghamshire: Colin Smythe; Totowa, N.J.: Barnes and Noble, 1986.

Scholes, Robert E. *The Cornell Joyce Collection: A Catalogue*. Ithaca: Cornell University Press, 1961.

Schwaber, Paul. *The Cast of Characters: A Reading of "Ulysses."* New Haven: Yale University Press, 1999.

Schwarz, Daniel. *Reading Joyce's "Ulysses."* New York: St. Martin's, 1987.

Schwarze, Tracey Teets. *Joyce and the Victorians*. Gainesville: University Press of Florida, 2002.

Scott, Bonnie Kime. *Joyce and Feminism*. Bloomington: Indiana University Press, 1984.

Searle, John. *Expression and Meaning: Studies in the Theory of Speech Acts*. Cambridge: Cambridge University Press, 1979.

Searle, Leroy. "New Criticism." In *The Johns Hopkins Guide to Literary Theory and Criticism*, edited by Michael Groden and Martin Kreiswirth, 528–34. Baltimore and London: Johns Hopkins University Press, 1994.

Sedgwick, Eve K. *Tendencies*. Durham: Duke University Press, 1993.

Selley, Peter. "The Lost 'Eumaeus' Notebook: James Joyce, Autograph Manuscript of the 'Eumaeus' Episode of *Ulysses*." Auction catalogue. Sotheby's London, July 10, 2001.

Senn, Fritz. Review of *A Bibliography of James Joyce Studies,* 2nd ed. *James Joyce Quarterly* 16, no. 1/2 (Fall 1978/Winter 1979): 181–88.

———. *Joyce's Dislocutions: Essays on Reading as Translation*. Edited by John Paul Riquelme. Baltimore: Johns Hopkins University Press, 1984.

———. *Inductive Scrutinies*. Edited by Christine O'Neill. Baltimore: Johns Hopkins University Press, 1995.

Shattuck, Roger, and Douglas Alden. "Searching for the True Text." *Times Literary Supplement,* June 10–16, 1988, 640–41.

Shillingsburg, Peter L. *Scholarly Editing in the Computer Age: Theory and Practice*. 3rd ed. Ann Arbor: University of Michigan Press, 1996.

Shloss, Carol Loeb. *Lucia Joyce: To Dance in the Wake*. New York: Farrar, Straus, and Giroux, 2003.

Silverstein, Norman. "Joyce's 'Circe' Episode: Approaches to *Ulysses* through a Textual and Interpretive Study of Joyce's Fifteenth Chapter." Ph.D. diss., Columbia University, 1960.

Slocum, John J. "Collecting James Joyce." *Gazette of the Grolier Club*, no. 33–34 (1981–82): 6–18.

Slocum, John J., and Herbert Cahoon. *A Bibliography of James Joyce, 1882–1941*. Soho Bibliographies. Vol. 5. London: Rupert Hart-Davis, 1953. Published in the United States as *A Bibliography of James Joyce [1882–1941]*. Bibliographical Series from Yale University Collections. New Haven: Yale University Press, 1953.

Slote, Sam. "Preliminary Comments on Two Newly-Discovered Ulysses Manuscripts." *James Joyce Quarterly* 38 (Spring/Summer 2001): 17–28.

———. *"Ulysses" in the Plural: A Survey of the Editions of Joyce's Novel*. Dublin: National Library of Ireland, 2004.

Slote, Sam, and Wim Van Mierlo, eds. "Genitricksling Joyce." Special issue, *European Joyce Studies* 9 (1999).

Smith, Simon Harcourt Nowell. "The Soho Recipe." *Times Literary Supplement*, no. 3217 (October 25, 1963): 876.

Spielberg, Peter. *James Joyce's Manuscripts and Letters at the University of Buffalo: A Catalogue*. Buffalo: State University of New York at Buffalo, 1962.

Spoerri, James F. "The Odyssey Press Edition of James Joyce's *Ulysses*." *Papers of the Bibliographical Society of America* 50, no. 2 (1956): 195–98.

Spoo, Robert. "*Ulysses* and the Ten Years War: A Survey of Missed Opportunities." *Text* 10 (1997): 107–18.

———. "Joyce Scholars, Editors, and Imaginary Readers," *College English* 60 (1998): 330–35.

———. "Copyright and the Ends of Ownership: The Case for a Public-Domain *Ulysses* in America." *Joyce Studies Annual* 10 (1999): 5–62.

Staley, Thomas. "*Ulysses*": *Fifty Years Later*. Bloomington: University of Indiana Press, 1974.

———. *An Annotated Critical Bibliography of James Joyce*. London: Harvester Wheatsheaf; New York: St. Martin's, 1989.

Staley, Thomas, and Bernard Benstock, eds. *Approaches to "Ulysses": Ten Essays*. Pittsburgh: University of Pittsburgh Press, 1970.

Stanzel, Franz. *Narrative Situations in the Novel: "Tom Jones," "Moby Dick," "The Ambassadors," "Ulysses."* Translated by James B. Pusack. Bloomington: Indiana University Press, 1971.

Steinberg, Erwin R. 1973 *The Stream of Consciousness and Beyond in "Ulysses."* Pittsburgh: Pittsburgh University Press, 1973.

Tanner, Tony. *Adultery in the Novel*. Baltimore: Johns Hopkins, 1979.

Tanselle, G. Thomas. "A System of Color Identification for Bibliographical Description." *Studies in Bibliography* 20 (1967): 203–34.

———. *Selected Studies in Bibliography*. Charlottesville: University Press of Virginia, 1979.

Thornton, Weldon. *Voices and Values in Joyce's "Ulysses."* Gainesville: University Press of Florida, 2000.

Tindall, William York. *James Joyce: His Way of Interpreting the Modern World*. New York: Scribner's, 1950.

———. *A Reader's Guide to James Joyce*. New York: Noonday Press, 1959.

Todorov, Tzvetan. *Grammaire du Decameron*. The Hague: Mouton, 1969.

Topia, André. "The Matrix and the Echo: Intertextuality in *Ulysses*." In *Post-structuralist Joyce: Essays from the French*, edited by Derek Attridge and Daniel Ferrer, 103–25. Cambridge: Cambridge University Press, 1984.

Tymczko, Maria. *The Irish "Ulysses."* Berkeley and Los Angeles: University of California Press, 1994.

Valente Joseph. "The Perils of Masculinity in 'Scylla and Charybdis.'" In "*Ulysses*": *En-*

Gendered Perspectives, edited by K. Devlin and M. Reizbaum, 111–35. Columbia: University of South Carolina Press, 1999.

van Hulle, Dirk, ed. *James Joyce: The Study of Languages*. Brussels: Peter Lang Verlag, 2002.

van Voorhis, John W., and Francis C. Bloodgood. "*Ulysses*: Another Pirated Edition?" *James Joyce Quarterly* 9, no. 4 (Summer 1972): 436–44.

Veeser, H. Aram, ed. *The New Historicism*. New York: Routledge, 1989.

Vesala-Varttala, Tanja. *Sympathy and Joyce's "Dubliners": Ethical Probing of Reading, Narrative, and Textuality*. Tampere, Finland: Tampere University Press, 1999.

Wales, Katie. *The Language of James Joyce*. New York: St. Martin's Press, 1992.

Warhol, Robyn R. *Gendered Interventions: Narrative Discourse in the Victorian Novel*. New Brunswick, N.J.: Rutgers University Press, 1989.

Warner, Michael. *The Trouble with Normal*. New York: Free Press, 1999.

Wawrzycka, Jolanta W., and Marlena G. Corcoran, eds. *Gender in Joyce*. Gainesville: University Press of Florida, 1997.

Weaver, Jack W. *Joyce's Music and Noise: Theme and Variation in His Writings*. Gainesville: University Press of Florida, 1998.

Weir, David. "A Womb of His Own: Joyce's Sexual Aesthetics." *James Joyce Quarterly* 31 (Fall 1994): 207–31.

White, Hayden. "The Absurdist Moment in Contemporary Literature Theory." In *Tropics of Discourse: Essays in Cultural Criticism*, 261–82. Baltimore and London: Johns Hopkins University Press, 1978.

Wicke, Jennifer. "'Who's She When She's at Home?': Molly Bloom and the Work of Consumption." *James Joyce Quarterly* 28 (1991): 749–63.

Wilde, Oscar. "The Critic as Artist." In *The Artist as Critic: Critical Writings of Oscar Wilde*, edited by Richard Ellmann, 398–422. New York: Random House, 1962.

Williams, William Proctor, and Craig S. Abbott. *An Introduction to Bibliographical and Textual Studies*. 3rd ed. New York: Modern Language Association of America, 1999.

Wilson, Edmund. *Axel's Castle: A Study in the Imaginative Literature of 1870–1930*. New York: Charles Scribner's Sons, 1931.

Wimsatt, William K., Jr. *The Verbal Icon: Studies in the Meaning of Poetry*. Lexington: University of Kentucky Press, 1947.

Wollaeger, Mark A. "Between Stephen and Jim: Portraits of Joyce as a Young Man." In *James Joyce's "A Portrait of the Artist as a Young Man": A Casebook*, edited by Mark A. Wollaeger, 343–56. Oxford: Oxford University Press, 2003.

Wollaeger, Mark A., Victor Luftig, and Robert Spoo, eds. *Joyce and the Subject of History*. Ann Arbor: University of Michigan Press, 1996.

Woolf, Virginia. *A Room of One's Own*. 1929. New York: Harcourt Brace Jovanovich, 1957.

Woolmer, J. Howard. "*Ulysses* at Auction with a Preliminary Census." *James Joyce Quarterly* 17, no. 2 (Winter 1980): 141–48.

Zizek, Slavoj. *Looking Awry: An Introduction to Jacques Lacan through Popular Culture.* Cambridge: Harvard University Press, 1991.

Ziarek, Ewa. "The Female Body, Technology, and Memory in 'Penelope.'" In *James Joyce's "Ulysses": A Casebook*, edited by Derek Attridge, 103–28. Oxford: Oxford University Press, 2004.

Contributors

Sheldon Brivic is a professor of English at Temple University. His most recent books on Joyce include *The Veil of Signs: Joyce, Lacan, and Perception* (1991) and *Joyce's Waking Women: An Introduction to Finnegans Wake* (1995). He is currently completing a study of how Euro-American and Afro-American cultures have interacted with each other to shape the development of modern American fiction.

William S. Brockman is the Paterno Family Librarian for Literature at Pennsylvania State University at University Park. Bibliographer for the *James Joyce Quarterly* since 1990, he has published articles and essays on modernist bookselling and publishing history and is currently preparing a descriptive bibliography of the works of James Joyce.

Kimberly J. Devlin is a professor of English at University of California, Riverside. She is the author of *Wandering and Return in "Finnegans Wake"* and *James Joyce's "Fraudstuff"* and the coeditor of *Joycean Cultures/Culturing Joyces* and *"Ulysses": Engendered Perspectives*.

Gregory M. Downing teaches literature and culture at the Staten Island campus of St. Johns University in New York and is a Visiting Scholar in Comparative Literature at New York University. He has published a series of articles on Joyce's backgrounds in mid- and late nineteenth-century popularizations of scientific ideas about language, most recently "Diverting Philology" in *James Joyce: The Study of Languages*. He is currently completing *Universe of Discourse*, a monograph that will extend this work.

A. Nicholas Fargnoli is a professor of theology and English at Molloy College in Rockville Centre, New York; current president of the James Joyce Society; and founder of the Finnegans Wake Society of New York. With Michael Patrick Gillespie, he is coauthor of *James Joyce A to Z*; with Daniel C. Maguire, coauthor of *On Moral Grounds: The Art/Science of Ethics*; and with Michael Golay, coauthor of *William Faulkner A to Z*.

Michael Patrick Gillespie is the Louise Edna Goeden Professor of English at Marquette University. His most recent book is *The Aesthetics of Chaos: Nonlinear Thinking and Contemporary Literary Criticism*. He is currently editing the Norton Critical

Editions of Oscar Wilde's *The Importance of Being Earnest* and *The Picture of Dorian Gray*.

Michael Groden is a professor of English at the University of Western Ontario. He is the author of *"Ulysses" in Progress*; general editor of the sixty-three-volume *James Joyce Archive*, and author of numerous articles on Joyce, manuscripts, genetic criticism, textual criticism, criticism and theories of fiction, and computer presentations of literary works. His most recent books, both coedited, are *Genetic Criticism: Texts and Avant-textes* and the second edition of *The Johns Hopkins Guide to Literary Theory and Criticism*.

Ira Nadel, professor of English and Distinguished University Scholar at the University of British Columbia, is the author of *Joyce and the Jews*; *Various Positions: A Life of Leonard Cohen*; *Double Act: a Life of Tom Stoppard*; and *Ezra Pound, A Literary Life*. He is currently writing a biography of David Mamet.

Margot Norris is a professor of English and comparative literature at the University of California-Irvine. She has written numerous books and articles on Joyce's works and other topics relating to twentieth-century literature. Her most recent book is *Ulysses*, a study of Joseph Strick's 1967 film. She is the current president of the International James Joyce Foundation.

John Paul Riquelme is a professor of English at Boston University. He is currently editing *A Portrait of the Artist as a Young Man* for W. W. Norton and writing a book about Oscar Wilde's aesthetic politics and the origins of modernism in 1890s Britain. Among his works on Joyce are *Teller and Tale in Joyce's Fiction: Oscillating Perspectives* and an edition of Fritz Senn's essays, *Joyce's Dislocutions: Essays on Reading as Translation*.

Joseph Valente is a professor of English and Director of Irish Studies at the University of Illinois. His books include *James Joyce and the Problem of Justice*, *Dracula's Crypt: Bram Stoker, Irishness, and the Question of Blood*, and the edited volumes *Quare Joyce* and *Disciplinarity at the Fin de Siecle* (with Amanda Anderson). He is currently finishing a book entitled *Contested Territory: Race and Manliness in Modern Irish Culture*.

Index

The Florida James Joyce Series
Edited by Sebastian D. G. Knowles
Zack Bowen, Editor Emeritus